A Sacred Path

The Way of the Muscogee Creeks

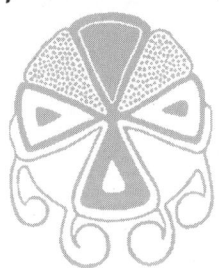

A Sacred Path

The Way of the Muscogee Creeks

Jean Chaudhuri and Joyotpaul Chaudhuri

© 2001
UCLA American Indian Studies Center
3220 Campbell Hall, Box 951548
Los Angeles, California 90095-1548

Publisher: Duane Champagne
Publications Manager: Pamela Grieman
Copy Editors: Pamela Grieman and Amy Ware
Assistants: Nam Nguyen and Benjamin Serna
Cover Artwork: *Creation and the Four Spirits*
    by Joydev Mahagi "Paul" Chaudhuri
Cover Design and Book Layout: Keeli A. Tebeau (Navajo)

Printed by McNaughton & Gunn, Inc.
Library of Congress Card Number: 00-109474
ISBN 0-935626-54-9

UCLA American Indian Studies Center
3220 Campbell Hall
Box 951548
Los Angeles, California 90095-1548

TABLE OF CONTENTS

ACKNOWLEDGMENTS

I have depended considerably on oral history in this work. The majority of the informants as well as the primary author have passed away. As a Creek, practically every Creek who has interacted with Jean Chaudhuri (Jean's maiden name was Ella Jean Hill, affectionate name Haya-atke/Hiyvtke—the line between night and dawn, or early dawn) is in a sense a contributor and the deep acknowledgment of Creek people is made. As a Creek, Jean herself was immersed in Creek values.

Because many of the contributors have passed away, part of the reason for writing this work is to ensure that this body of shared knowledge does not disappear. The late James Scott, who died around 1944 at about 110 years of age, provided many of the stories including the creation legend, the red stick/white stick legend of the social contract, the story of his own painful experience during the Trail of Tears, and additional insights into Creek ways. The late Billy Osceola of Brighton, Florida, provided many insights on Florida Seminoles. The same holds true for the late John Brown of Duck Creek grounds regarding the Euchees.

The late Netchie Gray also provided insights into Creek aesthetics, particularly costumes, music, and dances. Late parents Wilburn and Mary Hill provided their knowledge and information, as did the late Micco/Mekko Elmer Hill who had links to the Creek rebel Chitto Harjo. Jean's late aunts, "Ollie" Miller and "Ella" Hill also contributed. Among other contributors who are now gone are London Coker, Alfred Wilson, Max Beaver, the famous medicine man Dave Lewis, Sr., elder brother Clifton Hill, and a maternal uncle, Stanley Smith. Others who have conversed with us are Henry Harjo (now past ninety), whose father was in the Trail and whose grandparents died prior to removal. Additional contributors were Roosevelt Deerishaw (now more than eighty-seven years of age), Bessie Bell (now past seventy-eight), the late Ralph Heniha, Sr., Katie Holloway, the Coon family, the Hicks family, the Robert Hill family, Richinda Sands and the late Clifton Hill, the late Bunny Hill and family, Wootko Johnson, Peggy Chupco, Eziel Harjo, Christine Heniha, Mattie Bear, Louina and Cindy Jackson (seventy-five and seventy-eight years old respectively), John and Lewis "Doc" White (seventy-eight and eighty respectively), Cindy Hill, Ella Bender, two Florida ladies (twins who are over one hundred years old), various Florida Seminoles and Miccosukees elders twenty-three years or more ago, the Alice Snow family, Rachel Bowers

(Seminole), the Al Weiss (Alabama) family, and the Harry Long family. Given the participating interactions over time in social settings in a Creek way rather than formal social science interviews with tapes, the acknowledgments cannot be cited in the standard way.

We also acknowledge, with thanks, visits with the late Micco Tony Hill of Asilanabi, the late Willie Lena, and a brief visit with Micco George Thompson of Hickory Ground. Special thanks are given to Russell Thompson, *micco*/chief and *heleshayv*/medicine man, and Amos McNac, *empunayv*/speaker of Nuyaka ceremonial ground, for their encouragement in the project. Mr. McNac also assisted with the Creek glossary. He is a member of the Creek Tribal Supreme Court.

None of the Creeks or Seminoles are legally responsible for any errors in the manuscript. Per custom, that responsibility belongs to the authors.

Thanks are due to almost everyone mentioned in the acknowledgments for their encouragement. Thanks are also due to Carl Clausen, the archeologist, for sharing with Jean his insight into the historical Creek pathways and settlements in Florida. Thanks go to Byron Schneid for his map drawings and advice on geology. Also acknowledged is the assistance and support of our two sons, Joydev Mahagi "Paul" Chaudhuri and Jonodev Osceola "Jon" Chaudhuri. Paul did some of the key artwork and Jon shared his contacts and experience in working with the tribe and also his participation and interest in the traditional ways. Paul, Jon, and their cousin Lance Sands also had to adjust their lives during the elaborate fieldwork which took decades. Thanks also to Professor Emeritus John Mahon of the University of Florida for his encouragement, and reverence to the late Yale philosopher F. S. C. Northrop, who pointed toward a "philosophical anthropology" and who sensitized us to the links between concepts of nature and culture in both "aboriginal" and "modern" worlds. A deep *maddo*/*mvto* to all Creeks who have helped, including those who are gone, and a request for forgiveness for any errors of omission or commission for which the authors bear the sole responsibility.

Additional thanks for assistance in the processing of the manuscript go to the following persons: Sue Watson for earlier drafts, Catherine (Hill) Foreman for a picture of James Scott, Destine Pascual for various copying/computing, J. Wendel Cox, a postdoctoral research associate in Indian history and computing at Arizona State University, Pat Nay of Tempe and Arizona State University for final processing, Steve Walker, ex-chair and colleague in political science at Arizona State for his encouragement, and, finally, Professor Duane Champagne and Pamela Grieman, both of UCLA's American Indian Studies Center for their sustained encouragement and support.

Please note that many Creek words are italicized and used in this text. Usually, an English spelling close to the sound is used with the Creek spelling next to it in its first usage. The glossary at the end, which supplies both English and Creek spellings, should be helpful.

DEDICATION

To the late Wilburn and Mary Hill, the late James Scott who walked the Trail of Tears, Chitto Harjo, and those Creek leaders who struggled for the survival of the Creek ways under very difficult circumstances. Fourfold thanks (*mvto, mvto, mvto, mvto*).

Due to the passing of my coauthor and life partner after the completion of the draft manuscript, this dedication is also to the loving memory of Jean Chaudhuri (Haya-atke/Hiyvtke, Ella Jean Hill). Per tradition her remains were buried in the same place as her umbilical cord after birth.

Vnokeckv, mvto

THE MUSCOGEE CREEK PATH:
AN INTRODUCTION

The Muscogee Creek people historically were one of the largest groups of aboriginals in North America before Columbus and before new European diseases and epidemics, battles for survival, and the forcible removal from Georgia, Florida, and Alabama to Oklahoma in the 1830s severely reduced their numbers. They were core participants and inheritors of the broad Mississippian culture and core creators of the southeastern cultural umbrella before Columbus. There is a considerable amount of literature about their conflicts with the Europeans and later Americans. The literature is stronger with respect to the external elements in summarizing their movements, locations, and the actions of the Europeans and considerably weaker in capturing their aboriginal perspectives—the inner world of the Creeks.

This work, which has involved many decades of experience, participation, and research, attempts to close the significant gap in the literature and tries to share a credible and coherent understanding of the internal world of Creek values. The phrase, *the Creek mind*, signifies the world of values based on Creeks' understanding of nature and their culture; no disputations in social science jargon regarding the meaning of the mind is intended. Creeks often called, and traditionals even now call, this world of values the sacred path. As in the case of any discussion of values of a large tribe or community, there are regional diversities and differing shades of perceptions in different individuals. Many Creek stories have yet to be told. What is attempted in this work is to illustrate the coherence of the main pathway and the common dimensions of the Creek world.

This book attempts to convey Creek values and views and translate them into the perennial questions underlying social philosophy, including concepts of nature, genesis, the formation of society, gender relations, the system of decision-making and conflict resolution, religious views, the socioeconomic system, the relationship between the known and the unknown, perceptions of "outside" groups, and ultimately a sense of their own history. Despite the historical lack of a written language, Creeks had an elaborate and complex civilization. Capturing a sense of it involves a knowledge of the language and an in-depth understanding of what the keepers of the traditions were trying to mean and say. The Creek language is full of nuances, idiomatic expressions, and double and triple meanings; merely formal training in the language often misses the tacit assumptions and intentions of what social science patronizingly used to call "informants." The intention of this work is to illustrate the rich interconnectedness of the values of the Creek world, not to disturb the remaining traditional aspects of Creek life or to cause disturbance of that life by others.

A cornucopia of Creek stories, legends, and myths exists. When properly analyzed and understood and not trivialized into only children's stories, these stories, legends, and myths encapsulate within them the carefully nurtured values of the Creek way. Like many other value systems the Creek way points toward the ideal. Practice and behavior can fall short of the ideals that provide the normative cultural standards. To understand the Creek values at work is not an easy task. Apart from the need to know the language and have good oral history sources, several interrelated yet distinct principles appear to be important.

First, epistemological distinctions between Creek and European ways of describing entities must sometimes be infused into the inquiry, at least for illustrative purposes. Dictionary definitions will not do. For instance, mainstream Christian thinking conceives of a bracketed, reified, individual self and soul. Fundamental Creek thought also eschews the existence of atomistic permanent souls, selves, and entities. The Creek entities—"all my relations"—male, female, human and non-human, known and unknown, are all part of a continuum of energy that is at the heart of the universe. The continuum of energy and spirit, *boea fikcha/puyvfekcv*, and the ever-present principles of transformation and synergy illuminate the meaning of all-important entities in the Creek world.

Second, the pluralistic and decentralized nature of Muscogee (Creek) society has resulted in many regional differences in the details of the legends within the confederacy, as well as many versions of local and clan stories. The logic of the main legends is widely shared, but the details and spinoff clan stories can vary. Thus, many Oklahoma animal stories are known among the Florida Muscogee/Creek Seminoles. However, in addition to the presence of the familiar rabbit and bear in the Oklahoma stories, some of the Florida versions of the same stories will include more frequent appearances of the alligator.

Third, changes in Creek society caused by the sustained clash with the dominant society make for a difficult task in preserving the oral history and therefore much of the Creek perspectives on their history. On top of the dislocations and fragmentations of violence, war, and rebellion come the varying perceptions of at least four contemporary factions of recent and contemporary Creek society who adhere to varying fragments of Creek values. There are the deeply Christianized Creeks, many of whom have not formally learned or have forgotten or suppressed many Creek beliefs and may wander back and forth to and from traditional practices. A second faction includes mixed-bloods for whom one or both sets of clan lineages are now missing or unknown. They presently appear to number at least half the Creek population. Even in the early days of European contact, through a combination of rape, liaisons, and intermarriages, a class of culturally alienated mixed-bloods developed. Their perceptions and interests were often different from that of most full-bloods. A third faction, the bureaucrats, possibly overlaps with the other categories. This faction follows the familiar behavioral patterns of a colonial bureaucracy emulating or attempting to emulate middle-class mores. The final faction consists of the unchristianized or very superficially Christianized Creek full-bloods who attempt to maintain Creek beliefs and practices in differing degrees. One can then add individual personality differences of character, intelligence, and knowledge over the layers of factional roots and Creek traits in order to understand the diversity of contemporary Creek values.

In addition to epistemic issues, regional variations, and cultural factions, a fourth caveat in understanding the Creek world is in the aesthetics of the legends and stories. The entire corpus of classic Creek stories and legends is intricately interrelated in both substance and form. In matters of substance, a story or legend can highlight a set of values without necessarily contradicting different ethical values brought out in a different story and context. Thus, in the creation story the turtle may play a benevolent role and illustrate the values of Mother Earth. In a second story, his shell may be crushed in order to show the effects of pride and the virtue of humility. As we shall see, these are not contradictory values.

In matters of form, a major story or a legend will often have a major story line. However, one event or interaction of characters can open up an elaborate network of interconnecting spinoff stories. The parts or spin-offs do not contradict the main story but may appear to do so to someone who is quick to reify and reduce. Thus, in the legends involving the emergence of man, the main story line involves the surfacing of the turtle, whereas spinoff stories may involve an eagle and a dove looking for land. Historically, aesthetically, and logically these are all chapters and parts of the same cosmological view. The final caveat is that even with our best efforts, areas of Creek values will remain unclear because of the loss of the best Creek minds in the wars, the massacres, the Trail of Tears, and the erosion of language and oral transmission. Continuing the erosion is the massive and rapid urbanization that began with the end of World War II.

The full-blood storytellers, using Creek language through the late forties and early fifties, were the intellectual guardians of a major watershed in Creek history. They were connected with the Trail of Tears themselves or in their immediate family circle. Based on their legacy and with appropriate genuflection to the literature, the subsequent chapters in this book attempt to show the inner coherence of the Muscogee concepts of nature, religion, community, gender relations, ritual, intergroup relations, governance, the system of production, conceptions of health and the magic of nature, and, finally, the unfolding and unraveling of their experience with the coming of Columbus.

LINKS TO THE COSMOS:
MOUNDS, SUN, MOON, AND STARS

Concepts of nature are deeply interrelated in most traditional philosophical and cultural systems, in contrast to western culture which, at least
since Descartes and Kant, has tended to distinguish between the world of
science and the world of culture. The relationship between nature and
culture is very deeply interconnected in the Muscogee Creek world.
However, the terrors of the European invasions, the killing of the Creek
historians and priests, the forced migrations, and the creation of colonial
America and the United States resulted in gaps of knowledge and erosions
of ritual elements in the Creek way of life. Despite these losses, the important connections between Creek conceptions of nature and culture are
clearly evident in what we know of their history and in the core elements of
contemporary traditional values.

Astronomy, chemistry, and botany, from a Creek point of view, are integral roots of Creek values. Creeks were deeply interested in living in
harmony with nature and therefore paid great attention to the details of
nature as well as to the construction of ethical, medical, political, and social
rules. Nature was not merely external, to be examined and conquered;
rather, humans were part of it and had particular trusteeship responsibilities
for caring for the rest of nature. Unlike in biblical civilizations, in Creek
cosmology there was no fall from grace; traditionally, Creeks conceive of
themselves as being in the equivalent to a Garden of Eden, charged with
taking great care with all the rules of nature. Now, as in the past, Creeks
pray for all their relations—seen, unseen, and unknown—a single cosmic
string of energy runs through all.

In studying the rules of nature, the Creeks had their specialists: the calendar priests (those who understood the stars), those who understood plants and animals, and those who understood diseases and their cures. Such specialization did not result in permanent castes and hierarchies. The specialists' authority was contextual; the medicine man, for instance, did not lead in war strategy directly. His or her authority was exercised in the context of medicine, and perhaps only one kind of medicine. Similarly, in matters of astronomy neither scientific nor related political authority was centralized. Designated inhabitants of each regional ceremonial ground knew enough about the positions of the sun in order to make their own determinations regarding appropriate festivals or tasks. No great pharaoh or great living human sun exists in the traditional Creek world of authority. Perceptions of nature were cross-checked with the perceptions of other trained observers, thus providing the seedbed for a decentralized but cooperative political system and network.

The Creek conception of the cosmos bears similarities to other traditional societies that placed great importance on the sun and the relationship of the sun to other objects in space and time. However, the uniqueness of the Creek views provides the key to Creek values which had similarities, but also great differences, from the detailed conceptions and values of other American Indian tribes and societies.

THE MOUNDS AND THE SUN

The Creeks were at the center of the mound builder's culture in the south, southeast, and midwestern United States.[1] Their oral history abounds with stories of mounds of various shapes—round, rectangular, oval, flat-topped, conical, and even serpentine. In their oral Creeks were extensive travelers, not merely for trading purposes but also for ritual and natural pilgrimages. They traveled by boat in the Gulf of Mexico and took regular journeys north through the Mississippi Valley into the Midwest and Ohio regions. Again, given the confederated nature of Creek society, they generally had good relationships with such tribes as the Shawnees in the north, which persisted through the rebellions against the Americans in the time of Tecumseh, whose mother apparently was a Creek.

The famous but abandoned Cahokia mounds in St. Louis may possibly have been part of the Creek world as part of the umbrella of Mississippian Valley culture. Certainly, the evidences of astronomical research at the Cahokia remains and the Creek oral history relating the importance of mounds for observation and ritual interactions with the cosmos and their cosmological views have their parallel. Certainly, the mounds in Georgia, Alabama, and many other parts of the southeast were located in known Creek country just before Columbus. The post-Columbus Creeks are the most logical centerline descendants of the mound builders of the so-called Mississippian culture. Some of the values of that tradition, in a diffused manner, were spread among the other southeastern Indians.

Many of the mounds served as the observatories of the Creeks. High, flat areas with various arrangements of long poles provided the necessary elaborate sets of empirical readings for answering the basic astronomical questions that Creeks traditionally were interested in. From oral history alone it is clear that they were interested in the "true" or polar north, south, east, and west; these directions provided important paths or sets of values. Even now, the four logs of the ceremonial fire (which is related to the sun) must be laid according to the four cardinal directions. The four arbors in contemporary ceremonial grounds are also lined up according to the four cardinal directions. After abandoning the mounds, single poles and their shadows and also the North Star aided in fixing the directions.

The elaborate mounds and multiple poles of the past provided much more information than the directions. However, even in abandoning the mounds, possibly in response to massive flooding or other disasters, the Creeks maintained their central information system regarding the sun. Even now, every ceremonial ground has a central pole. With one pole rather than the multiple poles on mounds, one can find the polar north and then infer other directions. The eastern sun's longest shadow in the morning and the western sun's late afternoon shadow of the same length gives us an angle and also a triangle. If this angle or triangle is bisected or halved at the pole, the bisecting line points exactly to the north away from the pole.

Additionally, by laboriously drawing the circles between morning and afternoon shadows of the same length, one can find the full length of the sun's apparent "journey," that is, the summer and winter solstices. The sun "hesitates" or "visits" at the horizon for four days, a confirmation, in addition to the directions, of the sacredness of the number four. Creek ceremonies, rituals, healing practices, and medicine-making often use the number four or multiples of four. The number four is important in space (cardinal directions) and in counting time as well. Daytime is counted into four equal sun-related parts, and the word for the times of the day, even now in the days of watches, derives from a term for the sun, *hassi/hvse*.

The oral history of the Muscogee Creeks repeatedly refers to the historical importance of the mounds, *gun halwa/kvnhvlwv, igan halwaji/ekvnhvlwv, igan halwa/igan ekvnhvlwuce*, for more measurements and ceremonies related to the sun beyond what the remaining poles provide in contemporary ceremonial grounds. The earlier astronomy is reputed to provide additional information about the passages of the sun and the relationship to other heavenly bodies.

The Cahokia mounds in East St. Louis and possibly the Incinerator Site in Ohio show some parallels to Creek curiosities.[2] While many southeastern groups shared some similar features, the Creeks easily provide the most elaborate, continuing, and consistent examples of southeastern thinking. The Cherokees are relative latecomers into the southeast in their journey southward from the Iroquois areas.

The mound numbered seventy-two by archeologists at Cahokia appears to have defined a "carefully calculated north-south center line at Cahokia."[3] All of the mounds "appear to have been laid out according to an astronomical plan designed around the cardinal directions."[4] At number seventy-two at "sunrise on the winter solstice the shadow of the post would fall right along the axis of the mound." As the sun rose and moved south, the shadow would move north of the ridge. On the summer solstice, the setting sun would cause the post to cast its shadow along the axis of the ridge in the opposite direction.[5] The lineup of the two shadows, if marked, constitutes a straight line.

With what historians of astronomy classify as the apparent annual motion of the sun, the line will gradually circle *counterclockwise* in the Creek world or the northern hemisphere. Therefore, for the Creeks the apparent "motion" of the sun is counterclockwise around the earth. As the late Micco Tony Hill[6] (a relative of Jean Chaudhuri) of Asalanabi ceremonial grounds pointed out, in following the path of the sun, the Creek stomp dances move counterclockwise around the ceremonial fire, which symbolizes the sun. Many other tribes' dances, including those performed at contemporary intertribal powwows, in contrast, are clockwise in their motion. For traditional Creeks, since the empirical cosmic central reference point is the sun, the aesthetics of the dance follows the counterclockwise annual motion of the sun. Not only the sun but the entire network of seven bodies—the sun, the moon, and the five then-known planets—*appeared* to follow a similar counterclockwise direction.

Since the sun, the moon, and five planets are key bodies in space, this contributed to other Creek conceptions of natural authority—such as possibly the seven *miccos* (*mekko*/chief of specified function) of Creek tradition. The seven visible stars of the Pleiades provide another set of seven spirits. The number seven also shows up in the key idea of seven directions, another key Creek concept of space. The seven directions include the four cardinal directions. The fifth would be the center of the observer—the *boea fikcha/puyvfekcv/fekcv*, fire within spirit, or energy. The sixth would be downward into the earth. The seventh would be upward toward the sky. The seven points or coordinates provided the temporal spatial framework, while the cyclical "motion" of the sun in measured multiples of four provided the temporal framework of Creek life.

In addition to their curiosity about the "motion" of the sun, moon, and the planets, Creeks also observed the equinoxes. The two equinoxes and the two solstices mark the beginnings and ends of the four seasons of observable nature. In the northern hemisphere of the Creek lands the shadows of the poles in the autumn equinox point due west at sunrise and due north at sunset.[7] The Cahokia mounds also appear to confirm the interest of the mound-builders in the equinoxes.[8] The thesis of a possible Creek connection at Cahokia is bolstered by the presence of several Creek characteristics.

These include first the idea of mounds; second, the use of cedar posts and postholes; and third, the finding of "carved and polished stone disks that may have come from the southeast."[9]

Other excavated sites such as the Incinerator Site in Ohio[10] and the Crystal River Site in Florida[11] also appear to confirm the symmetries of Creek beliefs and practices. Even the serpent mounds of Ohio and elsewhere may be ritually linked with Creek science and Creek values. The Creek oral history repeatedly mentions that the Creeks traditionally went north to special mounds for pilgrimages in spring and autumn. Creeks regarded the mountains, rivers, and valleys as having been created by giant serpents or snakes accompanied by the trembling of the earth. The earth trembles in many Creek stories dealing with the cycles of creation and destruction. The work of the snakes realigns the fundamental elements of Creek physics—water, earth, fire, and air—which are different forms of energy as we will see in subsequent chapters. The creation of the mountains is an important link in the energy cycles of the evaporation of water and the regeneration of the earth by rain. This is discussed in greater detail in a subsequent chapter on agriculture.

Mounds are in part symbols of this link—platforms for studying the sky "scientifically" and placating nature ritually. *Gun halwa or igan halwa* (high place) and *gun halwaji* (little high place) are terms that are used interchangeably for mounds. The fascination with mounds is primarily associated with the Creeks and other culturally related tribes, not with the Iroquois, Siouan, or the Kiowa and Comanche groupings.

The southeastern precursors of people later on called Creeks had elaborate mounds and temples.[12] In the lower Mississippi Valley, as part of the "Coles Creek" culture, were temples that "were a repository of images of the supernaturals."[13] The migration of the Creeks to Georgia was accompanied by the creation of many mounds—not as large, perhaps, as the ones in Cahokia but reiterating the importance of mounds nevertheless. With the repeated survival challenges and the coming of the Europeans, the physical presence of mounds began to diminish—remaining today only in legends, stories, rituals, and ceremonial symbolism. The mounds keep shrinking, but in the transformations one catches a glimpse of their importance. Until quite recently, in Christianized Creek burial grounds in Oklahoma, they made elevated mounds, platforms, and structures reflexively.

Serpent- and snake-like mounds in some areas could well be physical evidence of the Creek conception of snake-like forces working in nature. Contemporary geologists speak of S-forces, which are sidewinder-like seismic forces. P-forces are rollercoaster-like, sinuous forces and stop-and-go forces that move like repeated snake strikes. The Creek conception of snakes creating the formations of the earth are early parallels of these geological conceptions. Some of the snake-like mounds could have honored these forces as well as acting as sites for storage and observatories of natural phenomena. These forces of nature are still celebrated and imitated in various snake dances and doubleheader snake dances in the contemporary Creek stomp dance repertoire. The oral traditions of the Creeks refer to visiting the pilgrimage sites to the north and also making contacts with other tribes around Florida and the Gulf of Mexico. The connection of mounds is suggestive in some of these interactions, at least in the oral tradition.

THE MOON AND THE SUN

In addition to the sun being a strong male force in nature, providing energy and shaping concepts of space and time, the other bodies in the heavens also help to shape Creek life. The moon is female, but she too has a special energy. The moon also assists in determining time. The Creeks, like many other societies, used a combination of a solar and a lunar calendar. Given the measurement problems involved in coordinating both solar and lunar sequences, this gave the leeway of authority to village *miccos* in consultation with calendar priests, *hilis haya-s/heleshayv*/medicine men, and others to specify the details of the timing of the dances, the celebrations, and other events.

As in so many other societies, the moon was associated with the counting of the menstrual cycles, with changes in men's temperaments with respect to women, with the timing of some ceremonies, and with other elements and events in nature. The moon has important female energy and had an important role in the timing of the lives of women. Menstruation was not "evil" in the Creek world. It was a time for withdrawal from sex and interactions with men, but also for great empowerment of women. During the withdrawal period, while the men were shut out, the real educational development and empowerment of women took place. So much of anthropological work has depended on male "informants" that the woman's world and its crucially important role in the Creek world is repeatedly and deeply misunderstood and missed. The later discussion of Creek women in this work will expand this theme. It is sufficient to point out that the entire educational system and instructions from women elders took place in these menstrual lunar cycles.

Creek stargazers, astronomers, or *miccos* attempted to understand lunar eclipses. Fascination with and fear of eclipses were common in many traditional societies. For the Creeks, however, lunar eclipses were meaningful acts of sheer beauty. They spoke in terms of love—of the bashful female moon putting a veil over a private tryst with the male sun and then devouring the sun with love. The Creeks knew that after enticements (partial eclipses) the final tryst, that is, the full lunar eclipse and its special relationship with the sun, occurred once every eighteen years and, according to oral history, special ceremonies occurred at this time. This was the Creek equivalent of the Babylonian and Hindu/Buddhist *saros* cycle allowing for differences in meaning for a year. If we use contemporary definitions of a year, the full lunar eclipse cycle takes a little longer than eighteen years. The shift to Gregorian and modern calendars also results in shifting meanings of a year. The "metonic" cycle counts nineteen years as the time between cycles.[14] But if we stick to the Creek tradition of counting months by "moons," then observationally a full lunar eclipse occurs once in eighteen years. Counting months by lunar measurements gradually results in a disjunction between the lunar months and the timing of the four seasons—spring, summer, fall, and winter—which are determined more dominantly by the behavior of the sun. The sun-based shifts of the harvest, however, again become correlated with the lunar monthly cycles every eighteen lunar years, hence, the importance of the full lunar eclipse as a coordinate for calculations of time.

The importance of the eighteen-year cycle is corroborated by Creek stories. A generation is an eighteen-year cycle—after that, a new generation or "spiritual regeneration" occurs. In Creek beliefs when the "wedding" of the moon and the sun takes place every eighteen years, a new set of spirits is created which invigorates the earth under the blessings of the seven *miccos* of the Pleiades. It is in these eighteen-year adjustments that the creative "miracles" of new spirits and energies are infused in nature and in human societies and cycles.

The astronomical calendar conceptions and the eighteen-year adjustments of lunar and solar calculations have their counterpart in Creek stories. This tricky adjustment is one of the reasons for the birth of the trickster in the person of the rabbit. Chapter eleven will develop this theme of magic and trickery in more detail. We concentrate now on the role of the rabbit in the tricky eclipse connections between solar and lunar journeys.

Originally the rabbit was not regarded as a trickster but as a member of the little animal world. Rabbit came to the ceremonial grounds and asked the people to join their circle around a fire. However, suddenly the fire seemed to go out and it became very dark. There was some confusion and people sensed that Rabbit was running away with a large bag. They caught Rabbit, and in that process Rabbit stumbled. When Rabbit stumbled, first the moon came out again, followed by the sun. People from that time on regarded Rabbit as a trickster and his stumbling created the broken, separate rhythms of the lunar and solar cycles which are connected with new energies every eighteen years. But since then, we always have to be aware of the tricky rabbit when trying to understand the regularities and the intervals in the cosmos. In another story, Rabbit was near a mound and was given a flute by an earth spirit so that he could make sweet music to bring complementaries and male-female unity together; this points toward the tricky marriage of the sun and the moon at full eclipse time.

The creation of the moon, the stars, and the earth is also represented in creation legends and is discussed in a subsequent chapter on the Creek genesis. The moon, when in its phases related to full eclipses, was supposed to "swallow the sun" in a symbolically sexual union of male and female energies. Out of these unions new energies were released into earthly and human affairs and new versions and ideals of the "perfect man" and the "perfect woman" were infused into human life on earth.

THE STARS

As we shall see in the chapter on genesis, other heavenly bodies, especially the stars, were created out of the interactions of the sun and the moon. In addition to the moon, these other heavenly bodies fascinated the Creeks, both in astronomy and in the construction of values. The Milky Way was an important collection of energy, functioning in the Creek view of life as a sacred white pathway between earth and the ultimate energy or great universal spirit and *ibofanga/epohfunkv*. It provides the last path to cross in life's journey before we return to the original source of energy. Legends and stories also included the Taurus and Pleiades systems, with Taurus figured as a buffalo and Pleiades figured as seven spirits. The big and little dippers— seen as boats rather than dippers—were integrated into the stories.

Astronomy was only one part of nature. Creek life and values were shaped deeply by their perceptions of aboriginal botany, physics, chemistry, and other guideposts to the work of the sum total of energy and spirit, Ibofanga. In later chapters, we shall see the impact of astronomy, botany, physics, and chemistry on the Creek genesis, the social and economic system, and Creek religion and magic.

Despite the growth of modern scientific theories, the behavior of repeatedly observed empirical phenomena and their implications still holds true for the same reference points. Modern science has marched on to larger generalizations that supposedly have absorbed the truths of traditional theories. While this may be mathematically true, the nature-culture balancing and the insightful, ethical elements of a world like that of the Creeks have not been carefully transferred into contemporary times. From the perspective of many traditional elders, modern living has thrown out the baby of wisdom with the bathwater of an older science, and displays a deepening chasm between nature and culture. Modern living, therefore, to many traditional Creeks, goes hand in hand with the revenges of traditionally conceived nature in crises of the environment and the far deeper accompanying crises of the spirit.

The perceived danger, according to and in terms of Creek prophecies, is that if we do not live in natural and cultural harmony, destruction by fire and flood is likely. Those who live in harmony will return deep into the earth and Mother Nature for regeneration. For others, the journey to regeneration takes considerably longer and is possibly scary.

NOTES

1. For a broad discussion, see especially Chapter III in Ruth M. Underhill, *Red Man's America: A History of Indians in the United States* (Chicago: University of Chicago Press, 1953).

2. For a good review of the astronomical significance of the Cahokia and incinerator excavations, see Ray A. Williamson, *Living the Sky: The Cosmos of the American Indian* (Norman: University of Oklahoma Press, 1984), 236–268. In addition to Williamson, the authors are indebted to Daniel Matlaga of the Department of Physics and Astronomy at Arizona State University, whose keen interests include historical astronomy, and Byron Schneid, a practicing geologist with an interest in planetary geology. For another discussion about Cahokia's contributions, see Jack Weatherford, *Native Roots: How the Indians Enriched America* (New York: Fawcett Columbine, 1991), 6–18.

3. Melvin Fowler quoted in Williamson, *Living the Sky*, 242.

4. Williamson, *Living the Sky*, 243.

5. Ibid., 244.

6. Conversation with authors, July 1993, Asalanabi grounds. Micco means "chief."

7. For a general guide on observing the shadows in autumn see Deborah Boyd, "Eye on the Sky," *Astronomy* 21:9 (September 1993).

8. Williamson, *Living the Sky*, 246.

9. Ibid., 241.

10. Ibid., 250–256.

11. Ibid., 258–262.

12. See Ruth Underhill, *Red Man's America*, 42–43.

13. Ibid.

14. For comparative definitions of *saros*, metonic, and other calculations of solar and lunar eclipse cycles and the calculations at Stonehenge, see Gerald S. Hawkins in collaboration with John B. White, *Stonehenge Decoded* (Surrey: Delta, 1965), especially 178. For the return of the positions of the solar seasons after each *saros* cycle, see Anthony Aveni, *Skywatchers of Ancient Mexico* (Austin: University of Texas Press, 1980), 66–82.

Muscogee Genesis:
The Creation of the Earth and
the Emergence of the Clans

The creation myth of the Muscogee Creeks is a complex, sequential, and evolutionary story with many subsidiary stories, chapters, and spinoff themes. It is a major door to the Creek mind with lots of peepholes, each of which offers an interesting but partial glimpse of the Creek value system. Unless properly interconnected, many of the fragments and spin-offs can give a misleading view of the entire symphony of creation and trivialize the content into children's stories or fragments. Without delving deeply into appropriate oral history, many of the holes in this elaborate jigsaw puzzle cannot be filled.

A major source of field notes on Creeks is the classic work by John R. Swanton, which deals with aspects of the large creation legend only briefly.[1] Before describing fragments of the myth, he repeats the story of the earth as an island and then notes the following: "I have been told that there was once a long myth of this kind, most of which has been lost."[2] Swanton also draws upon fragments recreated from the non-analytical, somewhat haphazard, earlier collection of Creek stories in the archival manuscript of W. O. Tuggle entitled *Myths of Creeks*.[3] Many of Tuggle's tales are Uncle Remus kinds of stories, most of which appear to be adaptations of Creek stories which became diffused in African American and Anglo folk stories. This creation legend, however, is more than a child's story. It is a powerful theology and is symbolically honored and entwined with Creek traditional ceremonies even today. While there are some regional differences in details, the main logic of the myth and the analytical comments proceeds as follows.[4]

IN THE BEGINNING: THE CREEK CREATION MYTH

Four elements were the instruments of the ultimate and singular universal spirit, Ibofanga: fire (later formed into Grandfather Sun), master of breath or wind (Hesagedamesse/Hesaketvmese), water, and earth. Christians make Hesagedamesse into the Christian God, whereas traditionally he was, and to contemporary traditionalists remains, just an assistant to Ibofanga. The first two elements were male principles while the second two were female. Fire in the form of light, or the sun, was above. The wind or breath or air was all around. Further below was water, which was regenerated by the interaction of heat and air as part of a cycle of evaporation and rain. Below the water was what was to become earth as we now know it.

Deep in the womb of the earth was darkness, a land of dreams and desires of knowing. The reference to darkness is important. Some Creek informants apparently have told interviewers that Creeks came from the west or that they poured out of the earth. To understand these metaphorical fragments we should note that in Creek values, darkness or blackness is the color of the west. So coming from the west and coming from darkness are equivalent. Creek conversations abound with double meanings. In the dark world of desires and dreams, incomplete but living things like seeds were stirring, desiring knowledge and completeness in the womb of Mother Earth. Mother Earth was covered by water, and the interaction and dialogue between earth and water resulted in further development, flow, and infusion of energies into embryonic living things.

At this point, we will avoid spinoff stories, which include the story of a snake-like creature that went through a hole at the bottom of the ocean and shared information with others about various underwater worlds, thus pointing to the existence of multiple worlds. The main legend continues with the stirring of living things in the mixture of the earth and the water, which constituted the beginning of the second world where the light was still very hazy and living things bumped into each other yet managed to communicate and where enlightenment continued. Living things thirsted for knowledge, and earth and water wanted to release the pent-up development of energies in the muddy underworld. The living creatures wanted to break through the muddy world into greater light. Crawfish volunteered to lead the way through the mixture of water and earth, but could not completely be freed from mud.

At this point the turtle, an early earth form and amphibious creature—versatile in water, mud, and land—led the way. All the creatures climbed up on, in, and around the turtle's back and the huge turtle gradually emerged through the mud and the water into the third world of a dim light, fog, and air. All the living things poured out onto the top of the turtle—the great transporter in the journey of birth and enlightenment.

The continuity of the Creek values for traditionals exists in contempo-

rary unconscious links to the creation legend. In contemporary Creek ceremonial grounds, after the earth is dampened with sprinkled water, the
micco's assistant calls out, *loja loja/loca*, a symbolic call to the turtle for
assistance in the ritualized journey to enlightenment in the stomp dance,
which begins in darkness and finishes with the light of the rising sun. After
the beginning of the initial rituals the women dancers still enter the grounds
today with the turtle shakers or equivalents on their legs—another contemporary symbolic link to the legend of creation. Turtle was the original transporter to the world of light and knowledge. Designated people will again call
to the turtle, *loja, loja*, in order to encourage the female dancers and the
journey of the turtle. The turtle's journey, after all, began in earth and water,
which are female spirits and energies.

The third world that was reached on the back of the turtle was
surrounded by a fog above; of course, there was the water around and the
earth below. The living things had more energy and light than they had in
the mud below. But they still did not have clear vision. Since there was at
least air around, they sought the assistance of the birds in their midst who
were and still are now in their appropriate element.

The thread of a theory of evolution of mud creatures, ocean creatures,
animals, and birds can be seen running through the creation legend and the
journey to the knowledge of the world. Gradually the various species differ-
entiate but they are all interrelated. Indeed, the concept of community
extends to all things and is inclusive in nature in the traditional Muscogee
value system.

Two birds, an eagle and a dove, representing protective but peaceful
seekers and messengers, were delegated the authority to explore the environment. They went out for the sacred four days and returned. Some scattered versions of the story about seeing earthworm deposits here and there
exist, but the main thrust is that because of the presence of the thick fog, the
eagle and the dove could not penetrate the barrier just as the crawfish had
not succeeded in getting through the mud. More energy was needed at this
stage. The energy linkages clearly show the Creek conception of aboriginal
physics. The linkages get more and more powerful yet balanced at each
stage. After all, fog itself is a product of the interaction among water, air, and
some heat.

Given the impasse with the fog, the living creatures chanted to the
totality that was out there, the comprehensive spirit, Ibofanga, for help. But
Ibofanga (neither male nor female) was impersonal and busy. So help in the
form of an assistant, Abokta/Vpoktv, a form of male energy, appeared. He
is called Hesagedamesse, the giver and taker of breath.

Hesagedamesse was and is the master of energy in the form of breath,
and breath gives the beginnings of motion and life. Other forms of energy,
such as the sun, were and are needed. The combination of breath and the
sun energized the other elements of the universe, including spirit water and

mother earth in a balanced way. The first two elements are male while the last two are female. So now after the first level of earth has been transformed into the second mud, the primitive living things journey to the third level above the water on turtle island and await the further work of Hesagedamesse, the giver of breath.

Hesagedamesse, in turn, has several assistants or subsidiary forms that blow (wind, air, oxygen) energy in different strengths. Again, the continuity of the Creek mind can be seen: blowing and the related infusion of energy still appear in a variety of contexts in the contemporary Creek world. The blowing into and the bubbling and energizing of medicine by a medicine man with a reed into a bucket or container is one example. The gentle blowing of a healer into injured areas of the body to aid the natural flow of energy by a little pressure is another. The past traditional blowing of conch shells and then buffalo horns is a third. Even in post-Columbus Christian adaptations, Creeks used to blow conch shells before moving to the use of buffalo horns, cow horns, and then the modern swinging and ringing of bells in churches. Some old Creek churches have held onto, without using, conch shells for blowing. Deep lower abdominal breathing in the singing of contemporary Creek churches and the spontaneous ringing of the bell to designate unity of the spirit by a spiritually energized person are some cultural fragments of the work of Hesagedamesse, the master of breath who helped the original Creeks in their journey on the back of the amphibious turtle as they waited, lost in the fog.

Hesagedamesse's assistants include breath in the form of several winds. Depending on the method of counting, there are four or five winds, the fifth being a "sacred" synthesis of the first four and appropriate for removing the fog and providing a clear (oxygen) environment for our turtle island sticking out of the mud and water.

The four basic winds include Boja/Puca, grandfather, the tornado, which appears when the physical conditions are there. Tornado would have destroyed the fledgling community. The second form is a gentle wind which can blow evenly. The third is a blowing storm wind, and the fourth is a little twisting "dust devil" that is silly but does not harm; it is illustrative of the "silly" aspects of life. Different degrees of male energy make up each of the winds. Hesagedamesse sent a special, gentle, evenly blowing wind from the east to remove the fog from turtle island. While some other eastern tribes also have turtles in their myths, the Creek myth has its own unique logic.

The removal of the fog constituted the fourth world in the creation odyssey of humans. In this fourth world, living things began to create complementary groupings—among humans, clans. The divisions of labor and clarification of all the relationships of nature and society emerged in this stage. Striving for cooperation and harmony was needed for continued survival after the gift of Hesagedamesse. When the breath-giver's sacred wind blew the fog away, the living things "saw" the panorama of nature's beauty for the first time. The gentle wind blew away also some of the debris, including living matter that was not stable or carefully handled, into the water around the earth/turtle island. These debris and cast-offs were the source of the rise of sea monsters' pollution and other evils in nature. The legend here is instructive of the dangers of the handling of waste matter, the creation of rot and stagnation, and the sources of evil pollution in the waters. Evil is in the continuum of the universe and arises when proper balancing of the elements is lost.

The Creation of the Sun

The blowing away of the fog exposed the living things to an intense light, another form of the energy of Ibofanga, the macroscopic atom that comprises the universe where the games of life and death occur.

Living things were initially exhilarated by the intense light. But soon it became evident that just as the darkness of the underworld was one extreme, perpetually intense light was another. So the living things held a great council to confer on the problem of the sustained intensity of light. All living things initially could communicate in an intuitive, vibrational language. Some, like the bear, argued for the return of darkness so he could sleep more. The wise deer, however, suggested a compromise between day and night so that a balance between reflection and rest on the one hand and growth and activity on the other could occur. The deer pointed to the alternate circles of white and black rings on the raccoon's tail and suggested a parallel reality of night and day. Hesagedamesse understood the needs of living things and began to respond to the needs.

Theologically, at this point several things can be pointed out. The conversations with Hesagedamesse were intuitive and integrated in character. There is no disjunction between "I" and "thou," soul and spirit, creator and created epistemologically speaking. Ibofanga's energy and, therefore, the *abokta* or assistant Hesagedamesse's breath is in all. Thus, the vibration or "communications" in one part of the universe has meaning in the others. The general and the particular are related by energy. Energy and mass are interchangeable in the Creek world.

Given the transformation principle, Hesagedamesse intensely rubbed his hands, causing friction, shifting cool energy to hot in the manner that Creeks originally used to rub sticks to create fire. The friction drew much of the waves of energy, including light, into a concentrated ball of fire as a heat and light source was gathered in one place.

Hesagedamesse then set the concentrated energy, or ball of fire, into motion by blowing it gently into space, thereby creating the sun and also thereby controlling the source of light.

The Creation of the Moon

Then by gentle kneading of energy and matter that was not fiery, that is, mud and water, the moon was created as a cool ball and set into motion with a balanced breath of Hesagedamesse. Grandfather Sun and Grandmother Moon were created and related to each other. Similarly, other planets were set into motion to further balance the family led by the sun and the moon to visibly circle around the earth island.

Thus, Hesagedamesse took into account the nature of living things: the rain, thunder, and spirit water. Continuous, uncontrolled, intense, and ever-present light and heat could burn the plants and animals. Intense, ever-present bright light could also dry up the mists, the rains, and the presence of water in many things. So the centralization of Grandfather Sun and the balances with the moon and the planets created a balanced system, male and female, each with an element of the other so there can be continuous balanced growth and development of living things.

Stars in the Sky

A beautiful spinoff story then poetically speaks of the creation of the stars. Mother Earth got into an argument with the sun, saying that the sun needed to stay a little longer so the work on earth could be finished. The sun scolded her, saying that daylight was enough. So Mother Earth reached for the sun to force him to help. Fiery bits of energy stuck to her fingers. She quickly stuck her fingers into the surrounding water and flung her hands and fingers upward with a sweeping and arching motion across the sky. This created the stars in the skies which are hidden when the sun is out, but creates the sparkling of the stars and the fiery meteors and fragments racing across the night sky. The touches of light at night enable the loose ends of the day's work to be finished. Similarly, there are bits of cloudiness and darkness in daytime, softening the dominance of the sun and enabling the cycles of rising vapors and rains to do their work.

The beautiful astronomical legends give us a picture of the balance of male and female energies, thereby showing the patch of darkness in light and light in darkness, all circling in the search for harmony in motion.

The legends provide a humanities parallel of the science of the Creeks which also sees the search for a balance between the four elements and the synergy linking the cycles of the dynamic energies of the earth, the water, the sun (fire), and the sky (air). This is no romantic pipe dream but the vision of an *earth-centered* culture with sacred trust responsibilities. The earth-centered physics involves exchanges between and transformations of various forms of energy and the cycles of energy exchanges among soil, water, nutrients, animals, sunlight, air, and rain in an environmentally balanced manner.

The removal of the fog and the balancing of the energies around earth so that the emerged living things can survive is the essence of the fourth world. The remaining challenge was the development and emergence of the fifth world where under Ibofanga's umbrella and Hesagedamesse's watchful eyes the divisions of labor and functions were set into motion and the architecture of law and the social order were designed.

THE FIFTH WORLD: THE COMING OF THE CLANS

The key puzzles of the first four worlds of the Muscogee Creeks closely fit each other if the Creek conceptions of the four elements, the seven directions, the time-space continuum of Creek astronomy, the loving ascension of body, mind, and spirit, and the gender-balanced dynamics of the relationships of nature are seen as shaping the creation and development of the cosmos. The fifth world deals with the proper preservation of the created world. Here, too, as in the first four worlds, there is an integrated Creek conception that should not be confused with the Greek *logos*, the Judaic dialectics of "I" and "thou," or the patriarchal or hierarchical systems of authority in various parts of the world.

The fifth world of the Creeks begins with the demarcation of the clans and the linking in a revolving network of specialized functions and obligations, including the trusteeship of nature. Specialization did not create a system of caste, although social science often looks for hierarchies. Neither the creation legend nor the traditional Creek practice created superior-inferior sets of clans. The Creek view involved a decentralized set of clans with mutual dependencies that hold forth the ideal of effective specialization within a non-European conception of democracy, loose federalism, or confederation and freedom.

The specialization of the clans in the fifth world created many details in each clan's history. The beaver clan passed on the beaver traditions in their oral history. The bears, the winds, the birds, and all the others did the same with their clan stories. Consequently, even today many bears know more bear stories than beaver stories and vice versa. There are snake stories, deer stories, and many others yet to be told.

Each of the clan stories has its own principles about the history, roles, and obligations of the clan. The number of the clans and the decentralized and diverse nature of Creek society sometimes bewilder outsiders about the relationships of the stories. The true clan stories told by knowledgeable elders of the clan are all connected to the same central worldview as encapsulated in the main trunk of the creation legend. Some regional differences in the details of the story also appear again, given the decentralized socialization patterns of the tribe. Also among the Creeks, as with any other people, degrees of expertise on tribal and cultural history can vary.

In any case, the process of assigning clans began after the removal of the fog. Prior to the coming of the light, the "sight" and knowledge of living things were muddled. Things bumped into each other. Groups associated with each other did the best they could but their knowledge of each other was limited. However, when living things adjusted to the light and the sun they began to understand each other's nature better. Then, with the intuitive supervision of Hesagedamesse and the assistance of Mother Earth, the divisions of labor and the clans began. Mother Earth understood the functions that each organism performed in its early stages, and with the removal of the fog by Hesagedamesse new and harmonious social roles could be assigned in the new world of light.

Human beings already existed together with other living things. Human beings were not animals. However, animals and plants were relatives since they were all part of the recycling of energy. Humans began to be assigned to or were associated with the animal or plant clan with which they shared the greatest characteristics. Even now, when Creeks ask other Creeks what clan they belong to, they are literally asking, "What do you stick to?"

Twelve clans were created at first. A host of other clans were gradually added under the umbrella of an animal or plant, rooted in nature so that all the complementary functions of society remained balanced and clear. The people who provided the leadership in sensing the arrival and importance of the fog-clearing east wind gravitated toward the first gathering of the wind clan, which had some characteristic functions such as being able to foresee and predict the changes in nature, literally "which way the wind blows."

The bear was the gatherer of medicinal plants and berries and was, therefore, the leader in the way of medicine. So those who helped with healing, sickness, and wounds in the days of darkness followed the way of the bear. Those who could integrate a variety of building skills into a cooperative effort gravitated toward the beaver clan, since the world of the beaver is a balance between individuality and community cooperation in building dams and homes.

Birds can fly over great obstructions in their travels and carry information over great distances. So those who showed a nature and talent for running and carrying messages gravitated to the bird clan. The wolf is familial and protective (Grandfather Wolf, Creeks call him), so those with a protective instinct gravitated toward the wolf clan. Those who could detect that slightest distinction and watchfulness with respect to plants and also danger gravitated toward the deer clan.

The small animal and potato clans were added much later than the first twelve clans, representing the evolving natural and social worlds. After the first round of assignment of clans, new clans were added with changes in the membership of the Creek confederacy and changes in migration and regional development.

A series of additional legends provides the legitimacy and the content of the traditional governance of the tribe, the laws of the tribe, and the customs of the tribe. Key legends include the epic story of the battle and conciliation of the red sticks and the white sticks warriors, which illustrates complementary functions of government and society. A story about three spirits provides the foundation of the "natural laws" of the tribe which include environmental protection responsibilities and the primary virtues of love, faith, and compassion. A number of corn women legends pinpoint the notion of unity in tribal diversity, communal obligations, the nature-culture links, and the sanctity of Mother Earth.

In addition to the red stick/white stick legend and the corn mother stories, a third body of animal, snake, and vegetation stories illuminated the maxims of the tribe, which assisted the socialization of young people into the tribal values. Thus ended the symbolic journey of the Creeks from their gestation in the womb of Mother Earth and the beginning of the instruction and responsibilities of her children.

The first caveat in the long and instructive Creek genesis is that if natural harmony is not maintained, Pojasa/Pucasv, an assistant spirit, and Hesagedamesse revisit the earth from time to time and the energies of the elements, particularly fire and flood as well as quakes and storms, will destroy the linkages and possibilities of newer worlds.

Despite the cultural erosion of some elements of the traditional Creek world, the benchmarks of the creation legend underlie the cycles, the sequels, and themes of the stomp dances, including the preludes and postludes of the rituals on the traditional ceremonial grounds where the fire still burns and the call of the turtle is still heard—*loja, loja, loja, loja.*

NOTES

1. John R. Swanton, "Social Organization and Social Usages of the Indians of the Creek Confederacy," *Forty-Second Report of the Bureau of American Ethnology to the Secretary of the Smithsonian Institution, 1924–1925* (Washington: United States Government Printing Office, 1928).

2. Ibid., 487.

3. Manuscript in the archives of the Bureau of American Ethnology. No clear citation is available.

4. The myth has been discussed with many elders listed in the acknowledgments, but the main source for the full narration was the late James Scott of Okemah, Oklahoma, who narrated the myth to Jean's parents first and later to Jean and her brothers in the 1930s and 1940s. As in the oral tradition the story was repeated many times in order to commit it to memory.

WAY OF THE SPIRIT:
THE FIRST PRINCIPLES OF RELIGION

In the Muscogee Creek cosmos, all living things consist of particular combinations of body, mind, and spirit. When these are not in harmony, one is truly lost and healing becomes necessary for the entity to continue. The body, mind, and spirit are related in an ascending order, with the spirit being the highest. When our spirit (*boea fikcha*), or ceremonial fire, dies, we wither and die. Thus, while illnesses of the body and the mind occur, the greatest tragedy is the death of the spirit, which is difficult to regenerate because it has moved on to a different journey.

There is, however, a single, unifying principle in the universe that links every manifestation of body, mind, and spirit. This unifying principle is energy. That energy is the fundamental principle of the universe the Muscogee Creek deduced independently of any other known source. Even though the Creek tradition is oral rather than written, the cosmology, the unifying principle, and the detailed derivations from the principle make for a nexus of scientific, theological, social, and aesthetic theory that is as complex as those of the great written traditions. An understanding of the Muscogee Creek way would dissipate much of the stereotypical and conventional distinctions between supposedly aboriginal, preliterate, simple, and superstitious societies on the one hand and complex, modern, literate, and rational societies on the other.

The energy that exists throughout the universe is both static and dynamic, potential and kinetic. All the manifestations of energy are combined into one single entity, a macroscopic atom, if you will, which traditional Creeks reverentially regard as the most sacred thing, Ibofanga, which covers everything and within which both rest and motion exist.

Ibofanga is above us all and is the unifying principle in the entire energy field which is existence. The field includes links between various entities. The links may appear to be linear at times in the short run, such as in the marriage of a man and a woman, but ultimately and in the long run, Ibofanga is circular in character. Creation and destruction, sending out energy and the return of energy, is all part of the comprehensive energy field and reciprocity that is Ibofanga. Ibofanga's work is so sacred that it is almost sacrilegious to disturb it. Ibofanga is not personalized; it is neither male nor female, though it is the source of male and female energies and all the other reciprocal energies alike. Ibofanga is seldom mentioned in Creek prayers; it works through assistants. One depends on the various assistants of Ibofanga for personal consolation and assistance—such as Hesagedamesse, the master, the giver and taker of breath. It is he, Hesagedamesse, who is mentioned most frequently in Creek prayers and stories. Christians, not understanding Ibofanga, have symbolically transformed Hesagedamesse and appropriated it as God, the Holy Spirit.

There is no imagery involving Ibofanga—it is the ultimate unifying principle of both Creek physics and Creek theology. Nor is there any dualism in ultimate reality beyond the perishables of human, plant, and animal life. Ibofanga is too busy creating, resting, and recharging to be personally involved in the warp and woof of daily affairs. Ibofanga, however, has set in motion laws that govern the universe. Ignoring these laws ignores the principles of Creek science and, therefore, causes disruptions in nature, imbalances, and disease.

The principles of nature include harmony, the bonding between seemingly different elements. The bonding has the element of *eros*, of what Creeks call *anogetchka/vnokeckv*, which is love,[1] hence, the predominance of the values of *eros* and love in Creek approaches to both nature and society. Nature is something to be loved—not conquered. *Logos* and the mind are not enough in Creek values. It is the symbolism of the *heart*, of sensitivity and feeling, that is the physiological analogy used again and again in discussions of Creek values. Very traditional Creeks will talk about *figi/feke*, the heart, which provided the terminal for exchange of *boea fikcha* energy in the field of energy that belongs to *thakko boea fikcha*, the grand energy or spirit, which ultimately Ibofanga, which is the sacred name and not even to be mentioned. It is all-pervasive and invincible. There are no Creek curse words involving Ibofanga.

Various cultures, in their physics, attempt to understand nature in terms of interactions between fundamental elements. So it is with the Creeks. The dynamics of Ibofanga's energy operate through four major elements: air, fire, water, and earth. These elements are *not* material atoms. The form of the energy gives them their personality. These four fundamental elements, with different combinations of energy running through them, account for all the phenomena of the universe. These elements, in turn, are not fixed material entities because they are constantly transformed by energy—the principles of transformation and reciprocity are important keys to the Creek mind.

Without proper understanding of Ibofanga and the four elements, all Creek metaphysics will be regarded as only magic and superstition. Nature, however, with its tricks and quirks, does not appear always as rational. Rabbit the trickster and the clowns of human societies represent these quirks. Some (but not all) of these quirks, and the implications resulting from human failure to work for harmony, are the major sources of evil.

Many cultures have favorite numbers that are used for metaphysics, ritual, and belief. For the Christians it is the trinity, for Hindus it is a combination leading to 108, for Daoists it is eight or sixty-four. For the Creeks, four and multiples of four provide the important numbers and appropriate ratios—in the organization of symbols (four-log fire), in their ethics (four pathways), in their practices (four-day ceremonies for the dead) and four or eight days for the busks/dances. Fours and multiples of fours connect the *external* phenomenal world of the Muscogee Creeks.

IBOFANGA AND THE ASSISTANTS: MALE AND FEMALE

Ibofanga is such a sacred entity, it is not to be disturbed. Because Muscogee Creeks almost never mention Ibofanga by name, personal prayers are more likely to be made to one of the assistants such as Hesagedamesse—the giver and taker of breath. Yet Ibofanga remains as the absolute, unifying principle of the universe encompassing all of the elements, all of the laws, and all other entities, seen and unseen. While violation of the natural laws established by Ibofanga has its chaotic consequences, Ibofanga does not personally intervene in specific problems. However, the unwavering and all-encompassing presence of Ibofanga is the major distinctive religious center of traditional Creek thought and illustrates the unity amidst the diversity—no simple animism here. To broadly categorize the aboriginal Creek mind as simple pantheism or animism would be a major analytical error.

In contemporary times, knowledge of Ibofanga has dimmed in certain aspects of the Creek world. Christian churches, in varying degrees, have sought to eradicate traditional Creek beliefs. Of course, they have not always been successful since Creeks sometimes unknowingly bring in the concept of Hesagedamesse again and again into Christian prayers and hymns. Because Hesagedamesse has the element of a personalized spiritual authority, Indian Baptists accept "him" as the equivalent to the Christian God. But Hesagedamesse as an assistant to Ibofanga remains somewhat different to the traditionalist from the God of the Puritans, the Baptists, or the Catholics.

The traditional Creek ceremonial grounds of today contain several key reference points for Ibofanga. Every ceremonial ground has a tall, wooden main pole pointing straight upwards as a bridge from the mortal to the immortal world of Ibofanga. Also, after the symbolic synthesis of the four elements of earth, water, air, and fire, the first "friendship dance" involves the joining of hands and singing which includes a mystical humming of the sound *iyabi/eyuppe*,[2] the recognition and honoring of Ibofanga. It is at that point that the external and internal dimensions of the Creek community are in the most attainably perfect harmony in this life.

Ibofanga, the greatest of all *miccos* or rulers, is connected to the empirical world through the work of four assistants or *miccos*. The four major assistants of Ibofanga include Hesagedamesse (the wind principle); Pojasa (the fire principle); the water spirit, Wewafulla/Yewvfullv; and the earth spirit, Igana Jaga/Ekvnvvcakv, or holy Mother Earth. The first two are male principles and the last two are female principles. The four are involved in the cyclical dance of life (and death). As the giver and taker of breath or life Hesagedamesse therefore controls the energy links in all living things. Pojasa, his assistant, controls the conservation and entropy principles. Pojasa directs the wise conservation of energy and talent in all living things. If conservation laws are violated, or if the appropriate use of talent and energy does not take place, Pojasa withdraws the appropriate power or ability. If the balance of nature is disturbed, it is the principle of Pojasa which results in the erosions and debilities and revenge of nature in the floods and collapses on earth. Pojasa is not arbitrary; it represents a balanced scale of natural justice.

The Creek world below the genderless unifying energy of Ibofanga includes a complex array of balances of male and female principle spirits and elements. Male and female are active and reactive principles, and yet there is an element of calmness in the male and an element of power in the female. Parts of trees can be male while other parts can be female. Given the dynamics of life, its essence is a striving for balance. Balance is not permanent. Hence, human beings in their assigned responsibilities of trusteeship in nature must be an active force in understanding the flow and male/female dynamics of nature. Hence, the Creek world is not a lazy world; it involves work within nature's boundaries.

Hesagedamesse is a male and active principle, sometimes referred to as the "man above."[3] Christian Creeks often attempt to fuse the imagery of Hesagedamesse with the fundamentalist Christian God. Pojasa/pucasv is also male and is often symbolically a grandfather; even the word *poja/puca* includes the meaning, grandfather. Hesagedamesse assisting Pojasa parallels the principle of entropy and the taking away.

In addition to the two male principles are two major female principles in this world. The two female principles are represented by the earth spirit and the water spirit. The earth spirit assumes different forms such as the grandmother or corn mother, who provides precious corn from her body. The water spirit also shows up in different forms throughout nature, emerging out of the rivers, lakes, streams, and the ocean. Thus, "below" the genderless all-pervasive energy of Ibofanga inhabit the various male-female principles that are the sources of knowledge and power of nature.

The four major principles represent the minds of nature under the spiritual umbrella of Ibofanga. The Creeks conceive of existence as the descending hierarchy of spirit, mind, and body, with the spirit providing the overarching unity to the rest. The spirits provide the mind of nature, the principles of nature at work. These principles of nature, in turn, work through energy links between four major physical elements in nature—fire, wind, water, and earth. Many traditional societies in the old and new worlds have regarded these four as the major elements. However, the way the four elements are energized by mind and spirit is a distinctive feature of the Creek view of life. Without energy and mind, the elements would be inert and static—fire can go out, be strong or be weak—so can wind, water, and earth.

Fire and wind are predominantly male and are more strongly linked to the male Hesagedamesse and Pojasa. Earth and water are predominantly female and contain female spirituality for the most part. All the seemingly animistic plural spirits are linked through Hesagedamesse, Pojasa, water spirit, and earth spirit and integrated into the comprehensive spirit of Ibofanga—the first principle of Creek religion.

NOTES

1. See note 2 in chapter 10 for a comparative discussion of the meanings of love.
2. Per Micco Hill of Asalanabi.
3. So characterized by Wootko Johnson, mentioned in the acknowledgment.

THE FORMATION OF COMMUNITY:
THE MASCULINE ELEMENTS OF WHITE STICKS
AND RED STICKS

The major legends and myths of the Muscogee Creek tribe, unfortunately, often appear as fragments in the literature, thereby making it easy to miss much of the logic, the meaning, and the sheer poetry and aesthetics of the conceptions of the natural and social order. As we have seen, much of the full creation myth of the tribe has suffered from this fate.

One major spinoff of the creation myth, when properly rendered, is a story of epic proportions. Like several other traditional epics, such as India's Mahabharata, the red stick/white stick epic contains the symbolism of war and peace, links between theology and human psychology, and links between psychology and political theory. Out of the mists of the creation legend came the concept of the clans, and out of the mists of the red stick/white stick story come the concepts of linking psychology to the social order. This includes the functions that bring the clans together. When properly narrated by a Creek storyteller in a traditional setting, the red stick/white stick legend has the dramatic proportions of classical epics. Standard histories of Creeks routinely refer to red stick/white stick groupings among Creeks but do not link them to the major epic. Occasionally, writers refer to the ball game myth as it relates to the structure of the tribe, but they have not analyzed the myth in depth; perhaps this is due to the lack of in-depth insider information.[1] The ravages faced in the preliterate Creek/European encounter have altered the quality of the narrative, which used to be told by the storytellers in old campgrounds between the dances or in educational sessions within the family.[2]

The red stick/white stick legend, in essence, deals with the lesson that in building social systems a series of seemingly opposite human psychologies, chemistries, and functions have to be blended. Ultimately, opposites can play complementary rather than contradictory roles in building a community. The red stick/white stick balance is one of a series of apparent dualisms that are reconciled and synthesized in the work of the great spirit Ibofanga. The metaphors of the Creek world have many parallel dualisms of male/female, east/west, life/death, north/south, and mind/body among others that appear in different contexts, all carefully linked. The creators of historical Creek ideas were not ego-driven and did not leave any individual authorial signatures. The Creek Homers remain unknown. Nevertheless, the links between the major metaphors and symbols demonstrate careful attention to the flow of ideas and details. The dualist symbols of red sticks and white sticks do not point towards permanent ontological dualism. All of the major dualisms have an element of each in the other (as in day/night) which works towards a unified purpose in nature and society.

There has been considerable confusion among non-Indian historians about the terms *red sticks* and *white sticks*. Sometimes the terms are mistakenly and confusingly applied to Creek clans, Creek towns, or Creek settlements. The Creek creation myth, which includes the origination of the clans, does *not* indicate any permanent groupings of the clans into exclusively white stick or red stick clans or *talwas/tulwv-s*. Nor are towns or regions totally and exclusively designated as red stick or white stick towns in any of the legends, myths, or stories in the oral history of the Creeks. A *talwa* may have a lot of red sticks gathered there at a given time and be loosely called a red stick town. Similarly, a Creek peace town may be loosely called a white stick town, causing some confusion on the white stick/red stick functional distinction.

Some towns happened to have more red sticks than white sticks, specifically during conflicts with and defense against the Europeans. Some towns were designated as peace towns, and since white is also the color of peace, the peace towns were confused as white stick towns. Actually, peace towns were places of refuge, renewal, and healing, and they provided sanctuary for persons with a variety of troubles. And they were protected by red sticks.

The red stick and white stick designations were applied in two interrelated ways. First, the red sticks and white sticks were people who as individuals displayed different psychological traits and therefore were differently suited for differing communal functions. Thus, these traits were utilized for two governmental functions. Red is the color of active life, while white is the color of reflective life. Those individuals who showed an extroverted activism were designated red sticks, whereas others with a more reflective quality were labeled white sticks in pre-removal days. One brother could be a red stick and the other a white stick. Red sticks gravitated toward the tasks related to the security and defense of the community, while white sticks tended toward the performance of the more civil functions of the community. Although the red stick/white stick labels were not applied to women, the substantial character differentiations spilled into the woman's world. Red stick-type women played active roles in clan leadership and policy issues. White stick-types gravitated toward herbal knowledge and other quiet functions.

Naive observation, superficial analysis, and mistranslations have created a confused baggage with respect to the role of the red sticks and white sticks. Careful attention to the details of the mythical and epic battle between the red sticks and white sticks can clarify the roots of the distinctions and illuminate a neglected corner of Creek culture. Red sticks (active) and white sticks (reflective) are psychological characteristics that can be found in the nature of different individuals. In contrast, membership in clans and townships is traced genealogically. Clan descent depends on the clan relationships primarily of the mother, secondarily of the father. Town membership primarily depends on the identifications of the mother's town prior to marriage and the wife's town after marriage. Red stick/white stick distinctions are individual distinctions though family influences can sometimes prevail. In pre-removal days the same family could, in principle, have red stick and white stick members. Clan elders could pinpoint the predominant characteristics of a child during the child's growth just as they could determine whether a child is likely to be a medicine man (*hilishaya*), a warrior (*tustenagee/tustvnvkhe*), or future-teller (*owala/owalv*).

Red sticks are more likely to gravitate toward assuming one of the multitude of security roles—*tustenagee* or a *yahola/yvholv*. White sticks are more likely to gravitate toward the "social services"—medicine man, a *micco*'s assistant, a peace *micco*, a cheerleader, or a prophet. As one of Gilbert and Sullivan's operatic songs state—every boy and girl alive is born a little liberal or conservative. The Creeks also traditionally thought that everyone was a little red or a little white—tending toward activism or reflection. Again, as the red stick and white stick epic points out, these are twin characteristics that strive for harmony rather than being eternal, intrinsic, and permanent contradictions. Harnessing the individual's energy is the key to harmony in a community.

THE HARMONY OF THE PSYCHES: THE RED STICK/WHITE STICK EPIC

Traditionally, Creek storytellers told the mythical story of two twins on earth, both of whom were youthful, curious, playful, and competitive. One (later to be white stick) was more gentle than the other, more aggressive twin (later to be red stick). The later-to-be white stick twin preferred the contemplative night and the moonlight, while the later-to-be red stick liked the active daytime and the sunlight, though both were energetic and their capacity for leadership and vision were parallel and similar. Like all living things, they were composed of energy in the form of body, mind, and spirit.

In their instructions, they were told that in exchanging their energies they should strive for balance. Twins do not represent good and evil, but the balance of qualities. However, in their playfulness one day, they wrestled and wrestled until they were exhausted. They both fell down, collapsing in their exhaustion, tired in their body and mind. Their spirits at this point journeyed upward into the mists and clouds—thereby symbolizing a Muscogee vision quest. As in the creation legend, wandering through the fog is a prelude to knowledge. As they became aware of their surroundings far from familiar territory, they became apprehensive.

The more aggressive, power-oriented twin volunteered to go in the direction that was comparatively darker (reddish) in search of medicine and urged his brother to go in the direction where the light was whitish and clearer. Darkness is not evil but a source of medicine, reflection, and power. They both agreed to meet back at the misty middle and then they went in two opposite directions. The dark side beyond the mists vibrated with the sounds of thunder and flashes of lightning—various energies clashing in the night. The exchanges of energy were not harmonious.

In the darker side, the first twin came upon some spirit people engaged in martial training with sticks and in playing the Creek double-stick ball game, a two-handed version of lacrosse. They told the twin that preparation for conflict was important. They had not yet had the opportunity to fight and they did not know exactly who their enemy was, but they were ready, since the stick ball game with two sticks and the ball was the little brother of war. From time to time, they would hurl their weapons across the mist. The twin was amused, and he told the people that he and his brother knew stick ball games and that they were not holding the ball right. The people were disbelieving and set up a challenge match of skills. The people lined up eight of their best players, only six of whom hit the skull atop the pole at the center with their ball. The people then gave the twin eight chances to see what he could do. By twilight time the twin hit the mark eight times in eight tries. The people marveled at his skill.

The second contest of skill involved being able to remain submerged under water. The best warriors showed their skills. The twin laughed and showed them how to save their energy by using a strong hollow reed from a clump of reeds that were reddish from interacting with the soil and the elements. He stuck the reed a little out of the water to draw the air into the mouth while submerged. The people murmured that the red stick twin was wiser than he looked and their respect increased.

The third task involved jumping across wide gaps. This entailed being very skillful (*dahopgee/tvhopke*). The people were skillful in stepping back from a chasm and jumping across it. The twin (*abokta/vpoktv*) suggested that there was a better way. The people laughed—but their chuckles and laughter were getting weaker with each demonstration of the twin's skill. The twin said, "You shouldn't just step back and jump from a standing start; keep running continuously and you will achieve a smoother elevation and

greater distance. There will not be time to step back during a real battle."
The prestige of the twin again increased with his achievement.

In the process of completing all the tasks and the conversations afterwards, night had fallen. During the night conversations, the people talked
about the fourth task of a warrior—to get someone's heart (*chafigi/cufeke,
figi/feke*=heart). The twin balked at the idea, saying that one should not do
that without the guidance of a medicine man who could perform a purification ceremony (a "white" function) afterwards. Besides, the twin said, as a
tustenagee "warrior" he should be leaving since there was no medicine man
and it was almost dawn. He also wanted to get back to his brother.

The people were reluctant to lose a skillful and potential leader. They
tried to grab him and hold on to him. He slipped out of their grasp and kept
running towards the daylight. The people of darkness retreated after
encountering the bright dawn. The twin made it back to the agreed-upon
meeting place—the middle ground with diffused light and mist. This parallels the spot in the Creek creation myth where the fog preceded the discovery
of the role of the clans. Here, too, the mist is the beginning of the twins'
journey toward blending darkness and light in order to learn the role of
balancing functions and psychological characteristics in life and in the
community.

While the first, more active twin (red stick) had journeyed into the dark
side beyond the mist, the second more contemplative (white stick) twin journeyed toward the opposite side, beyond the mist. Here he came into a beautiful land where there was full daylight and beautiful gardens, plants, trees,
and herbs. He began to inspect and collect some plants and herbs. Animals
and birds were also present, but they were irritated by the intrusion of the twin
into their world, so some of them descended on him showing their irritation.

The twin's nature was such that he did not want to engage in conflict
and he knew that he should not escalate the irritation of the birds and the
animals. His natural instinct was to bring about harmony by his actions
rather than conquest. The twin began to "talk" with the birds gently. He
began to scatter some of the selected plants and herbs to the animals and
seeds to the birds. He also cut a whitish hollow strong reed which he fash-
ioned into a flute to charm the animals—a "white stick." They seemed paci-
fied. This section of the story illustrates the irritation and illness brought by
the animal and aviary worlds and the roles of plants and herbs in healing.
Herbal warriors can battle the "animal" and "bird" diseases of the body—
botanical forces balancing the zoological forces.

After the pacification of the animals and birds, the second (white stick)
twin came across a body of water. Note the comparative quiet of this aspect
of nature compared with thunder, rain, and turbulence experienced by the
red twin on the opposite side beyond the central mists, where both the journeys began.

When the second twin reached the body of water, he began to study the fish and collected some fish so that he could bring some fish and some of the plants back to his brother in the misty meeting place. The sun was setting, so he thought it was time to leave. However, a host of people descended on him, asking him who he was and what he was doing there and why he had been talking and chanting to the plants, the animals, and the fish. The twin explained to the people how he and his brother had wrestled and were exhausted in mind and body—leaving the spirit to wander up into the mists. This in itself is symbolic of "sleep," sublimation, dream, or vision among the Creeks where the spirit, not "soul," goes on a journey of reflection and learning.

The twin showed the people the importance of herbal medicine, of the spiritual medicine of the flute, and of chanting to heal conflicts in the biological world. The people were fascinated with the twin, his medicine, and his control over the four worlds—plant, animal, bird, and fish. They wanted to hold on to this "white stick" medicine man. They warned him about the dangers they had faced when darkness came. Another group (the reds) from the other side of the mists regularly caused confusion. Arrows and missiles would fly and there would be thunder, lightning, and clashes of various forces. Since the second twin had been singing "medicine" songs, they wanted the songs to heal and strengthen them and wanted him to stay.

The twin, however, pointed out that he had to hurry back to his brother since darkness was almost upon them. The people tried to prevent his escape and gave chase. The twin ran toward the mists. But the people stopped in the mists because they were intimidated by the forces of the dark side emanating from the other side of the mists.

The second twin found his brother sleeping in the mists, awaiting their reunion. The second twin had the whitish flute (stick), while the first twin had the reddish reed (stick) in his hand. The twins compared their experiences in their journey and their escapes. In their dialogue they both concluded that they could help each of the two worlds and mediate the problems each caused for the other. One world was full of active energy but faced conflict without adequate "medicine," while the other had the medicinal resources but lacked the organization to deal with external conflicts and the extraction of medicine. Both twins assumed that their leadership could resolve the problems. However, life is not that easy, as we shall soon see.

The twins knew that both had lots of energy, but each had varying degrees of knowledge in organizing physical and mental skills. Together, they could be awesome. They both decided to go first to the people in the dark side beyond the mists and assist them in bringing about harmony in their lives. When they reached the dark side, they could see from a distance that a ceremonial dance was underway and that the chants were asking for a skillful leader to come their way. They also were asking for a return of a leader they had previously seen and chanting, "We want Red Stick" repeatedly.

The twins began to compare their perceptions. The second twin asked the first "what kind of reed or stick did you make and bring out?" The first twin said that it was a branch of a tree without any medicinal roots of any kind growing out of it or attached to it. The second twin asked, "What color was the reed when you were submerged with it in order to show them how to breathe while hiding under water?" The first twin said, "Sort of reddish." Well, said the more logical second twin to his more emotional brother (representing the dualism of reason and emotion respectively), "The people are apparently clamoring for you—*red stick*, that is the appropriate label for you."

Red Stick asked his brother for more details about this brother's journey as they moved away back to the misty area, away from the people chanting for a *micco-abokta*, a leader or assistant. The second brother pointed out that the people he had encountered wanted a medicine leader and an organizer. He said that he had used a stick or "reed" from the rootish branch of a white birch tree to fashion a flute for the songs and that he had also found medicinal roots. The first twin said, "I bet they have a name for you too— probably white stick." The twins agreed that the two groups should be brought together. They journeyed together to the bright daylight area beyond the mists.

There, too, was a ceremonial chant in progress. "Spirit come back—you brought medicine songs with you—and you played your flute. White Stick come back." The twin brothers slipped back into the neutral misty grounds and began discussing what ought to be done.

They agreed that the dark side people and the white side people should be brought together. Red Stick pointed out that there needs to be a fight before the groups accept each other. White Stick rolled his eyes and said, "No, let's get them to a council where they can talk with each other and find mutual benefits in association." Before they knew it, the twins were arguing with each other about the relative merits of fighting and consulting in building a community out of competing chemistries. White Stick argued that fighting wastes energy whereas Red Stick argued that talking alone cannot reconcile bottled-up energies. "First fight it out, then talk," was the essence of Red Stick's message. They went back and forth in their arguments four times, without breaking an impasse. Red Stick was already labeling the people in the dark side as red sticks and saying that he could lead them easily into battle. White Stick was reluctantly left to guide the opposite "white sticks." He thought, "I am a good person—I need to keep trying for peace." He tried to tell his brother, "How can you lead the red sticks to peacefully form a community?" The red stick brother was impatient. He said that the "red stick people" were ready for a fight and he could easily lead them to the great confrontation he thought was necessary.

The white stick brother began to cry softly at the thought of the confrontation and was concerned about reconciliation, and so he put his mind to work, considering the realities of the energies of the red stick people and his red stick brother. The white stick brother began to negotiate the rules of "war," so as to bring about minimal harm. Given his rational abilities, he was able to quiet his red stick brother sufficiently to bring about some key concessions and rules.

Total war would devastate both the red sticks and the white sticks and the survivors would not be envied by anyone. Thus, the white stick suggestion—a *symbolic* war, limited in scope, weapons, and by rules—was the best that could be done. The twins picked an intense version of the stick ball game—the little brother of war—for the confrontation between the red sticks and white sticks. The location of the confrontation would be at the heart of a sacrificial mountain, the flat, somewhat center field atop a mountain (mound). The red stick twin insisted that the battle was to be continuous—without a break—and that four key weapons could be used, ball sticks, clubs similar to the sticks, blow guns, and bows and arrows. Only *sofki/sofke*, the famous Creek soup made from parched corn and drippings percolated through wood ash would be allowed for nourishment to either side. After these preliminary minimum agreements, the red stick twin marched off to organize the eager red sticks while the white stick brother sadly had no alternative but to do his best with the white sticks.

The red sticks had gathered at the ceremonial grounds and when they saw the red stick brother coming, a tremendous chant went out—he is coming, he is coming—let's bring him to our council. When the red stick twin arrived at the council, he wasted no time in taking charge. He did not give the people a chance to talk; such is the nature of aggressive, warlike conditions. The twin informed the people of the nature of the four weapons to be used, the location of the battle, and the conditions agreed upon. He warned them that, despite the rules, many would be hurt and some would die in the impending battle. He pointed out that he had war medicine and that his leadership and medicine could scatter the enemy. However, he warned the red sticks to leave his twin brother alone, never to touch him.

Some of the red stick warriors considered the red twin arrogant; others came to his defense. After debate, they reached a consensus. They agreed with a shout that they would follow his leadership since he appeared to know something about the other side and they didn't. Further, they wanted the healing medicines and resources that the other side reputedly had. They were still worried about marching to war since the ground on the dark side was riddled with deep fissures and splits and was bombarded with thunder and lightning.

The red stick twin said he knew a special song to bring the ground together and end the fissures in the earth. He sang his song, "*igana dilesas/ekanv telesvs*, earth come together." To his own surprise the ground heaved and sealed the deep splits. Even today, traditional Creeks speak of gulfs and distances in the earth being brought together by the vibrations (songs) and movements in the earth. The twin ended his talk by saying that whoever won the battle on the sacrificial mountain would dominate the other side and there would be peace and harmony afterwards. He had confidence in the readiness of the red sticks for battle.

Concurrently, in white stick territory, a council was listening to the wisdom of the second, white stick twin who was beginning to assume the leadership of the white stick people. They would rather have had the twin teach them the civil functions of healing, of botany, and of medicine rather than go to war. The white stick twin began talking to the people. "My brother is my *abokta*, my twin. He is basically a good person but sometimes unkindness emerges from him. Usually he tries for harmony. I really do not want us to fight—I realize that you really want to learn the medicine songs and learn about nature." The people, however, wanted him as a leader of the white sticks and to prepare for an attack by the red sticks.

The twin reluctantly and humbly took charge. He instructed the people not to hurt his brother. Further, he said, they must make sure that the red sticks were definitely going to do battle. So to test intentions, the twin had the people assist in making a medicine bundle with four feathers and four medicines in it. The bundle was to be attached to an arrow and shot into red stick territory. Said the twin to the white sticks, "My brother will sufficiently recognize the medicines. One is for peace within oneself. If they take it, they will negotiate. The second is for healing various types of wounds if they are injured. The third is to make you forget, in this case, aggression. The fourth is to separate people and keep them away—this medicine probably was once used to keep you white sticks away. We all emerged from the same mother and there was no gulf between us. My brother has the mind of a rabbit—darting from here to there—full of various tricks. He has joined the earth together and he is ready for a fight. Our best archer needs to send the medicine bundle. We need to make another effort to solve our problem; it is affecting us all, including my brother and me. The two of us are at our best when we are together and we are also of one mind and spirit. Let us shoot the medicine bundle." The best archer shot the arrow with the medicine bundle into the red stick camp.

The red sticks were astir upon receiving the bundle and were curious about its meaning. The red stick twin leader told them that the bundle contained a message. Realizing that the red sticks lacked a full-fledged medicine man, he asked whether there was anyone who knew anything about medicine, because if the bundle was not handled properly the contents would crumble and the message would be garbled. One person stepped up and volunteered—he knew a little bit about medicine and, therefore, made "bad" medicine—but at least he would be more careful than the rest. The red stick twin asked him, the "assistant," meaning the incomplete or bad medicine man, to open the bundle. When it was opened up, the twin saw the contents and explained its meaning.

The red sticks grumbled about the overture since their emotions were already boiling. The "assistant" crushed the bundle in anger. The red twin realized that there was then no stepping back for the red sticks. He attempted to moderate their anger by telling them that he would not lead them to battle unless the ground rules of battle were accepted. The red sticks grumbled about the rules and said that it would mess up the effectiveness of battle, but seeing that they would be leaderless, they agreed to the previously announced ground rules about the choice of weapons, the location, the timing (no breaks), the refreshment (*sofki/sofke* only), and above all, not hurting his white stick twin brother. The red stick twin then turned to the "assistant" saying, "Since you crushed the bundle, you need to send a message back." The "assistant" red stick sent bad medicine messages back including bird feces, sumac venom, *fakka jadi/fakke cate* (red earth—a symbol of death), and a lock of hair. The bundle was accompanied with vulture feathers, unlike the peaceful eagle feathers which had accompanied the message from the white sticks.

The white twin was depressed upon receiving the negative message of the red sticks. Still trying to avoid a fight, he tried several delaying tactics. He asked the reds for the specification of the age limits for fighters that would fight in the rectangular mountaintop arena. The reds laughed at this query. The red twin took up for his brother: "Don't underestimate him—he is a strong medicine man—he is just trying to clarify so that unnecessary injury would not occur. Let's send a message back." The red stick brother then suggested sending the message back. The battle would be fought with *tustenagees/tustvnvkke* only—young warriors—children, women, and older people would not be hurt. The "assistant" reluctantly agreed but sent the message in the form of a young man's hair lock accompanied with feces. The whites were further disgusted. However, the white twin still was able to have them send a third bundle to the reds consisting of an animal skin, requesting drawings of directions and details of protocol on the approaches and allocations of the areas of the mountain for each side.

The red sticks thought that this was primarily a ploy for time but their leader—the red twin—interpreted it as an appropriate request for clarification. The red twin proposed that the two sides would come in separate files from the west, facing east. The red warriors, taking a southern route, then would occupy the southern corner of the east side of the arena and have their ceremonial fire in that corner. The white warriors, taking a northern route, would march in eastwards and gather at the northern corner of the east side of the arena. Note that all the connections of the four major colors, the directions, and the accompanying values match the essential conceptions of the Creeks in these matters. The white supporters would gather on the north side and similarly the red supporters would gather on the south side. The whites would have their own ceremonial fire in their corner. There were also to be four conch shell blowers in each of the four corners to make any necessary announcements related to the fight. The fight would continue until the exhaustion of the last man.

The whites agreed to these rules in their council meeting. It should be pointed out that both whites and reds, while they were each "led" by a twin, nevertheless made their decisions by consensus in assemblies. The decisions were made through sequences of leadership, speeches, responses, debate, discussion, and then consensus.

The white twin successfully persuaded the white sticks to send one last important message, which illustrated the reflective, community-building quality of the white twin. Normally in a Creek stick ball game, women and children form vocal cheerleading groups for each side. The last white stick request had two parts. First, the young white stick and red stick women and children would be combined and seated on the east side of the arena. Second, all the clan mothers would be seated together on the west side of the arena with the best mourners sitting behind them. Note several important points about this request. The clans had already been created before the resolution and synthesis of the white/red values in the Creek historical tradition. Further, the mothers would have their backs to the west and darkness and look towards the east where the sun and therefore life begins. The young women cheerleaders face the west since their journey begins with the east and proceeds to the west. The clan mothers are not divided into red and white groups. Clan lineage symbolically provides an umbrella, however fragile at times, over the psychological differences of the reds and the whites. Being an *owala* (prophet) the white twin could see that uniting the clan mothers in one group rather than separating white and red clan mothers, cheerleaders, and wailers/mourners would provide latent seed symbols of unity that would play a role in uniting the tribe. He was also persuasive in pointing out that there would be so much pain that distinguishing between cheers would be difficult and that cheering in unison would sound powerful.

The red sticks, again, balked at the suggestions of the white sticks, wondering, "Why should our women and children share their pain?" The red stick twin spoke out persuasively in the council, "Let's not get distracted by these compromises; you wanted to fight, which can be and is imminent. Let's get on with it." The red stick is not as rational as is his twin brother and does not fully understand the long-run implications of the compromises. This is precisely why in Creek symbolism the white sticks provide the long-run community-building and peace, while the reds provide the activism, the security, and the energies for battle.

The red stick twin gave the final call to his people: "Be prepared. Have your blow guns, arrows, clubs, and sticks ready. And take war medicine." But his assistant pointed out that they did not have a full-fledged medicine man and the assistant only knew how to make some bad medicine. This made the red twin wonder in his own private way, "How did I get into this predicament—separated from my brother whose helpful medicine was always there? I do not fully understand all the implications of what is happening. I am a natural fighter but I wish that I was not separated from my brother. Perhaps one day we will be united; however, I have now a battle on my hands."

In the meantime, the white twin was even more saddened by the impending battle, but since at least the white sticks looked up to him, he distributed healing medicine to the men for use when they were hurt. As the sun set on this day of immense negotiations and preparations, both sides gathered around their fires for the night, awaiting the battle that would begin at dawn.

THE BATTLE

With dawn's early light on the next morning, traditional water drums began to beat. Even the water drums seemed to work with the elements—water, air, fire (sun), and earth. Water drums have a deeper resonance than other drums with skins stretched over logs. The various scaffolds, including those on which the dead would be laid, and the battle structures were set up around the sacred mountain. Flurries of activities by equipment handlers, *sofki* (corn soup) makers, conch shell blowers, and various other assistants were taking their places as people frantically got ready. The cheerleaders, the wailers or mourners, and the clan mothers all took their designated places in the amphitheater. Then with the continued drumming, separate files of red stick and white stick warriors began their marches up the hill from two different directions—the red sticks entering the arena from the southwest side and the white sticks from further north. Both files paraded eastward in the arena and were greeted by the cheers of the young women on the east side of the high amphitheater. Reaching the east end with the whites on the north side and the reds on the south, they stopped and turned toward the west side of the arena; a startled murmur swept through the ranks. Sitting on the west side was the solid group of mothers and mature mourners. The fused symbolism of impending death and maternal concern was overwhelming. They began to be concerned about the future of the building of a community.

The "assistant" (bad) red medicine man lifted up and showed "his" medicine bundle, which was really the white bundle that he had crushed during the negotiations on protocol. Unwittingly, he caused some confusion and concern—such is the power of crushed (bad) medicine. The warriors were distracted by worrying about the women and children. The warriors then began to sing their death songs. Some vultures, many eagles, and other birds were flying over the arena in the "heart" of the mountain—essentially a rectangular amphitheater. Vultures signify death while the eagles signify wisdom, peace, and a soaring of the spirit. There are various spinoff stories about each of the other birds flying at various stages, but the main point is to remember that various birds played varying roles as messengers.

After the death song, a healing song vibrated throughout the arena, followed after a wait by a song for health and long life—pointing toward possible survival and the restoration of community. With the ending of the three chants, four (the sacred number) medicine men began to circle the central arena, counterclockwise, as Creeks do. Four conch shell blowers blew powerfully on their shells four times. Traditionally, Creeks blew on conch shells on various occasions, both for spiritual and for signaling purposes (which also has a separate spinoff story).

The medicine men spoke to the crowd before and in the intervals between each of the conch shell blowings, a total of four times to each section of the crowd. The messages were essentially the same each time: "This impending battle may not solve anything. This is not our way. To fight among ourselves is not the best path. However, people must speak according to their duties; ours is to urge peace and harmony, but sometimes we are not listened to. However, we must speak the truth. Today we will see whether fighting, talking, or a blend of both is better. We shall see." Then the fourth and last round of the shell blowings filled the arena with sound followed by the death chants of warriors and the assembly. A spirit of sadness permeated the entire arena. After the death chant, a healing song began and it soon began to rain.

In the midst of the rain the warriors entered the center of the field and faced each other. Then the fighting began as sticks and clubs, darts and arrows flew fast and furious in the air. The rain began to be accompanied by thunder and lightning, and the "gods" or "spirits" of thunder, lightning, and rain vibrated throughout the arena, throughout the battle, which lasted eight days continuously from dawn to sunset. The major elements were all at work in different forms: thunder, lightning, rain, and earth trying to soften human folly but nevertheless allowing humans to learn their own lessons. Gradually in the rain, the poisons and venoms were washed away. The increasing mud and rain made the footing difficult; the warriors could not get leverage for serious blows. What injuries occurred were treated by roving medicine men trying to bring about peace. The mud and the slipping and sliding made the clubs, sticks, arrows, and darts ineffective. The more the warriors tried, the greater was the difficulty with the work of the elements. Eight days of aggressive energy expenditure and the work of the elements resulted in increasing exhaustion. On the eighth day, the sun came out and the men lay all over the arena totally exhausted. With the coming of the sun a healing chant began to rock the arena.

The chanting spread as the exhausted warriors began to stir. The red stick twin and the white stick twin came toward each other and embraced, happy that they had found each other again. While people were hugging and chanting, the rising creative spirit uplifted everyone's morale and there was the coming together of a community based on reconciliation and love. The twins' spirits were lifted and they rose from the mists to tumble to earth again, knowing the way of balancing and cooperation in human affairs. Spirit, mind, and body were once again infused with cooperative and community energy. Thus ends the story of the battle between the red sticks and white sticks and one important symbolic stage in the creation of community. All-out war was to be replaced with less lethal play for the resolution of disputes in the communities—when mediation and arbitration failed. The futility of total war was to be replaced with the "little brother of war," the stick ball game. The ending provides the link to other stories just as the creation story and the red stick/white stick stories are linked in the chain of Creek thoughts and values.

The creation and red stick/white stick legends are often told in bits and pieces, and with cultural erosion the danger of losing the logic of the stories as well as the full stories themselves is imminent. These stories, together with all the other stories, contained the essential seeds of preliterate Creek culture and thought. Telling the stories and pointing out the implications of the ideas provided the basis for the early education of Creek youth. The storytelling, tutoring, training, and disciplining were analogous to our contemporary efforts to teach the modern myths and legends of evolution, the quarks, the black holes, the "big bang," and the nature of "our" universe.

While Jean Chaudhuri heard elements and confirmation of Creek stories from various elders, the setting for the stories shows a last frontier of the Creek educational world. The core storytelling for Jean was done by relatives, including her late father, and even more deeply by the late "Grandpa" James Scott who was on the Trail of Tears from Georgia to Oklahoma and lived to be around 110 years old. Sometimes the story would be told at home, more often outdoors. A frequent occasion would be while resting during a horse and buggy journey from the home in the "country" to the big city of Okemah or other nearby areas in Oklahoma. Wilburn Hill would gather sunflowers to pick off the petals and make the flowers and stems into various shapes and forms. In the evening, playing with natural objects, hands, and flowers, shadow puppetry would be performed on bedspreads behind a fire with the enchantment of the storytelling and interpretations of Grandpa Scott—heightened by the drama of creative visuals, for instance, the releasing of fireflies from a jar at sunset to illustrate the Creek myth of the earth mother creating a firmament full of stars with bits of the energy of Grandfather Sun.

The red stick/white stick myth shows the emergence of varying active/reflective psyches; their misunderstandings, their dialogues and conflicts, their resolution and superordinate importance of the values of community. The myth was reenacted ritually in resolving conflicts that went beyond debate. Communities and bands resorted to the "little brother of war"—the stick ball game which avoided intentional death. The myth is rich in the symbolism and values of the tribe, and each major one is a chapter in the Creek story of treasured values. Myths provide an important internal dimension of the Creek world that is not reached by dependence of the basic body of English, Spanish, French, and American documents or the retelling of the episodic observations of outsiders and travelers in Creek country. The Creeks kept no written records, but their storytelling and oral history skills deeply compensated for the lack of a written record. Interpretations and inferences from archeology and European documents or scattered statements by "informants" to reporters who did not speak the language give us, at best, an incomplete understanding of Creek values and their world.

The white stick/red stick myth illustrates the functions and roles of white stick and red sticks in Creek society and the blending of the varying dual functions of reflective/active, civil/military, conflict/communication, and security/social services in Creek government and society. The blending was done in different ways in Creek history. The overriding values of assemblage, debate, and the search for consensus were important. There were general all-inclusive community assemblies and also assemblies of red sticks (warriors) and white sticks (*miccos* and their *aboktas*). Sometimes these would be labeled as the "house of warriors" or "the house of kings." The meanings would vary depending on time, circumstances, perspectives, and degrees of Anglo influence. The classic myth, however, provides the historic standards for understanding the dynamics of red sticks and white sticks in Creek society.

NOTES

1.   See Brent R. Weisman, *Like Beads on a String* (Tuscaloosa: University of Alabama Press, 1989).

2.   The late James Scott is the major source of our version, though the version matches the fragments left of other versions that emerged in conversations over the years. Scott's grandfather told it to him before setting off on the Trail of Tears with other relatives. The grandfather heard it from his grandfather, which traces it directly back to at least the 1700s.

The Formation of Community:
The Feminine Principle

The masculine and feminine principles are always conceived in harmony in classical Muscogee values. This holds true in cosmic principles, in social structure, in the division of labor, in botany, pharmacology, and in government. While the matrilocal Creek system of familial descent is widely understood, much of the rest of the body of female principles and their equal complementarity to the male has become ambiguous because of post-Colombian forces.[1]

Since the coming of the Spaniards into Florida, the story of Creeks has been a story of cultural survival on the run. The role of the red stick warriors in the battles for survival caused dislocations in normal family patterns. The Spaniards, and then the Anglos, began to deal with the male *miccos* and "chiefs" since they appeared to be equivalents of European authority figures and made for "efficiency" in cessions and transactions. Mixed-bloods rapidly began to emulate the hierarchical forms of the Europeans, and missionaries also began to impose patriarchal symbolism in dealing with the Creeks and Seminoles. Further complicating these forces was the work of various types of "scholarly" commentators who had built up a formidable but incomplete conception of Creek society because of the almost universal dependence on male "informants." Sailing through these muddy waters is not easy. But if the compass marks of Creek cosmology, legends, and oral history, including the stories of women, are used, we are more likely to understand the fullness of Creek culture and gender relations.

COSMOLOGY AND THE FEMALE

Nowhere in Creek cosmology is the female principle held in permanent subservience to the male. The most important principles are neutral and genderless. Ibofanga, the macroscopic atom—the heart of all synthesis—is genderless and eternal. Ibofanga, when in movement, works through his creative *abokta* (assistant) which is the dynamic energy—Hesagedamesse, which is male, but there are major complementary female water and earth spirits. Neither *yeekchida* (the principle of empowerment) nor *boea fikcha* (the fire within), which operates equally through males and females, is biased toward any gender.

Hesagedamesse, the dynamic principle of the comprehensive Ibofanga, works through sets of equally balanced but specialized male and female principles. The sun, the thunder, lightning, wind, fire, and the red sticks/white sticks are primarily male. However the moon, the corn mother or spirit (Ojiboya Fikcha/Vcepuyvfekcv), the water spirit (Wewa Boea Fikcha/Uewvpuyvfekcv), the Holy Mother Earth (Iganaajaga/Ekvnvvcakv), and the heads of clans are all female—with their own empowerment. Without the equal cooperation of the female forces there would be only chaos and conflict in the universe. Without water (female) life would not be possible. Without the world of nighttime, the moon, the stars, the cycles of growth, nutrition, reflection, and regeneration would not occur. The equal female role in the environmental cycles is also matched by the equal yet distinct role played by the substantial and balanced female principle in human affairs. The essence of some key oral history myths clearly denotes the substantial and balanced feminine aspects of natural and social authority.

MYTHOLOGY AND THE FEMALE

A spinoff mini-story in the long creation myth illustrates the important role of women in the human world matching the female principle in the physics of things. Turtle, the female earth mother, nurtured and carried the Creeks in their journey to light. Turtle shell rattles are worn by the women dancers in stomp dances. When the fog cleared in the creation myth and knowledge began to broaden the human clans, societies began to form. The people started making the early classifications of the first clans such as the wind and the bear based on the links to the fog-removing wind and to medicine. But the process was far from complete when a spirit woman—transformation of Mother Earth—emerged and began to play a major role. As earth mother, she knew intimately the original root identities of each and every person and living thing. She was the carrier of the seeds and she knew better than anyone the order, identity, and offspring of her children. The mother feeds the children in her womb; she is the source of power, food, mother's milk, and is the gatekeeper of the herbal and medicinal world. Each band and group in turn symbolically feeds from a nipple of Mother Earth.

Various spinoff stories link the earth mother with the authority and knowledge given to human mothers who end up being the heads of each clan. The bear mother knows her cubs and similarly all human organizations (clans) will trace their lineage predominantly on the mother's side.

In addition to the earth woman story, a whole series of myths about the corn mother and the fundamental female empowering gift of agriculture and food exists. In one story, corn woman (spirit in feminine form) emerges out of the earth after the end of thunder and rain. She is in motion, slowing down sufficiently to instruct the people. Rays of light shimmer in waves, and rays of beauty surround her as she waves her hands. Corn woman, or corn mother, gives the gift of corn to the people with instructions that if they are careful in nurturing nature they will never go hungry. As she climbs and reaches the top of a rainbow, corn woman is well into scattering seeds of multicolored corn on all sides of the rainbow. In her discourse she points out that like the multicolored corn there are many different kinds of humans. If they follow the rules, they too shall be fed. Knowledge of and the attempt to work with diversity appears to be a Creek characteristic and provides the seed of confederacy.

Clearly, this legend points out that corn is not just for Creeks and that the bounties of nature should be properly shared, provided the nurturing balances of nature are maintained. The corn mother has many children scattered over the earth. This corn woman story and its companion stories establish the authoritative role of women in compassion for the needy and in the management of agriculture. In the Creek traditional world it was the women who took care of needy families and also made the key first decisions on the planting of the corn and beans.

Another corn woman legend (too long to repeat here) presents the corn woman transformed into a grandmother instructing a young boy about the rules of agriculture and the necessary work ethic. Again, the authority figure here is female.

The female principle is illustrated in yet another story which deals with the themes of peace and community associated with the coming of a rainbow. In the myth, the male spirits of thunder and lightning were fighting and rumbling in the sky, and stormy rain swept the land. The earth was disturbed and the animals were afraid. A huge snake struck out toward the sky in response to the disturbances of lightning. Tired of the fighting and the male disturbances of nature—spirit woman—a female principle—rises, waves her hands from the center outward creating the rainbow, and decisively "slams" the rainbow between the opposing forces, bringing about a quieting of the conflict. Mediation and conflict resolution is a female principle in the myth of the rainbow.

The myth of the clan mother, the corn mother, and the rainbow all illustrate some of the different yet fundamental and distinctive roles of women in Creek society. The myths and the cosmological conceptions are supported by a whole series of Creek traditions, social structures, and practices underlying the importance of the female principle in the traditional Creek world.

MENSTRUATION AND WOMEN

Overgeneralization about traditional societies sometimes obscures the logic and perception of specific societies. For instance, the generalization about aboriginal fear of menstruation is a barrier to a detailed understanding of the unique Creek way. A proper understanding will point away from simple fear to a deep respect for women and their menstruation.

Feminine power is enormous in the Creek view of life. In the Creek legends a story about the placement of four virgins in the four embankments of a defensive mound or structure reveals the power of the women, who by their presence are able to weaken the opposing warriors.

Feminine menstruation is regarded as sacred, natural, and pure. The puritan biases of Anglo society, even among its early social scientists, have turned the values of respect into fear even among those Indians who have been assimilated into Anglo ways. However, because it is natural it is not ignored. A series of rules and practices brings the symbolism of menstruation into harmony with the balance of nature. Thus, relatively contemporary Creeks point out the ways of cleanliness for a menstruating woman. A Creek menstruating woman was to bathe downstream so that nature would readily absorb the menstruation materials in natural recycling. This is different from modern "absorbents," which are not easily reclaimed and not properly recycled in nature.

Conventional historians, depending on some informants, have only one part of the story dealing with the prohibitions for men during a woman's menstruation. These masculine prohibitions include not walking in the pathway where a menstruating person has recently traveled. Men should not go into or near the separate women's house where women will stay during menstruation. Men should not have sex with menstruating women—nor should they touch her, look at her, have lecherous thoughts about her, touch her personal things or drink from her cup. The known aspects of men's prohibitions create a negative aura of taboos and misconceive the ever-present balance of the Creek world. To understand the balance, one must see it from within the oral histories of elder traditional women who are generally outside of the predominantly men-to-men talk of anthropologists and historians except for some fleeting and superficial conversations.

The cosmic and legendary spiritual "powers" of women are particularly concentrated in women at menstruation time, when all the gifts of nature and society are showered upon her. Women are the keepers of many of the Creek traditions, and it is during menstruation time that in Creek tradition the woman's role was defined in great depth. These were truly holy days during which the dynamics and flow of nature were at work—particularly given the Creek reverence for *jada/catv* (red/blood) which is life. *Jada* was a reminder that the life force was at work in a specialized way and that special attention must be given to this force which is symbolized again and again in the use of the color red in the aesthetics of the Creeks—in certain directions, clothing, rocks, facial makeup, and war paint among other things.

Clan mothers were notified directly when a woman began menstruating, while the men, in general, knew it indirectly. The clan mothers would announce among themselves that the girl would need twenty-one gifts during this period of her isolation in her special house with her own things. In this special house, in her special period, she was most receptive to education about both nature and culture. Menstruation was a time for the most intense possible continuing education for the seed bearers of the culture. A full understanding of the role of female education has declined, contributing to cultural erosion among many assimilated Creeks.

When the twenty-one gifts were collected the relatives got together to divide their labors in ensuring that all twenty-one gifts were in place. The material inventory was as follows: (1) personal cup; (2) spoon; (3) bed mat and covers; (4) three buckets—one for clear water, a second for herbal water, and a third for specific herbal baths; (5) chair; (6) straw hairbrush; (7) new change of clothes; (8) medicine bag; (9) clay prayer (fire) urn; (10) medicine bundle including an eagle (peace) feather, a rock, and other items; (11) new shoes; (12) moss for cleaning; (13) a clan symbol of the mother's side, for instance, a bear claw for the bear clan; (14) a special rock; (15) two eagle feathers (not in the bundle); (16) broom; (17) house; (18) grape vines; (19) herb box; (20) six baskets of different sizes; and (21) a reed.

These twenty-one items constitute the classic materials needed for an intensive period of learning as in the old adage, when the student is ready the teachers will come. Ideally, eight designated mentors arrive at the house and exclude all others, thereby avoiding all other social distractions. Each of the eight mentors is a specialist in one of the eight key disciplines. The period of instruction begins and ends with the blowing of a conch shell; the blowing links the learning ceremonies with that of Hesagedamesse, the giver and taker of breath and life.

The eight mentors from the eight specialties are as follows: (1) a fortune-teller—given the intuitive denotative logic of the traditional people, the fortune-teller was really a refined logician who could show the future implications of actions and thoughts; (2) a medicine woman, who would instruct in diagnosing and curing illness. Grandmothers managed the initial triage and primary health care of the family prior to any referral to a specialist or medicine man's home if and when it was necessary; (3) an herbalist who would teach the identification, care, and picking of plants, since women had special roles in horticulture; (4) a voice controller who would help develop the full range of the Creek voice for speaking, trembling, cheering, mourning, and other functions; (5) a teacher of family ethics who would lead the novice through the myriad connections of obligations and privileges in the clan and family networks; (6) a teacher of songs who would teach the necessary repertoire of songs. After all, women provided and performed the key earth blessing rituals (separate from the main stomp). The blessings of the corn, the water, the earth, and the ribbon dances,[2] the women's first dance in ceremonials, the turtle dancing, the clan songs, and many other songs were part of the exactly memorized repertoire; (7) a mentor for animal tracking, so that the woman would be safe in the forest or in the wilds; and (8) finally, a mentor to teach the mother's role, since the mother is the chief educator of the Creek child.

This entire complex of feminine education, ritual, power, and beauty has been missed by most historians, and the traditional older women have largely kept it to themselves. But ignorance about the feminine role obscures an understanding of half the Creek traditional culture. The decline of this understanding was hastened not only by the conflicts with invaders but also by the enforced patriarchy of Christian missionaries—the early Spanish Catholics followed by the Presbyterians, Baptists, and Methodists. The erosion of culture was also increased by the killing of most of the holiest and most knowledgeable medicine men in the wars and in the period of removal. It is often understood that Creek women had a more powerful role than women did in many other tribes. Vestiges of their power remain informally within families and even in churches, despite the missionaries. But the architecture and beauty of the Creek feminine world is only dimly understood in current times.

The balance of male and female principles permeates all Creek thinking. The balances, therefore, involve the division of various powers, functions, and privileges. The purpose of the divisions is not rooted in any suspicion of evil, "witchcraft," or female inferiority, but in the complementarity of their potential contributions to cosmic and social harmony. After all, harmony is not automatically a given in the Creek view but is an aim that is to be striven for in every institution. The authority of women in classic Creek values is considerable. Representatives of clan mothers sat in the councils of the tribe before Columbus, according to the oral history. However, clan mother representation was eroded with the coming of the mixed-bloods, the missionaries, and the mimicking and imposition of European ways. Some of the vestiges of power also adhered to women in the traditional stories.

One of the first dances in the stomp honors the women, as women possess all the earth blessing ways. Women and men play balanced roles in the doubleheader stomp dances: women honor the earth, wearing turtle shells, while men honor the fire in the stomp dance, in female/male complementarities. Women also dance the "ribbon" dance, in which the current use of ribbons is a symbolic adaptation of the earlier use of various animal tails.

Women traditionally were in charge of directing agriculture involving decisions on what and where to plant. They also directed those men (including "gay" men) who worked in the fields with them. Women traditionally made the decisions to help needy families and to care for minors who fell through the cracks as a result of family tragedies.

The clan mother societies served as boards of directors on many policy issues including the treatment of prisoners, violations of social laws, and judgments on various sanctions such as death or banishment. Traditionally, there were several powerful women's societies in the Creek tribe. The clan mother's society in each community sent representatives to the council and also served as a separate board for arbitrating disputes. In addition to the clan mothers' society, there was the group of "beloved women," a larger group of women who were in the "autumn" of their lives. The beloved women complemented the "beloved men" group, which was composed of persons who had completed the cycle of being warriors and active administrators.

Beloved women provided guidance on medicine, women's education, storytelling, agriculture, and the culinary arts; on children and the examination of their qualities for further development; on songs; and on discipline. The beloved woman was in the third of the four seasons of a woman's life, complementing the four seasons of a man's life. The first season (spring) was the "age of learning," during which the development of the spirit on top of the important foundation of early childhood took place. The young woman was trained by the grandmother and groups of female relatives. The second season (summer) was the season of "spirit woman," the period of involvement in which the developed spirit was active and involved in the network of life and its relations. The beloved woman in her leadership roles appears toward the end of the accumulation of the experiences of the spirit woman, to be followed by the final stage, the age of wisdom which prepares one for the death songs and the final journey beyond this world.

In addition to the important role of women in the community, women play an authoritative role within the family. While both parents' clans are crucial in defining identities, the attachments to the mother's clan provide the more important affiliation for affections, education, support, and discipline. The mother calls on her brother rather than her husband in the disciplining of children, including their disciplinary "scratching." The mother is the major authority figure at home. It is she who nurtures the spirit of the child from conception through birth to adulthood, who sings and "talks" to her spirit children, even before they are born. The mother's milk is holy and is even mixed with some infant medicine among Florida Creek-Seminoles. Widowers often remain attached to the wife's family.

The woman traditionally plays an equal role in courting. Among the Creeks, it was not merely the men who could court young women with flutes, but women could answer with reed flutes. Women and men were partners in marriage, resulting in the uniqueness of the Creek myth of roles in a marriage. The ideal of the marriage involves the partnership of a "perfect woman" and "perfect man" in an "imperfect marriage." Perfect woman is the unmarried female who is ready for her first marriage. She has been through the age of learning and she soon will be a spirit woman. Perfect woman and man do *not* become one unit—since there is always complementarity. Harmony is never permanent—it is the striving for harmony that provides the beauty of a marriage in motion.

While women did not have overt red stick/white stick designations, they had similar role differentiations. Some would show and be recognized for active leadership in councils while others would share and be appreciated for their reflective spirit in education. However, the Creek women traditionally were physically active. They participated in sports, they ran and swam, and they did practically everything the men did except for being front-line combatants in war. Daintiness and faintness in spirit or voice were not the ideal feminine virtues in traditional Creek society. While men had the edge in actual fighting, women had the edge in actual authority. Together they worked towards bringing harmony in the midst of the imperfections of life.

Without the male force of the fire, life would be weak and blind; but without the earth mother, the water spirit, and the corn woman, all varying forms of the female principle, the stirring of life itself would not be possible. The creation myth begins with the stirrings in the womb of Mother Earth. Women played an equal but complementary role in the structure of Creek life.

NOTES

1.   There are many overgeneralizations and attempts to correct them with additional overgeneralizations regarding women's roles in Indian tribes. See Sherry B. Ortner, "Is Female to Male as Nature is to Culture?" in *Woman, Culture, and Society*, ed. Michelle Zimbalist Rosaldo and Louise Lamphere (Stanford: Stanford University Press, 1974). According to Robert Lowie, as paraphrased (p. 70), Crows believed women inferior to men because menstruation was seen as a "source of contamination." Whatever the Crow situation may have been, the Creeks did *not* create a gender hierarchy because of menstruation, though they had elaborate rules about the natural function.

One analysis of post-Columbus cultural exchange recognizes what it calls the loss of power by Creek women and the shift from gynecentric to patriarchal authority. See Sharryl Davis Hawke and James E. Davis, *Seeds of Change: The Story of Cultural Exchange after 1492* (Menlo Park: Addison-Wesley Publishing Co., 1992), 195–197.

Most standard documentary histories of wars, removal, and the skin trade miss much of the women's story in the Creek world. One recent author seems to be sensitive to this role but does not appear to have the relevant information or analysis to understand Creek women's roles in any depth. See Kathryn E. Hollan Braund, *Deerskins and Duffels: The Creek Indian Trade with Anglo-America 1685–1815* (Lincoln: University of Nebraska Press, 1993). Braund's characterization includes the following: "The role of women in the Creek decision-making process was completely ignored by European observers and is thus excluded from the written record ... there is mention of the Beloved Woman of Coweta in the historic record, and it is likely that most other Creek towns appointed beloved women ... the function and role of beloved women will never be completely understood.... They were among the most prestigious families. Beloved Woman of Coweta was allowed to speak before the town council.... There were other 'official' positions for women in Creek society, though their titles and responsibilities have been lost to history.... Some women accompanied Creek war parties, but their status and functions remain fuzzy.... Even if they did not occupy official roles in government, enough hints remain to show that women were a potent political force, especially in matters of war and peace and clan retribution" (Braund, 22–23).

2.   Ribbon dances used animal tails and pelts in early times.

AROUND THE CEREMONIAL FIRE

The contemporary Creek stomp dances retain the heart of Creek culture, despite the erosions at the edges that have occurred through the protracted conflicts with European values, the terrors of invasion, wars, removals, the creation of Oklahoma statehood, discriminations, rural brutalities, and Christian missionary activities. In pre-removal days dances were held throughout the year but four of the dance festivals provided the cardinal points. The most important of the four was the *buskida*, the annual green corn dance.

In the contemporary world, the *buskida/posketv* remains as the most important festival and occurs in late summer in eastern Oklahoma. In addition to the green corn celebrations, there are other dances whose dates are specified for each ceremonial ground by the leader or *micco* of the grounds. There are, among others, ribbon dances, crane or feather dances, buffalo dances, and the more common stomp dances, some of which are social.

The stomp dance has spread as a contribution to various intertribal celebrations and social events. When performed in a traditional Creek ceremonial ground, the stomp dances are a cultural reaffirmation, despite the loss of lands, and are community social, cultural, and religious events. Beyond the various details lies a profoundly integrated celebration of Creek traditional values that is not easily self-evident to casual observers who may not be familiar with the Creek view of life.

Concepts of community, spiritual renewal, reaffirmation of equality and freedom, the blending of the four physical elements of nature, the four mind/spirits, the energy of Ibofanga, the role differentiations, and the revisiting of the entire creation myth are all blended into the contemporary, traditional Creek stomp. In spite of the external changes, ancient Creeks would clearly recognize the continuities of Creek values that show themselves in any single Creek stomp night on a traditional ceremonial ground, that is, one uncorrupted by alcohol or social partying.

Prior to the day of the stomp and the morning after the stomp, various cooperative tasks are undertaken, including the cleaning of the grounds and the gathering of wood, water, and various other material necessities. There are also the internal organizations and celebrations with friends, visitors, and relatives in each of the family camps on the grounds. In addition to the stick ball games and supplementary events of the stomp dances, the *buskida*—green corn dance ceremonial—includes important component rituals: making vows, renewals, rites of passage including scratching, and the ceremonial eating of the green corn for the first time in a year, after appropriate fasting. The green corn celebrations constitute a symphony of the entire combination of Creek values and practices. But every stomp in addition to the green corn ceremony contains the links to the Creek cosmos without the additional details of the *buskida*.

The four elements, the four spirits, the four paths, the seven directions, and the all-encompassing Ibofanga are represented in the stomp ceremonies. The initial four logs in the central fire pit symbolize the "four log religion," with the logs facing exactly east, north, west, and south. Today, many logs are piled on, but the underlying four logs remain in the ritual. Underneath the logs, the base includes a mixture of earth and water. The lighting of the logs, originally with rubbing sticks, represents the spark of the fire from Grandfather Sun. The breath of Hesagedamesse—air—makes the growth of the fire possible. The stomp dance grounds have "architectonic" rules and structure that are not always self-evident to observers. The central square is surrounded by a circle which includes the arbors. Then there is an outer, sacred quasi-circle which includes the central pole and the ball field. These are lines of ritual inclusion and exclusion depending on the persons involved and the timing. The semicircular camp houses are just outside of this circle.

The central fire also reminds one of the seven directions of the Creeks: east, north, west, south, down, center, and up. The four logs point to the first four directions. The base and the rocks in the earth point downward, the smoke moves upward, and the fire remains at the center. Symbolically, this parallels the Creek conception of self, which includes four external sacred paths, each with its own values, sometimes represented with colors. Internally, the Creek spirit is rooted downward to Mother Earth, the fire of energy burns in the center of the person, the spirit spirals upward in the Creek mind, and it exits through the top of the head upon death to join the spirit and energy linkages with the rest of the cosmos. There is no permanent bracketed individual soul here, no Lockean *tabula rosa*, no windowless monad of Leibniz, no Hobbesian or Marxist material atom, and no spiritual atom of Bishop Berkeley. Nor is this a scattered set of reified animistic spirits. Symbolically, the spirit within is in harmony with the spirit without.

In the stomp dance fire, the wood represents the sacrifice of the plant world. The sacrifice of the animal world is represented by the offering of the deer tongue, now substituted by a cow's tongue in some ceremonial grounds. The humans have their own fasting and cleansing ceremonies topped by the "taking of medicine." All families of living things play a role in the ceremonies.

The stomp begins at night—represented by the color black, night is a time for reflection, the prelude to creation, and the beginning of a new journey. The moon is feminine. Gradually, through the gathering of energy throughout the night, the final integration of active energy takes place at dawn with the first appearance of the male—Grandfather Sun. The infusion of the sun's rays activates all the medicine and energizes the spirits of the individuals and the community and a new journey begins. Male and female are harmonized and the wedding of nature and people is complete.

The four elements—earth, water, fire, and air—play a role in the sequence of the dance as well. The earth is lovingly cleaned and prepared before the dance. Water is ceremonially sprinkled systematically through the dance area. Superficially, it is to keep the dust down; symbolically, it represents the unification of earth and water. In addition to earth and water, the element of fire is directly present at the center of the dance, while clean air envelops the presence of the other elements and is further nurtured by the songs, the shouts, and the breathing of the participants. The joining of the forms of air and oxygen acknowledges the presence of Hesagedamesse, just as the spirits of earth, water, and fire are acknowledged.

The deepest acknowledgment of all is the recognition of the ultimate unifying spirit, Ibofanga/Epohfvnkv—clearly, peacefully, briefly, and without disturbance. At the beginning of the dance the men and women line up facing each other—male and female—and chant the *iyabi*, the call to the one great spirit Ibofanga. Then male and female, though different, unite together equally to honor the spirit and energize the community in the first dance which is a friendship dance in which everyone holds hands and circles the fire in an unbroken chain without a beginning or end. The dance path is counterclockwise, paralleling the sun's journey from east to west. A person points toward the rising sun with the right hand while facing north, also moving counterclockwise. Subsequent dances will then assign different roles and the dances, at the signal from the dance leader, will contribute in different ways, but the first friendship dance captures the exact relationships of Ibofanga, the spirits, and the elements.

The gathering of vision will proceed throughout the night, and then with the first rays of sunlight the "medicine" is fully energized and a vision dance, *obanga-hadjo*, takes place followed by a closing friendship dance of greeting and farewell prior to the next spiritual rejuvenation in the cycle of life.

Given the erosion of the economic and governmental foundations of Creek culture, the gatherings at Creek ceremonial grounds[1] remain one of the most tangible current links to the logic and values of the Muscogee world. When the current elder *miccos* of the grounds pass away, the quality of the future core of Creek values will depend on the wisdom of the future *miccos* who take their place in leadership in many things including the ceremonial grounds.

NOTES

1. For an anthropologist's description of ceremonies, see James H. Howard, *Oklahoma Seminoles* (Norman: University of Oklahoma Press, 1984), 104–180.

Ethnicity and Diversity in Creek Traditions: Natives, Mixed-Bloods, African Americans, and Whites

Traditionally, the Muscogee Creeks had their own unique ideas of ethnicity and diversity. The Muscogee views were deeply rooted in their conception of selfhood, which in terms of ethnicity and diversity were both universal and inclusive, and which linked the self to the cosmos. The concern for "all my relatives" included the human, zoological, geological, and botanical worlds. The core of this natural circle of community included all humans.

While the notion of humanness did not include Europeans and Africans until the arrival of Columbus, they were included in theory by implication and in practice after Columbus. The Creek "universalism" rested on different logical grounds than that of the Roman Stoics and the philosophical Catholics. The values rested on the Creek notion of love, a deeply contemplative and disciplined non-European eros—without the common vulgar sexual connotations of the Greek principle of Eros.[1] The root of the love is compassion because the spirit of Hesagedamesse, the breath-giver, is everywhere. Race, ethnicity, and gender cannot block the path of the universal energy. The exchanging of energy is life—the blockage of energy is death. And the traditional Creek always chooses *jadi/cate*, life, which also means "red" and "blood."[2]

The myths surrounding creation, red sticks and white sticks, perfect man and perfect woman, and all other major myths and stories constantly speak of the spiritual eros in the exchange of energy, of *anogetchka*, or heartfelt love, as the basis for existence. Nowhere in the Creek legends are racial features identified as the key to superiority or even to Creek identity. Of the Creek distinctions that existed, the most important was the one of speech. Humans speak differently from animals, though early in their evolution they spoke the same language, according to the creation myth. Those who spoke Muskogi were the Muskokalgi; the rest were people of different speech.

The "others" or "people of a different speech" were also children of Hesagedamesee. Where possible, other tribes were to be brought under a confederacy of equal partnership among communities. This is exactly what the Creeks did with the Euchees, Miccosukees, and other groups whose speech was different. No people were intrinsically eternal enemies against whom total war was to be directed. With respect to tribes that were outside the confederate circle there was a shifting continuum of friendship, athletic rivalry, or other forms of conflict.

The contexts in which hostilities could occur included the death or infliction of injury on a kinsman, intentional destruction of the sacred tangible symbols of the tribe, the intentional destruction of Creek agriculture, and hunting or violation of Creek laws of nature, including destroying the environmental balance. Creek values did not take balance for granted. Even though all were children of Hesagedamesse, it took constant effort to maintain the dynamics of harmony between spouses, between tribes, and between people. The way of the white sticks and the eagle, of consultation and negotiations, was better than the way of the vulture and of death. But if negotiations did break down, Creeks understood that down the road ball games could be tried. Ultimately, war could result.

Creeks developed their own laws of war. Despite anecdotes to the contrary, traditional Creek values did not sanction carrying decomposed parts of the enemy's body for adornment—that would violate Creek conceptions of personal cleanliness. War was always followed by cleansing ceremonies, and unabsorbed aspects of the spirit of the enemy were not welcome. The "heart" of the enemy was a different matter since it represented concentrated energy. Symbolically and ritually, Creek warriors could possess and absorb the enemies' hearts in war. They could also sacrifice hearts.

No permanent enmity was part of the Creek way. Relatively speaking, the most persistent difficulties of the Creeks with other nations involved the Cherokees, who were pushed southward by the Iroquois Confederacy and who kept treading on Creek territory. The Cherokees were a very diffused and decentralized group—Creeks would have conflicts with some bands, war games with others, and peace and even intermarriage with some of the rest. Hostilities with the Cherokees involved either the violation of the laws of nature, including the taking of excessive game, or of murder. The hostilities with the Cherokees took on a broader nature as Cherokees lined up with the whites against the Creeks after Columbus, through the battle of Horseshoe Bend with Andrew Jackson, and finally through taking opposite sides during the Civil War. In the latter, many Cherokee and mixed-blood Creeks aligned themselves with the South while most of the full-blood Creeks, who rejected slavery, aligned with the North after initially seeking neutrality.[3]

In addition to the sporadic cycles of hostilities and interactions with the

Cherokees, the relations with whites were also strained. While no intrinsic racial hatred of whites was evident, sustained, intense, and penetrating bitterness arose from the disturbances of the sacred land and the unremitting search for resources accompanied by genocide on the part of the whites. The massive and in many ways fateful, if not culturally fatal, impact of Creek/white interactions caused a bitterness among full-bloods against white culture. However, the roots of their bitterness lies in the loss of land and a way of life and white values, not in a dislike of a certain skin color.

An entire class of mixed-bloods developed as a result of Creek-white contact.[4] The mixed-bloods were sometimes the product of willing liaisons but more often, according to the oral history, the product of various forms of force. Many mixed-bloods strove for acceptance by the more powerful white world as they adopted the materialism of the white world. Losing their clan identity, since at best they had only one clan link rather than two, and not being socialized into the clan protocols, alienated them from the full range of Creek cultural interactions. If mixed-blood children bonded early with Creeks, full-bloods fully accepted them. However, if this bonding did not occur, fractional Creek blood could not prevent the alienation caused by the perceived love of violence, greed, selfishness, and betrayal among the Scottish, Irish, and English mixed-bloods, a fissure between full-bloods and mixed-bloods that began in the eighteenth century and continues to this day.

The early attitude was best captured in the oral history and traditional rendering of a speech by the great Creek hero, the earlier (prior to 1860s) Opothleyahola. Speaking of the mixed-blood betrayals of Creeks, Opothleyahola acknowledged that they too, including Alexander McGillivray, were children of Hesagedamesse, but calling on the latter he cried out, "Oh, Hesagedamesse—you can forgive them—you made them— they are part of the same energy that you gave me—but I cannot forgive them."[5] They are part of the same human chain, but they were unforgiven because of their actions.[6]

The cosmopolitan values of the Creeks disposed them toward creating working relationships with other tribes, bands, and groups. Their values, as expounded in the red stick/white stick legend, pointed out that building harmony is not easy or automatic. Strife, due to miscommunication, is always possible and often probable. The Creeks underwent many skirmishes and battles but they were always looking for confederated alliances. They were possibly more oriented toward balanced, decentralized, yet nonetheless systematic alliances than any other tribal group in North America, with the possible exception of the Iroquois, with whom the Creeks usually had a distant but friendly relationship, particularly concerning trade. The exact tribal membership of the Creek confederacy was not always openly discussed since it varied and secrecy had its advantages in war. But the Creeks, through rumors, messengers, and with other markings on a feather stick, knew the current membership of the confederacy at all times.

In addition to the face of the confederacy in war, the Creek trading relationships were extensive, as they traded north for rapidly vanishing wild rice and ginseng, and south for copper and other supplies from tribes in Mexico. The Creek fall pilgrimages took them north up the Mississippi Valley and into the Ohio mounds where they had ongoing relationships with a variety of tribes along the way, including the Shawnees. Southward and southwestward, Apalachicolas, Yamasees, Timucuas, and Natchez had varying affiliations with the Creeks. Even names like Timucuas and Yamasees are themselves corruptions of Creek designations. Thus, Timucuas were *dimitkosi/temerkuse*, people whose area lacked resources.

The various bands and tribes in the Southeast displayed varying physical features and varying languages and dialects. None of these intrinsic differences were barriers to membership in the confederacy—illustrating again the absence of racism and the acceptance of diversity among the Creeks. Once accepted into the protocols of the confederacy, none were slaves. Each community and region retained their autonomy. The central requirements were the civilities of the conferences, cooperation in war, cooperation in trade, and respect for the criminal code and the environmental policies of the tribe.

The need for working toward community, not only as specified in the red stick/white stick legend, but the sharing of the earth in peace with others, is an integral component in the legend of the corn woman creating and crossing the rainbow, which stopped the conflict of forces. In scattering multicolored corn on all sides of the rainbow, the corn mother's message is as follows: "There are many people of different speech on mother earth. I spread the multicolored corn in all directions that all may live." The bird in flight symbolized messengers, and sending messengers with eagle feathers was always an overture to peace. In contrast, the vulture was the harbinger of conflict and death. Eagle feathers were used not only in conveying peace to Native tribes, but to newly discovered nations as well. Thus, in 1734 Chief (*Micco*) Tomochichi gave an eagle feather to King George II of England, accompanied with the following declaration:

> These feathers are from the eagle which is the swiftest of birds. These feathers are a sign of peace and have been carried from town to town and we have brought them over to leave with you, oh mighty king, as a sign of lasting peace.[7]

Tomochichi's typically Creek openness was not to be reciprocated as Georgia settlers overran Creek lands.[8] This short speech fuses much Creek symbolism in it—the desire for peace, the role of the eagle, the consensus and decentralized civilities expressed from town to town, and the willingness to have a constructive nature respecting corn-sharing relationships with foreigners who were really intruders. The admonitions of the corn mother or spirit were to be heard in the four directions and pathways of the Creek fire. Even the

Cherokees, who were sometimes enemies, had a right to live and grow corn. Nature has its strange pathways and even the enemy can survive. The begrudging acceptance of the Cherokees' right to existence is contained in the famous Creek legend of how the Cherokees got fire. Essentially, the trickster rabbit tricked the Creeks and stole some of the fire from the Creeks and gave it to the Cherokees and the Choctaws. The message is not one of the need to put out the Cherokee fire but to accept the quirks of nature, where uncomprehendingly even the enemy lives and survives, sometimes quietly and sometimes noisily, even though their communal origins are perceived as a gift of the tricky aspects of nature, personified by the rabbit who does all kinds of tricks with varying consequences.[9]

When conflicts with other tribes occurred, both the martial valor of the Creeks as well as their respect for laws and the value of freedom came into play. If the enemy was perceived as having deeply violated Creek principle, Creeks could be, and often were, mean and cruel combatants, tearing out the hearts of enemies and torturing some of them to death, with Creek women joining in. However, the meanness was balanced with three important aspects of their values and their perceptions of humanity. First, they were capable of great forgiveness after an appropriate waiting period following a conflict. Part of the Creek oral history tells the timeless story of a band of Indians in Alabama who had murdered Creeks. The Creeks chased the band in revenge all over the Mississippi Valley and into Ohio and back. However, after a period of penance and rapprochement, the band was forgiven and accepted as completely equal partners in the Creek confederacy.

The second relevant value is symbolized in the Creek conception of the "peace town," special towns which were truly sanctuaries where no violence could take place. Individuals, bands, the homeless, the pursued, the lawbreakers, people seeking peace away from conflict, runaway slaves, and even enemies could enter a peace town and they would have guaranteed sanctuary. The Creek laws governing peace towns[10] were enforced by the red stick security forces; whoever had taken refuge in a peace town was to be kept out of harm's way and they would have access to medicine and food during their stay. Chitto Harjo's continued bitterness at the white world at the turn of the twentieth century, among other causes, in part arose from the white disrespect for Hickory Grounds, which had been declared a peace town. Harjo went there with Creeks and joined a group of blacks who had already sought protection and refuge from Oklahoma posses.

In addition to the rituals of forgiveness during the annual green corn festival and the availability of sanctuary even for enemies, an important third value governed Creek relations with other peoples. This third value involves universal freedom which follows from the Creek version of eros and love. Because Hesagedamesse's spirit flows throughout the universe, one should never attempt to keep any part of the spirit world in bondage. The Creeks had no jails for Creeks and no prisoner-of-war camps for enemies.

However, the enemy could be killed and his spirit could rejoin the energy of the universe, at least in the Creek view. Of course, the prisoners' perspectives were likely to have been different. Although temporary pain may be inflicted before death, the spirit is symbolically never to be imprisoned. This does not suggest that Creek captives necessarily enjoyed their treatment, nor that the Creek rites of passage were painless. The Creeks kept no prisoners, and traditionally before the advent of white-Creek mixed-bloods and Southern white influences, they kept no slaves.[11] Even the slavery that existed later in Creek country initially and primarily involved propertied mixed-bloods imitating the ways of the Southern gentleman.[12]

The opposition to bondage and any form of slavery provided one of the reasons for clashes with white society. From the full-blood Creek and Seminole standpoint, the enslavement of blacks was wrong, and so full-blood Creeks and Seminoles often provided safe havens to runaway black slaves. The masters of the slaves would then often rally the white forces against Creeks and Seminoles, precipitating conflicts. Common gossip that Southerners spread about Creeks and Seminoles was that Creeks intermarried frequently with Afro-Americans.[13] However, actual examination of clan relationships for both parents and the Creek views of African Americans show the inaccuracies in the projection of Southern white values.[14] The traditional Creek and Seminole views on slavery arose from their feelings for all fellow human beings.

The Creeks and Seminoles were fairly conservative about marriages outside the tribal circles because clan relationships gave them a root or anchor and a series of privileges and obligations in the tribal society. Their commitment to universalism did not mean that they were prepared to abandon their community identity, and being without a clan on either parental side meant the erosion of community and the rise of atomistic individualism and alienation. After all, the community was not based on force but on a shared conception of selfhood as well as the network of clans.

When the Muscogee people encountered blacks, several alternative options were available to the blacks. They could rest in the peacetowns. They could be given a community of their own—black town, *lustee talwa*, to restart their lives. Many residents of such communities traveled with the Creeks on the Trail of Tears and provided the nucleus of Creek freedmen— blacks who had grown up under the Creek umbrella. Blacks in towns like Bowlie, Oklahoma, can trace their roots to this sort of association with Creeks. This did not mean that this category of blacks had a clan lineage. Of course, a black or any member of a Muscogee community was free to leave the community at any time.

Historically, non-Creek blacks have been adopted into the spouse's Creek family, and over time, the non-Creek could be adopted into a sponsoring elder's family. From then on, gradually the lineage would return to the Creek fold. Of course, all the black and white adoptions are post-Columbus events. Prior to Columbus, non-Creek tribals were also, from time to time, absorbed into the tribe individually or in groups. Some of the group absorption contributed to the evolution of additional clans, accounting for many clans not listed in the original creation myths. Those prisoners of war who were not killed were also adopted into the confederacy.

The eros-based compassion and love of freedom for all was a consistent part of the value system of the Creeks, and except for those specially mixed-bloods who adopted the values of the white Southerners, the full-blood Creeks generally and consistently attempted to act upon those values. The sheltering of slaves, the freeing of slaves, the Seminole wars (which involved many full-blood Creeks) are all examples of the Creek compassionate love of freedom. However, with the infusion of dominant white values in Oklahoma, some Creeks inconsistently and in a confused way mimicked Southern white racist terms and labels, often superficially.

The compassionate yet clan-based, distinct, disciplined relationship with blacks continued during Indian removal. This resulted in cultural sharing. Blacks adopted many of the folktales from Creek pre-Columbian legends with respect to the bear, the rabbit, the opossum, and other animals in their Uncle Remus variety of stories. Creeks in turn sometimes blended Creek songs on the Trail with the cadence and wording of black spirituals. Out of this sharing in Oklahoma history, spirituals mixed with black/Creek symbolism and rhythms were born.

After the Trail of Tears, the varying relationships between blacks and full-bloods and blacks and mixed-blood Creeks continued in Oklahoma. The mixed-bloods in McIntosh County, like the Cherokee mixed-bloods, picked up the white pretensions of status with respect to blacks, including slaves, while the Creek full-bloods in Hannah, Henryetta, and Okemah did not develop attitudes of superiority with respect to blacks.

The core of the Creek full-blood attitude toward blacks showed up after the Trail of Tears in the US Civil War, which for many full-bloods further confirmed the quarrelsome nature of white society. After initial attempts at neutrality, many full-blood Creek leaders lined up with the North on the slavery issue specifically after the promise of protection of Creek lands. The leaders included the great Opothleyahola/Opothle Yahola, who originally had opposed removal but had given in only when he saw his people starving. Opothleyahola rallied a band of Creeks to fight for the North. Though he lost a battle and his life in the process, he thought he was fighting for black and Creek freedom. The North had promised land and protection for "loyal" Creeks. But the promises were not delivered. Among the rank and file of the Opothleyahola band was the young full-blood Creek rebel, Chitto Harjo,[15] who was later to organize proudly but unsuccessfully the last organized tribal rebellion, commonly called the Crazy Snake rebellion, against the United States. Chitto Harjo had fought with Opothleyahola for the North and against black slavery and was personally close to black freedmen, some of whom had gathered in the peace town of Hickory Grounds, which was Chitto Harjo's home base. When the breakup of communal lands began to take place, Chitto Harjo refused to accept his allotment and urged Creeks to reject allotment. What few negative comments against blacks Chitto Harjo made dealt with his sadness about those blacks who were not Creek freedmen or associated with the Creeks but were being given Oklahoma lands. Meanwhile, many Creeks were fast losing their remaining communal land in the process of individualized land allotments.

The full range of Creek and black relationships deserves a separate and lengthier treatment. In short, both the inclusiveness of Creek values and the corollary of human freedom provided the core of the Creek full-blood attitude towards blacks. The repugnance to slavery can also be understood in the usage of the Creek word *stewonaya*, which indicates someone who binds you up or enslaves you—a negative term. After statehood, Anglo lawmen in Oklahoma were called *stewonaya*. A Creek disciplinarian was never called a *stewonaya* because putting people in shackles or imprisoning them was never a part of Creek traditional culture. Even torture prior to death was preferred in Creek values to being bound as a slave.

Taking vengeance by torturing individuals during war or at other times did not contradict the general Creek commitment to the values of freedom and inclusiveness. Acts of revenge and compensation were permitted in the decentralized systems of Creek justice. They could banish one of their own from the community because of legal violations. Although individual character varied among Creeks, as in any group, the general values of freedom and inclusion provided the framework for judging individual conformity or deviance. Deviance had its price. In one of the Florida battles dirt apparently was stuffed into the mouths of slain whites before their last breaths. When the Seminole braves fully realized the ethical implications of their own unnecessary brutality and the bottling of the spirit, according to the late and great Billy Osceola,[16] many began their death chant prior to their suicide or suicidal acts, rather than being taken prisoner in the likelihood of subsequent white revenge.

Whites provided the biggest challenge to the Creek values of inclusiveness. This was due less to race than to the association of whites with the dominant European culture which many full-bloods saw as an unabated onslaught since Columbus against Creek values, Creek lands, Creek dignity, and Creek lives. There was nothing in the pre-Columbus experience which prepared the Creeks for the forces of European expansion and the thundersticks, or weapons of war. Adjusting to other Indian tribes involved an entirely different chemistry because it allowed for clan and linguistic differences and authority patterns that could be fitted into a larger continuum. However, Europeans brought notions of individualism without perceived social responsibility, the pursuit of private property without communal sharing, the pursuit of dogma, ethnic and religious cleansing, pervasive violence and total war, new and unknown diseases, and new and strange tools, laws, and values. Creeks usually had to give in or be destroyed or both. The outcome of Indian-white contact left a legacy of bitterness in many full-blood minds so deep that it shows up in strange ways. One very elderly Creek, when asked about his family's experience on the Trail of Tears, in essence said with some agitation, "I asked my father about the Trail—he became excited and bitter as though a very dark cloud came over him. My father demanded to know why I was asking—could I do something about it? Since I couldn't—let the ghosts lie—it was obvious my father was as deeply disturbed as I had ever seen him."[17]

Other full-blood families told detailed and bitter stories about the Trail. In many full-blood families, the distinctions among Spaniards, English, Scots, Southerners, and Northern reconstructionists blurred, with all being called white, not in reference to color but to the common denominators of radically different European ways and the conceptions of the isolated self, of private property, and of linear time. Chitto Harjo linked all the agony to Columbus. Columbus would come again and again, in the minds of Chitto Harjo and many full-bloods, under the guise of various transformations such as the conquistadors, Andrew Jackson, Dawes and the supporters of allotment of Indian lands, and the ending of the short-lived days of the Creek and other Indian republics sandwiched between removal and statehood.

The Creek interaction with the white world is of sufficient complexity that it deserves separate and elaborate treatment. Good historical and ethno-historical treatments of the interactions abound in the literature. But these works are not primarily Creek interpretation of such interactions. Part of the difficulty derives from contrasting notions of scholarship and discipline. Anglo historians are compelled by chronology and the written word commingled with conjecture and recorded hearsay. The Creek disciplined elders were governed more by major spatial events and the disciplined perceptions of the keepers of oral traditions. In chapter 12, we will refer to some of the major Creek historical landmarks. However, some of the Creek "prophecies" and interpretations of the legends can provide a sense of the full-blood Creek view of European "white societies."

The Muscogee Creek way of life included key metaphors that were contained in the legends. Tribal towns had keepers of the history and the legends of the tribe. These key legends were then extended by *owalas*, intuitive logicians or prophets, who would point toward the implications of the legends for the future. Three elements of legends have been extended by prophets to the characteristics of Europeans or whites. These three include the creation legend, different versions of the great sea serpent legend, and the ungrateful snake legend.

The creation legend included a segment which pointed out that what was cast out in the creative evolution of living things ended up in the ocean, and highlighted the danger of subsequent pollution and evil arising out of the ocean. Some post-Columbus, full-blood prophets suggest that immigration from abroad is an example of the trickeries of nature, of the evil that comes from the ocean.

The great sea serpent legend, which describes the sudden emergence of a giant serpent from the ocean, parallels the relevant segment of the creation legend. The serpent was ferocious but unhealthy and it literally spewed out, like bunches of foam, groups of baby snakes that raced toward land to do havoc. *Owalas* sometimes interpret the serpent as representing a giant European galleon, or ship, from which invaders were sent to do evil. The snakes landed so fast that the Creeks did not recognize the danger ahead.

The main story of the third legend speaks of a snake that was ill, cold, and weak. Creeks, in their compassion, took the snake in and kept it warm. However, the snake kept getting bigger and bigger, concurrently with the disappearance of various villagers. The snake finally got so big that it devoured the entire village. The simple moral of the story illustrates the need for knowing and watching the snake before you let it into the house and trust it. But the simple moral matches the *owalas'* deeper interpretation which points out the dangers of feeding the monster of European civilizations which began with modest, disguised pretensions and grew with greed into a terrible and huge monster that ate up Creek community after Creek community.

When the three legends are combined and applied to whites, we can see that the full-blood Creek attitude toward whites has been somewhat different when compared to the attitude toward blacks, other tribes, and even mixed-bloods. This does not mean that the Creeks were racist with respect to specific white individuals. It simply shows that the fatal impact of white society was regarded as something far different and more devastating than the boundaries of previous extensions of the Creek values of compassion, inclusiveness, and love. The swallowing snake that emerged from the ocean as a mutation of living things began to smother the Muscogee way, village by village. The *owalas* point toward a tragedy of perhaps unintended but nevertheless massive consequences. There are different versions of the growing snake but they all have sad endings, as though a major cycle of creation was coming to a close and an uncharted but basically sad "sixth" world was in the making—one that Chitto Harjo valiantly, but unsuccessfully, tried to prevent.

NOTES

1. For a more elaborate comparative discussion of contrasting meanings of love, see Chapter 10, note 2.

2. Creeks often used colors to represent concepts, including directions, various virtues, and people, in no particular hierarchical order. *Iste-jadi* also refers to the red man, or the Indian, and is much more complex than a reference to skin color.

3.   See chapter 12 for a historical overview.

4.   Several works discuss, in different degrees, the presence of mixed-bloods in Creek society. Any serious discussion of Creek perspective on mixed-bloods is missing in most works that are immersed in the standard pursuit of documentary and written history. The Creeks did not generate documents nor did they write reminiscences. An exploration of the oral history and an appropriate analytical framework are important in understanding the perspective of a beleaguered people who lacked a written language. For a contemporary work that combines documentary sources with non-Indian rumors (such as the ancestry of Osceola) and conjecture but misses any settled Creek perspective, see J. Leitch Wright, Jr., *Creeks and Seminoles* (Lincoln: University of Nebraska Press, 1968), specifically 60–62 and 73–101. Since the Creek perspectives are missing, Wright appears to perpetuate early white confusion (74) about who was regarded as a Creek by Creek communities, rather than by settlers, hunters, or agents. Wright's work at times appears to perpetuate, without objective documentation, many southern white perceptions of Creeks and Seminoles—about Osceola's ancestry and conjecture that "Bowles" is responsible for all the Seminoles with the name of "Bowlegs" (60–61). Wright also fails to distinguish Creek values from the massive onslaught of colonialism which resulted in the rubbing off of Anglo values on some Creeks. Further, without an understanding of the classic Creek economy, he portrays the unregulated pursuit of deer as a Creek preoccupation (71).It would take a separate review to illustrate the errors of Wright when he speculates about Creek values. His work is much more valuable as a review of non-Indian documents about Creeks and Seminoles but needs to be supplemented with Creek views.

5.   Narration rendered by James Scott in Okemah to members of the primary author's family and to the primary author in Okemah, Oklahoma until his death in the forties.

6.   See Michael D. Green, *The Politics of Indian Removal* (Lincoln: University of Nebraska Press, 1982), 33–36. Green's work, like Wright's, is solid when it comes to tracing standard non-Indian sources. Its weakness lies in the absence of Creek perspectives and in the engaging of conjecture about Creek ways. Green, for instance, is erroneously convinced that the wind clan had a settled superior status among Creeks, accounting for the rise of McGillivray and McIntosh.

7.   David H. Corkran, *The Creek Frontier: 1540–1783* (Norman: University of Oklahoma Press, 1987), 87.

8.   See the historical discussion in chapter 12.

9.   See chapter 11 about the cunning and tricky element of nature represented by the rabbit.

10.   Most historians have confused the Creek town classifications, assuming permanent distinctions between red towns and white towns. Peace towns were sometimes called white towns because the color symbolized peace. Red sticks and white sticks were character designations, not town designations. When several red sticks gathered in a town during a war, for instance, the town could loosely be called a red town.

11.   Southerners were immersed in the values of hierarchy, status, and inequality represented by Sir Robert Filmer's *Patriarcha* which represented establishment English values prior to the Puritans. Some of Filmer's lineal descendants settled in Virginia. This perspective resulted in seeing "kings," "queens," and "princesses" among the Creeks and other southern tribes.

12.   Benjamin Hawkins was Jefferson's agent in Creek country who provided much information about Creek country colored by his perspective. He speaks of the "Queen of Tukabatchee," probably referring to an important clan mother. Interestingly, most of the Creeks with private property and slaves he describes are mixed-bloods. See Benjamin Hawkins "A Sketch of Creek Country In the Years 1798

and 1799," *Collections of the Georgia Historical Society* III: I (MDCCCXLVIII) (New York: Kraus Reprint Co., 1971.)

13.   The term *African American* is of newer vintage. Southern whites used earlier terms with derogatory implications. For Creeks and Seminoles as we have repeatedly asserted, *iste* meant person, followed by *hetki*/white, *lustee*/black, *jadi*/red; this provided more detailed identification of the person involved without any implication of genetic superiorities or inferiorities.

14.   Southerners used racial labels frequently as putdowns. From the Creek standpoint, intermarriage did not make for inferiority, though it endangered the understanding of the clan relationships. Many African Americans who had married Creeks and Seminoles were completely accepted. But other relationships presented African Americans as a protected class, as a member of a Muscogee family, or as a resident of *lustee talwa*, black town. See the late anthropologist James H. Howard's views: "Seminole Negroes played a significant role throughout the ensuing Seminole wars and the removal of Indian Territory and were fiercely loyal to their Seminole allies. This loyalty was reciprocated by all Seminole leaders. Until quite recently, Negroes continued to reside among the Seminoles, acting as interpreters and liaison with whites. There was some intermarriage, but in almost all cases the mixed offspring became a part of the black communities rather than the Seminole towns. Blood group frequencies, for example, prove that the modern Florida Seminoles have almost no Negro ancestry and observations of Oklahoma Seminole phenotypes indicated this is true for that portion of the tribe as well." James H. Howard with Willie Lena, *Oklahoma Seminoles—Medicine, Magic and Religion* (Norman: University of Oklahoma Press, 1984), 6–7.

15.   See chapter 12 for a more complete portrait of Chitto Harjo.

16.   See the acknowledgment after the preface for recognition of Bill Osceola's contribution to our understanding of Florida Seminole oral history.

17.   Roosevelt Deerishaw, who lived until his death in the late nineties, in Okmulgee, Oklahoma.

THE MUSCOGEE POLITICAL SYSTEM: THE AUTHORITATIVE ALLOCATION OF VALUES

To the extent that politics and government involve an "authoritative allocation of values,"[1] the Muscogee Creeks' governance system contained the related instrumental structure, roles, and functions of its value system. The absence of a written language should not obliterate the realities and specificities of the Creek normative order in their customary law and politics.

Among the larger purposes of the government, striving for harmony with nature and within the community were two of the most important tasks. As the red stick/white stick legend in chapter 5 points out, the Creek notion of harmony presents some unique features. First, harmony takes effort; it is not a given and does not occur automatically. Given the unpredictable elements of nature and the quirks of human nature, the search for harmony takes sustained effort in all social institutions. The interlinked circles of a largely egalitarian community had no fixed political vertical hierarchies nor any fixed conceptions of caste and class. As we have seen elsewhere, the role differentiations arose from the need for division of labor associated with complex social tasks. Further, the Creek non-acquisitive ideals avoided large economic gulfs between the rich and the poor. The poor were helped and the wealthy gained community affection by gift-giving and sharing their resources.

The beaver stories of the Creeks, by analogy, point out that the beavers in their natural world demonstrate individual harmony, through their specialized tasks, and community harmony, through their division of labor in helping individual beavers repair their lodging. In turn, the Creek gift-giving and giveaways kept the economic range of distinctions among individuals and families fairly small. Additionally, without individually owned property, there was no intragenerational accumulation of land in the Creek traditional world. Personal property was mostly burnt when one died or it was left with the dead in their final scaffolds or, later, their graves. The accumulation of personal wealth was never a driving value in the Creek traditional world. Instead, sharing and exchanging energy and developing talent within the "natural" order of things provided the substantial meanings for the good life.

Legends, particularly in the oral tradition, contain compressed logical seeds of value and culture. The classic red stick/white stick legend reminded the Creeks that actual harmony is never a permanent gift. Differences in perceptions, personalities, and interests present the perennial seeds of social conflict. These differences are never permanently obliterated but to be balanced through the social and political institutions. Similarly, nature's cunning—symbolized in the antics of the rabbit, the trickster, the "little" dust devils or pseudo-tornadoes, and the natural justice of *boja*, the grandfather tornado—illustrates the cyclical themes of harmony, conflict, constructive efforts, and the return of harmony in the natural order. Like the Greek Sisyphus, Creeks have to move many boulders again and again. However, unlike the dark Greek imagery surrounding the condemnation of Sisyphus to a life of absurdity, the Muscogee Creeks envelop the Sisyphean tasks with the ethics of vitality, sharing, and communal celebration, mindful of the trickery and revenge of nature. The key to this striving for balance is the social and political organization of the Creek way.

STRUCTURAL OVERVIEW: UNITY AND DIVERSITY

The need for balancing diversities led to organization however loose, rather than anarchy. While the federalist system created by the American founding fathers differs greatly from the Creek system, the vertical division of powers in the federalist system resembled the Creeks' structure at certain points in their history.[2] Traditionally, the Creek gathering of tribes has been called a confederacy. This is not inaccurate since there was, traditionally, a great degree of autonomy allotted to tribes and tribal towns, or *talwas*. However, the uniformity of the Creek conception of freedom, the laws of nature, the intratribal protocols on war, agriculture, diplomacy, sanctuary, environmental rules, and the criminal codes gave some substance to the central Creek set of governmental and normative umbrellas without a central bureaucracy.

If we view federalism from a monistic positive law perspective, we will miss the nature of the unwritten living law customary norms of the Creek system of governance.[3] However, if we look at the Creeks from a pluralistic perspective of law and sovereignty, the Creeks indeed had common norms of freedom, safe passage, environmental protection, conflict resolution, and external security. The administration of these norms depended on a decentralized system. Thus, the decentralized mobilization of red stick warriors provided the instruments of external defense. Similarly, the recruitment of expert runners, primarily from the message-bearing clan—the bird clan—provided the communication system for the Creeks.

THE CONFEDERACY

We refer to the larger Creek system, as is usually done, as the Creek confederacy. It helps to see it as the equivalent of an intuitively conceived federalism: a middle way between simple federations or alliances and a Madisonian constitutional federalism (not the more centralized Hamiltonian federalism with the bureaucratic trappings of implied powers). In keeping with the Creek spirit, Creeks acted out of their sense of obligation derived from clan, familial, functional, communal, tribal, and consensual relationships. The obligations were binding both in war and peace except in the case of illness, special dispensations of elders, or the immunities derived from special individual "visions."

As a civilization without a formally written language, the Creek world compensated in their communications with a highly developed sense of oral dialogue, sign language, and drawings. Creeks traditionally used a now-obsolete southeastern sign language for communicating with non-Creek-speaking members and representatives of other tribes, as well as material signs such as eagle feathers to indicate peace or vulture feathers for war. They also used pictorial representations on skins; medicine men, for instance, regularly summarized their formulae on skins. The blowing of conch shells to communicate the results of conferences, the arrival or departure of messengers, and other bits of information were also part of traditional Creek culture. Creek officials generally were familiar with regional variations in the spoken languages of the confederacy. Specialized runners and relay teams of runners carried information from village to village and region to region. These runners knew the paths, which were kept secret in troubled times. While the runners were mostly men, Creek women, like men, were physically active and some accompanied male runners for sections of the way.

In the functional allocation of clan relationships the bird clan, as mentioned previously, bore the major leadership role for communications between the towns and regions. Members of the bird clan could recruit other relatives to carry out obligations but the responsibility rested with the bird clan. Throughout the inter-community communications, blending and balancing gender and clan relationships for serving a communal function was an ideal.

Membership in the Creek confederacy varied since, with the absence of slavery, tribes, bands, and towns could join or leave the confederacy. The confederacy was founded on the Creek legends and conceptions of pluralist dynamics and balancing in nature which predated the coming of Columbus.

The corn mother, in crossing the rainbow which ended the storms, scattered multicolored seed corn in different directions, representing her diverse children who must also follow the rainbow.

Part of the Creek tradition involved pilgrimages to and through various parts and groups of the confederacy—to the varying shrines and mounds. Then, there were specific reciprocal trading relationships and markets with various groups. The existence of the confederacy made the safe passage and the related protocols for long journeys, such as from Georgia to Ohio, possible before the coming of Columbus. After Columbus, with the intensification of the need for survival, the Creek confederacy became more dynamic in its security functions, while the pilgrimages and non-military functions began to decline. An example of the dynamics was the visits of Tecumseh, whose mother was reportedly Creek, to Creek councils in a somewhat unsuccessful attempt to expand the security and military relationships between the Shawnees and the Creeks against the whites. Gradually, however, with the ascending political roles of the mixed-bloods in Creek politics, particularly but not exclusively among the lower Creeks, the confederacy began to lose its legitimacy as groups such as the Seminoles began to deal with the whites in their own way.

Counting the number of members in the Creek confederacy is complicated by varying epistemological premises and classifications regarding the comparative meaning of terms like *tribe, band, township,* or *community.* From a Creek perspective, there were around thirty-three major members of the Creek confederacy at the time of European contact. Some of the thirty-three were counted without their own subdivisions, such as the Yuchie. In contrast, the larger Tuskegees had many subdivisions. Therefore, for some counts the subdivisions of major Tuskegee communities were also counted separately. When the subdivisions of major groups of bands and townships (such as Arbeka and Newayaka) were counted with the Yuchies, Alabamas, Coosas, Hichitee, and others, the membership could be said to be more than one hundred. Among the one hundred it should be remembered that many regional communities, in turn, had clusters of settlements, communities, and townships.

The confederacy did not have a capital in a European sense. They would decide an alternative township as a meeting place, either ahead of time or in communication through runners. Thus, they could call for a meeting in the Upper Creek region or alternately the Lower Creek region. The contemporary meaning of Upper and Lower Creeks has changed since pre-European times when "Upper" and "Lower" merely meant different geographical regions. With the arrival of the Europeans and intermarriages, additional meanings accrued to the originals. Lower Creeks included more mixed-bloods while the Upper Creeks, predominantly full-bloods, were culturally more conservative and resistant to white domination. Many aggressive red sticks gravitated toward the Upper Creeks, which contributed to the confusion among non-Creeks concerning the meaning of red sticks, who were sometimes mistaken as clans. Prior to Columbus, the core of the original confederacy involved the alternative balancing of the two main bodies of Creeks—the Upper and the Lower Creeks. The Upper Creeks lived in two major townships, Tukabachee and Arbeka, while the Lower Creeks inhabited Coweta/*koweta* and Cashita/*kasehta*. The largest Creek councils would usually alternate their meetings in these four major townships.

The non-Creek-speaking members of the Creek confederacy were not compelled to become Creeks. Many members of the confederacy knew more than one language, and the languages of other groups were not prohibited by the Creeks. Other groups also preserved their own legends, stories, and beliefs. However, what was expected was that in the conference grounds, council meetings, and in joint meetings the Creek protocol of respect for the *miccos*, the elders, the fire, and the other basic elements of the *chogothakko/cuko rakko* or the sacred grounds be respected by all.

As a result of the genocide by the Spaniards and later the English, some bands or groups began to disappear, with small remnants merging into larger groups in the Creek world, particularly after several generations of intermarriages. This was true of bands of Timucuas and Apalachicolas. The Trail of Tears also added to the merging of groups such as the Miccosukees, who over time became Oklahoma Seminole or sometimes Creeks. A measure of the conception of the confederacy, however, can be seen in some of the remaining fragments of the Creek view; the Yuchis, members of the confederacy, remain a tribe with their own linguistic history and cultural premises. Similarly, the Creeks and the Shawnee full-bloods of Oklahoma maintained, on the whole, a friendly relationship in Oklahoma through the 1940s and 1950s.

In their conception of political authority the Creeks recognized no racial, biological, or economic bases for authority. Nor did they have a theory of the divine rights of "kings" or *miccos*. The Creeks expected respect for the functions that key people performed and respect for the elders. When elders spoke on ceremonial grounds or in council, the youth would say "*Maddo*"(elaborate thanks) in a long, drawn out, respectful way. Some early settlers and naive observers would mistake the respect shown some elders, particularly *miccos* of townships, and mistakenly interpret the respect as evidence of monarchic authority or chieftainship.

The Creek conception of authority had two principle sources. The higher of the two sources was "the order of things" or the laws of nature, the rules that could be traced back from the four law-giving spirits, or elements, in nature and eventually to the first universal principle of the universe, Ibofanga. Out of the laws of nature come the rules for treating the botanical, zoological, geological, and astronomical worlds. This leads to the operational rules for agriculture, medicine, healing, hunting, preservation of natural resources, and pollution. These natural laws are fundamental and, therefore, deeper than the pronouncements of any *micco* or council. The natural laws, in turn, gave rise to three key Creek values of love, faith, and compassion which are the ideal requirements of Creek civil leadership. Even today, the *miccos* of the ceremonial grounds do not try to impress visitors with the extent or depth of their knowledge or power.

While the laws of nature provided the primary sources of authority, the secondary principle of democratic consensus or consent clarified and covered the remaining ambiguities of the political landscape. Creek democracy, however, was not mob rule—the process of consent included interlinked centers of decision-making, with checks and balances apparently intended to avoid the development of a permanent political elite. The decisions of community councils, regional councils, clan mothers, beloved men, and beloved women were all made by consensus, after conferences in which conflicting views were presented and open discussion and oratory was permitted and encouraged. The Creek conceptions of nature provided the general rules while consent helped define the details of policy.

Creek democracy did not imply the absence of individuality. Within the broad social framework a great range of individual activity and behavior was tolerated. First, there were many differentiated social roles in war and peace, and an individual's talent could be satisfactorily fitted to an appropriate role. Individuals were not forced to become medicine men, administrators, or *miccos*. With the appearance of appropriate qualities, people were guided towards the proper role, but they had to have the proper will or *boea fikcha*—the fire within. This respect for individuality was seen in the Creek passion for privacy. Creeks—contemplative by nature in their prayers and visions, in their crafts, or at home—were not afraid of being alone. The balanced love of solitude is a common part of the character of many mature Creek full-bloods, even today.

In addition to the blending of law with consent, and social requirements with privacy, Creek government blended another set of dual forces which were social-psychological in origin. This was the red stick/white stick phenomenon. In chapter 5 we have elaborated on the primary epic of the red stick/white stick battle and its outcome and implications. We turn now to its consequences for Creek government.

OF RED STICKS AND WHITE STICKS

Red sticks and white sticks were psychologically based labels which were applied to two different ends of the spectrum of personality possibilities—these were complementary twins or assistants or *aboktas*. Reasonability, analytical ability, patience, mediation skills, and scientific knowledge were some of the indicators of the white stick personality complex. Courage, strength, practical knowledge of nature and terrains, alertness, and a tendency towards activism and physical skills were indicators of a red stick personality. Obviously, no one exhibited 100 percent of the qualities, but one or the other was seen as a predominant trait. But both the complementary qualities were balanced by the common norms of the community and the laws of the councils, clans, and families.

Harnessing these twin physiological characteristics in Creek society took place in the balancing of civil and military or security functions. The white sticks took the leadership in performing the rich variety of civil functions and roles. The red sticks, in turn, took the leadership in the rich array of military, security, and law enforcement functions. The assignments of red sticks and white sticks did not mean that only red sticks could fight and only white sticks could govern. The assigned roles meant that it was up to the red sticks to mobilize for war or security—they could ask red sticks or white sticks for help. Similarly, white sticks were assigned civilian roles but they could recruit red sticks for communal tasks. The vestiges of the red stick/white stick phenomenon can be seen on many traditional ceremony grounds like Asilanabi (Greenleaf) even today. White stick types are the peaceful medicine men and the "encouragers" for the dances. Red stick types provide the security and the law enforcement, ensuring that drinking and other forms of pollution do not occur on the ceremonial grounds. But the red stick types also help haul water and wood when the civil authorities decide that these are needed. Today, a medicine man is not supposed to be an aggressive person while a ceremonial ground security person can be aggressive and firm in ensuring that the protocol of the ceremonial grounds is observed. Traditionally, the white sticks also excelled at conciliatory and mediational efforts. However, when the time arrived for the white sticks to insure the security of the Creeks, a red stick warrior could put on his war paint. He could paint half his face red (*jadi*/red/south/blood/life) and the other half black (*lustee*/black/west/death/reflective sleep). The warrior's signs indicated a balanced approach; he was equally prepared for life or death.

The red stick/white stick phenomenon has been widely misunderstood by historians who have used broad labels such as "red stick rebellion" or "red stick war," but such labels insufficiently explain the inner workings of Creek society. Since Creek society did not employ the Anglo-American statutory and common law approach to social order, much of the Creek governmental system has been understudied and underdescribed. Once English common-law principles began to be applied to Creek society by mixed-blood self-appointed elites, the erosion of traditional Creek government had begun. In Indian territory and in the state of Oklahoma, Creek constitutionalism mimicked the Anglo conceptions of law and government. The Creek normative content was captured less and less in the new structures of written "constitutions."

The Creeks traditionally had elaborately differentiated roles in both civil and military functions, much more so than most tribes. Many of the titled roles began to disappear with the European invasion, and some are therefore lost forever in the aftermath of the wars, the removal, and Oklahoma statehood. In the use of Creek terms, context makes a big difference. Thus the term *micco* appears again and again. Though loosely translated as chief or ruler or king, to properly understand the term *micco* the functional (civil/military) role, the jurisdictional (town/region) role, and the source of legitimacy (nature of the appropriate consensus of town and committee) must be made sufficiently clear.

CIVIL ROLES

Many of the civil roles withered eventually because of the extraordinary and sustained pressures from western civilization on Creek society, from the Spaniards to the present day. Once there was a role called that of the *ispokogi micco*, that of a priest. The role distinctions in Creek are horizontal and not vertical or "unequal." These priests provided leadership in dealing with Creek astronomy and its social implications, including the timing and rituals involved in the pilgrimages to the mounds. That entire function has evaporated and remains as fragments of oral history among the few reliable sources.[4] A *micco* represented a leadership principle, or concept, with contextual limitations and the *ispokogi* performed the astronomically related priestly functions in the Creek mounds. Contemporary *miccos* perform some of those time-setting functions, though the "mounds" are not the same. Sometimes, the ancient ones were referred to as *iste poggi/este pokv*, or "those that have gone before you." Some *miccos* were never persons but principles or concepts or "spirits," such as the seven *miccos* who governed the seven directions of Creek space. In contrast, the *italwa micco* was the determinant civil chief of a particular *talwa* or township. The *italwa micco*'s powers were accorded through consensus. He did not automatically report to the region's *micco,* whose powers derived from a regional council. The lineup of the *miccos* must not be thought of in hierarchical terms. With the coming of whites and white pressure on Creek society, aided by mixed-bloods, however, the conception of a linear hierarchy of chiefs began to emerge which contributed to the transfer and disappearance of Creek lands. The limited legitimacy of the disputed *micco thakko/mekko rakko*, or principal chief, can be seen in the execution (from the full-blood perspective) or the assassination (from the mixed-blood perspective) of William McIntosh, who had signed over Creek lands without consulting the network of councils. Without the consensus of councils, treaty-making by a *talwa micco* or a regional *thakka micco* was null and void in the Creek traditional way. It should be emphasized that we are describing the traditional norms of Creek governance before the rise of the mixed-bloods and the changes in legitimacy that followed. That legitimacy further eroded with the coming of European-style "constitutions."

The *micco* of each *talwa* had an *abokta* or assistant who was in charge of the internal workings of the ceremonies in the town square. The *micco* himself concentrated more on the external aspects of administration dealing with other *talwas*, visitors from other *talwas*, and making sure that the general features of the community consensus were being administered. The *miccos* and all other civil officers were the equivalent of executives. Policy-making by consensus was done in the communities and the councils. In addition to the *micco* and his *abokta*, a *talwa* would have a *yatika/yvtekv* who was an interpreter and an encourager for proper action. A *yatika* would generally know the nuances of several dialects and also know the tradition sufficiently to encourage the community and to explain to the community the linkage of specific actions to the logic of its historical and traditional foundations. Besides the *yatikas*, towns and communities would have *owalas/owalv*, the logicians who engaged in prophecy and showed the future implications of the current events. The *owalas* were the traditional prophets selected, trained, and honored for their vision. In addition to the *owalas*, there were *henihas/henehv*. A *heniha* administered public works—building an irrigation channel, constructing the community food storage bins, and other community activities.

A whole series of community roles were assigned, usually based on clan specialization. Bird clans provided the runners and the messengers. Wind clan members specialized in predictions about nature, including the weather. Bear clan members specialized in making medicine. The medicine men themselves were the *hilis hayas/heleshayv*. Townships also had a medicine speaker, an *asimbonaya/vsempunayv*, who would speak to the community about "the order of things," that is, what needed to be done holistically for general community health.

The roles described here illustrate the Creek love of functional specialization. None of these roles, including that of the town chief, was hereditary. A *micco*'s son, naturally, had a good opportunity to learn diplomacy and leadership from his father; however, sons do not always pick up a father's strength. Similarly, clans and families groomed their chosen members for specific roles, but fitness for office evolves unevenly and, ultimately, community acceptance determined whether one became a *micco*, a *heniha*, a *yatika*, or a *hilis haya*.

The elaborate governmental roles were not tied with the strings of law in the Anglo-American common-law sense. Therefore, like very traditional, community-oriented people, Creeks did not have nor did they need a separate, permanent bureaucracy. It could be said that the emphasis was on the spirit of the laws, and since the spirit was constantly shaped by Creek values and kept alive by the *yatikas*, the *asimbonayas*, the *hilis hayas*, storytellers, the *miccos*, and the entire network of community authority, no "recorded" statutes were necessary. Persons performing their assigned roles and educated accordingly made the system work.

The shattering of the specialized roles by the onslaught of European civilization began to undermine Creek government. Instead of the dependence on spirit, "modern" laws of the Anglo-American common-law variety started to replace the disciplined voluntaristic, communitarian social framework. Gradually the development of a "modern" Creek government took place. Although the titles sounded similar—*miccos* and principal chiefs and house of warriors—the framework changed and much of the spirit was gone. Mediation, exhortations, and moral obligation were substituted by adversarial interests, adjudication, and eventually litigation.

MILITARY ROLES

In addition to civil roles, Creeks also had a long list of military or security roles or job classifications. These roles were fully activated in war. Since the Creeks had a people's army as opposed to a standing army, however, these roles were also useful for special peacetime security tasks such as protecting the peace towns, evacuating civilians in disasters, and enforcing law in cases that required additional administrative strength. Again, we should recall from the logic of the red/white stick legend, that this war/peace dualism incorporated opposite sets of psychological traits and, further, that the striving for social harmony meant that there needed to be room to blend these two sets of manifestations of the human spirit.

In the military and security functions, as in the civil functions, there existed elements of a pyramid structure in the roles—again without a hereditary caste—that is, there were fewer *miccos* than *henihas*. Similarly, in the security structure there were more followers than there were leaders. However, the war leaders like the *miccos* were beholden to community consensus expressed through the relevant councils and committees. Thus policy-making and executive power were separated in Creek government but executive power resided in twin heads, the civil and the security (or war) chiefs. As in the civil functions, the war titles were given at appropriate times to the person. Thus, a Creek would have different names at name-giving ceremonies. For many, one of the names would be the civil role (*micco* or *heniha*) or the war role (*tustenagee/tvstvnvkke*).

The novice Creek warriors, normally the youngest people, belonged to the class called *tastikayalgi/tvstvnvkvlke*, the newly recruited warriors. Then came the rank of the *imalas*, who coordinated the rank and file. The more trusted (in war) among the *imalas/emvra* would become the *labotskalgi/rvposkvlke*. These soldiers and sergeants would belong to the broad group of the *imala lakalgi*. Above the *imala lakalgi*, who performed basic supervisory tasks, came the more permanent part of the military infrastructure—the shock troops, the *tustenagees* or *tustenagalgi*. Among the tustenagees were at least three gradations: the *tustenagee* proper, the "higher" *tustenagee thakkos* who could perform tasks of internal security, and the *tustenagi simiabaiyas*, who specialized in the strategy of external relations. Above the classes of *tustenagees* were the *yaholas*, the war chiefs, who were in charge of strategy and commanded the bands of warriors for each community. Among the *yaholas* from the various communities would then, by consensus, rise the equivalent of commanders-in-chief who earned special titles—such was the case of Obothleyahola (the intelligent commander) or Osceola (the *yahola* who has really taken the sacred *asi* or the black drink, has purged his impurities, and is truly ready for battle). *Yahola* would remain as a suffix for great war leaders, the prefix of whose name would capture their personal quality.

The war or security leaders did not constitute a permanent army in a modern sense. Normally, in everyday governmental affairs they would blend into civilian life and would be deferential to the *miccos* and *henihas* about the daily peacetime needs of the community. Only when conflict arose and the councils decided that defense was needed would the ranks of the *tustenagees* and the *yaholas* be activated. They would then consult with the most knowledgeable of the group of "beloved men" who themselves were once warriors, regarding strategy.

When the perceived security problem was local in character, with respect to an isolated band of Cherokees, the entire tribe was not mobilized. Local option among the appropriate and willing *talwas* prevailed with respect to the appropriate response. It is with the advance of European civilization that the nationwide mobilization of the warriors and runners became frequent and widespread in the interest of basic survival. Though the Creeks did not have a permanent standing army, the nature of the athletic activities of the Creeks—running and swimming, war games—kept the youthful security infrastructure of the tribe basically ready and prepared for battles when needed. Nevertheless, as we know, the eventual outcome of meeting the technologically powerful European juggernaut was the Trail of Tears and its aftermath. In war, particularly when avenging wrongful death, Creek men and women could display great aggressiveness and cruelty. Often, in the cleansing ceremonies after battles for survival, men displayed trophies and women beat the captured enemy.

During war, Creek decisions were made through elaborate steps. First there would be attempts at mediation and compromise. If diplomacy didn't work, symbolic war (that is, stickball games) was preferred to war. Only with the constant facing of the swords, the pikes, and later the thundersticks (guns) of the European forces did the war games begin to recede in importance as a method of solving disputes. The war games that resolved many intertribal and intratribal disputes could not perform the same function against an adversary whose aims and technology were entirely different from traditional adversaries like the Cherokees. The energies of the warriors—the *tustenagees* and others—like the energies of the civil officers—the *henihas*—were subject to the general decision-making system of the Muscogee Creeks.

THE FRAMEWORK OF DECISION-MAKING

The red stick/white stick legend and the creation myth provide the seeds of Muscogee decision-making, which, as mentioned earlier, was nonhierarchical in that it did not involve a vertical alignment of superior/inferior relationships. The symbolic roots of widespread dialogue and the eventual jelling of consensus and consent appear in the stories of clan formation, as well as in the discussion of the red stick council and the white stick council. Thus, the Creek executive function lacked an inherent source of authority outside the context of discussion and consent. However, the executive function with the civil *miccos* and the war *yaholas* were those of applying the principles agreed upon by the relevant council. As Swanton points out, a Tukabachee *yahola* stated in 1825 that he had no authority to sell land, there was no land to sell, and further, "What is not done in the public square, in general council, is not binding on the nation."[5]

Creek society was thoroughly infused with group discussions and meetings. Given the importance of the family and the clans, the discussions and decisions of the families and clans provided important aspects in weaving the social fabrics. Within the family, the mother played a dominant role and even her sisters—the *mamagee-s* or little mothers—provided surrogate authority in the absence of the mother. The father, ideally, was a skillful but loving teacher, but it was the mother's brother—the maternal uncle or uncles—who disciplined the youth, including conducting the dry scratching with garfish teeth on the legs and arms. Wet scratching was different and more ritualized and medicinal or related to initiation ceremonials and could involve a *hilis haya* or medicine man or *micco*.[6]

The family property belonged to the mother, though the father had his own personal belongings. The family structure was knit with a whole complex of clan and kin relationships. Age was not the only criterion in defining these relationships. A younger person from the father's clan could actually be the uncle of a Creek youth. These fusions of age and clan created the entire complex of the protocols of advice, assistance, respect, protection, humor, and ridicule.

Within each clan were also institutionalized groups of men and women, the beloved men and the beloved women. The beloved women or clan mothers of a clan, in turn, were linked with clan mothers of other clans to form a society of beloved women in each community. The matrilineal authority system of the Creeks meant that irrespective of the *de jure* formalities, the *de facto* authority of the women through the beloved women's groups was considerable. The women's groups equaled some of the most powerful committees in a democratic legislative process. A strong negative opinion expressed by the beloved women could veto any other policy recommendations with respect to community, agriculture, public works, land use, and other civil decisions.

Traditionally, the beloved women sent representatives to the community councils who could speak in the circles of decision-making in the round-houses. Their wishes could easily color the nature of the emerging consensus. Gradually, with the changes in socialization resulting from the wars, the imitation of the whites, and the rise of the mixed-bloods, male dominance began to edge out the beloved women in the public decision-making process. Vestiges of the power of women, however, can still be seen in the interactions at the gatherings of Creek traditionals and even in Creek churches.

Traditionally, before the rise of male dominance, the house of warriors and the beloved men had their own considerable but balanced powers. Within the clans they were involved in the executive aspects of clan activities. Thus, the beloved men of the bird clan would direct the youth who were the runners and messengers of Creek society. The beloved men in the councils would deal with the policy issues involved with the strategies of war, the conduct of war games, the negotiations within the confederacy, the conduct of hunting, the enforcement of the criminal laws, and conduct of the long pilgrimages to faraway mounds and shrines. The beloved men's committees too, like those of the beloved women, could veto certain points in the decision-making process. These veto points, or contextual power, functioned in the same way that committee deliberations do in congressional debates. Unlike the United States Congress or the state legislatures, however, actual policy-making did not involve pluralities or majorities. Final decisions involved the development of consensus at the end of the deliberation process.

John Calhoun, the leading spokesman of the Old South, spoke of the importance of consensus in the doctrine of the concurrent majority, wherein a minority had veto power over the majority. Calhoun's vision, however, excluded women, blacks, and Indians. In contrast, the Creek consensus involved developing synthesis in the views of institutionalized groups, of many specialized committees, and of women and men in relatively autonomous or decentralized *talwas* or communities, each with their legislative councils and executive miccos. While the clan system provided the conservative social framework, elsewhere we have elaborated on the absence of racism and the presence of a preoccupation with the value of freedom in the Muscogee way. The marriage of the male and female principles produced an inclusive community.

COMMUNITY AND GOVERNANCE

Each Creek community, or *talwa*, was autonomous in local government matters within the framework of "natural laws" dealing with crime and the environment. The details in the decision-making structure of other non-Creek communities in the confederacy differed. Our discussion centers on the Muscogee Creek communities.

While all of nature was revered by the Creeks, certain areas were particularly sacred or holy, *hithkida/vcaketv* (sacred place). Mounds were *hithkida*; so were the round or oval ceremonial grounds and the central square of each community with its sacred fire at the center. Creeks, like some other Indians, had winter and summer homes. Families were comparatively more on their own in the winter, while the summer was more communal in nature. These cycles also roughly paralleled winter hunts and pilgrimages, summer harvesting, and spiritual renewal. Yet even during the winter travels, their political and social roots remained with the relevant ceremonial grounds for each Creek. In Creek symbolism, everyone's umbilical cord is buried in one place on earth so Creeks traditionally always had a symbolic connection to the area.

Each ceremonial ground followed basically the same concepts of governance except for the special peace towns. The latter, as we have discussed in chapter 5, were traditionally places of refuge or sanctuary and separated from regular townships or *talwas/tulwv*. Refugees, runaways, homeless, and even the injured enemy could seek the solace of peace towns. Hence, the peace towns did not follow exactly the same governmental structure of *miccos* and councils, and depended on the survival and security support from nearby *talwas*.

Each *talwa* featured a roundish, or oval, ceremonial ground. Outside the ceremonial ground were rings of scattered homes or *huti-s*, for matrilocally extended families.[7] Additional structures such as storehouses were positioned near the family and community gardens. Around the ceremonial grounds were camp houses and huts where instruction, crafts, and visitations took place. The ceremonial grounds were the symbolic *chogo thakko/cuko rakko*, or the "big real home" grounds. Adopted elements of the spatial arrangements can still be seen around ceremonial grounds and even rural churches in Oklahoma Creek country today. The big house is a literal and somewhat inaccurate translation. A *chogo* traditionally was a spot in Mother Earth, and the true reference was to the place on earth rather than the structures above the earth which were more temporary. Today, the term *chogo* is commonly associated with the external structure of a home in common usage or in dictionary definitions. Within the *chogo thakko* ceremonial area was the central square, the Creek *polis*, where the ceremonies and dances were held. Each square, with its central fire, provided the spatial community link and center to groups of nearby *huti-s* or residential communities.

In the post-removal days of the tribe, the square remained as the vestigial central place for public meetings. Other gatherings occurred in camp houses and halls where decisions were made. However, in the classic pre-Anglo period of Muscogee life, the Creeks had additional regional conference centers where people from nearby *talwas* would gather for meetings. These regional council houses were sometimes also called the big house or *chogo thakko*. At other times, these roundhouses were called the *chogo biloxi/cuko polokse*, literally the roundhouse. Creeks would walk and later ride to these regional roundhouses, which could accommodate travelers overnight before the start of council meetings.

With the advent of the Creek and Seminole wars with the United States, the regional roundhouse became obsolete except for historical and traditional memory. The external elements of Creek life changed with the external forces that Creeks faced, but the core value structure remained deeply in the traditional cultural mind, often unconsciously. Yet the values represented by the roundhouse are very much part of the psychic world of the traditional full-blood. The principles of dialogue, specialized committee input, and the development of consensus when the *boea fikcha* or the spirit field was in flow can be seen in traditional Creek discussions and even in rural Creek church meetings, where someone would spontaneously go out and ring the church bell. In earlier days, the reaching of consensus would have been announced by the sound of buffalo horns. In very early days, before Columbus, the blowing of conch shells indicated the reaching of consensus in the roundhouse.

CHOGO BILOXI, THE ROUNDHOUSE

Roundhouses no longer exist in Creek communities except for attempts at the architectural imitations in the current Creek tribal headquarters in Okmulgee, Oklahoma, or the reconstruction by the late traditionalist and revivalist, Philip Deer, on his property east of Okemah, Oklahoma. The Creek roundhouse is repeatedly mentioned in the oral histories. Not every *talwa* had a roundhouse—smaller communities placed their councils around the town squares. The Creek roundhouses served several communities and settlements and were shared for regional conferences and council meetings. Creek roundhouses could hold hundreds of persons and were naturally round in shape both on the outside and the inside.

Recent excavations provide interesting archeological evidence about the concept of the roundhouse which was shared by the Creek tribal groups. In 1993, archeologists found the remains of the "earliest permanent European settlement in the United States" in St. Augustine, Florida.[8] A fort was built in 1565 "decades before the English established the Virginia Colony at Jamestown in 1607 and the Pilgrims on the Mayflower landed at Plymouth Rock in 1620."[9] The first Spanish settlement depended on the initial hospitality of one tribal band of the Timucua Indians, who were part of the Creek cultural umbrella. The Muscogee Creeks provided the dominant cultural umbrella in the southeastern United States.[10]

The Spanish wiped out a nearby French group and proceeded to dig in and "build" a fort. Essentially the Spanish, going beyond the hospitality of the Indians, took over the tribal Timucua roundhouse and converted it into a fort, placing a deep moat around the roundhouse. Seven months later, the Indians set fire to the roundhouse but the Spanish proceeded to build other structures and fortifications. The archeological evidence points to the Timucua Indian structure as "a large oval or circular structure with thatch roof that would accommodate up to three hundred people."[11] The Spanish settlement included about 1,500 soldiers and settlers. Their attempts to grow European crops failed, and in order to survive they had to adjust to the agricultural technology of the Timucuas in the sandy soil. The Timucuas were known as the *dimitkosi* by the Georgia Creeks. *Dimitkosi* and its corruption *Timucuas* simply refers to the poverty of the Timucua Indian region because of the nature of the soil. *All* of Florida was part of the broadly conceived Creek cultural area.[12] Florida was known to the Creeks as *gun fuski/kvnfvske*, a peninsula. "Gun" is derived from *igana/ekunv* which is "land" or "earth," while *fuski/fvske* means "sharp," that is, land that sharply goes out. In any case, the archeological evidence of the large and inter-village longhouses, big houses, or roundhouses confirms the oral traditional Creek historical references to the roundhouses being regional conference centers or gathering places for clusters of *talwas*. Thus, the square was the center of community government in a *talwa* while the roundhouse was the center of the region. The ebb and tide of regional government varied with external challenges. As we have seen, the center of the confederacy did not reside in one permanent "capital"; rather, the meetings of the larger confederacy would alternate among several regional centers, such as Tukabachee or Arbeka. The family, the clan, the *talwa*, the region, and the confederacy were the expanding concentric circles of governance. The roundhouse in its shape, size, and other architectural features incorporated many basic values of the Creek conceptual world. The general roundness symbolized the mother's womb, Mother Earth. As in the creation myth, there was movement and discussion among living things in the womb of Mother Earth prior to the journey into light and knowledge, symbolized by the sun.

The typical roundhouse faced east toward the rising sun bringing the dawn of knowledge, knowledge about what needs to be done. The creative force of the rising sun was thought to activate the gestation of energy-sharing that was supposed to occur within the womb-like roundhouse. The roundhouse was generally closed except for the one major opening toward the eastern sun and the opening on the top above the central fire. The male fire of the sun coming into the womb of Mother Earth provided the setting for the dialogues of the community. Through the dynamics of discussion, the Creeks believed, a truth for the community would be born. The materials for the Creek roundhouses and related structures blended with the variations in the regional material environments. In southern and warmer regions, thatched roofing was more readily available. In the north, increased use of mud and earth gave greater climate control in the roundhouses.

The ceremonial fire—paralleling the ceremonial fires in each of the squares of the *talwas* or communities—was situated at the center of the regional roundhouse. The fire pit featured a depressed hole at its base, which fortified the connection to earth and the earthward direction—one of the seven sacred directions. The fire itself was the center and one of the seven "directional indicators." A central hole in the ceiling of the roundhouse allowed the smoke and the heated air to rise upward to the third direction. The fire itself was kindled with four logs arranged in a cross with space in the center. Each of these logs faced one of the remaining four horizontal directions, east, south, west, and north. The vertical (up/down) and the horizontal (north, south, east, and west) planes and lines pointed to the fire at the center of the axis. For some ceremonies, four ears of corn would be arranged around the fire in a circular fashion, one ear of corn in each of the spaces between the logs. This central arrangement was particularly important during the busk, or green corn, celebrations in each of the *talwas*. The circular arrangement of the corn represented the spreading and sharing of the energy provided by the coming together of the four elements (earth, fire, air, and water) in the harvest. The central arrangement of the logs was a common denominator for Creek rituals in the *talwa* square and in the regional roundhouse. The internal circular seating arrangement is highly significant and has political and theoretical implications—the reconfirmation of the Creek egalitarian circles of community. Age has its wisdom and honor but in the process of sharing energy everyone participates, contributes, and is part of an even circle of equality. From each according to their ability and to each according to their needs was a traditional living Creek egalitarian principle.

The participating elders—the beloved men (and women, in earlier times)—entered the roundhouse from the right side of the entrance, circled it counterclockwise, and sat at the end of the circle next to the entrance. The youth, including the warriors, entered last and sat immediately to the right upon entering. The circle of the old to the young would then be completed because the opening created the closing of the circle by the energy of the sun. For major conferences, the participants took appropriate medicine, which was symbolically energized by the rising eastern sun. In the roundhouse, the ground would be cleaned and sprinkled with water and the fire would also be ritually fed with offerings. Whether it was a regional conference of the Creeks, or a meeting in the town square, the search for consensus or even sharing of energy was rooted in Creek philosophy of nature, its spirits, elements, and the bridges to social and political organizations.

The protocol of participation required deference to the beloved men and women, the elders. The youth were free to express their opinions but they also showed their respect for the elders by saying *maddo*, or thanks, in a deeply reverential way after an elder's speech. Those who came to the roundhouse conferences represented the *talwas*. Representation was proportional—the larger tribal groups sent more representatives—but the openness and the intensities of the sometimes fractional discussions and the importance of consensus gave everyone the opportunity to provide input into the decision-making process. The dynamic of balancing input from the communities, from the clan, and from specialized organizations was part of the process of developing broad public policy. Individuals who were not present at the council could also be heard if they had something to convey. The biological and clan relative systems were so extensive that if all else failed an individual could convey his views through a "relative" who would be present in a roundhouse or a *talwa* council meeting.

Throughout the world of Creek legends are series of twin stories in which the mother figure, sometimes Mother Earth, would give birth to twins, each with slightly different qualities. The common moral content of the legends denotes the need for balancing the diversity of human qualities so that out of the sharing of reciprocal but empirically different energies the unity of the spirit and the community would occur. The unity of the spirit also represented the vibration, voice, and spirit of Hesagedamesse. Achieving this unity, in turn, was celebrated in many ways, including using the sound of conch shells or buffalo horns. The red stick/white stick legend, overcoming factionalism with communication, is one such twin story, but many others point towards the dual balancing qualities of the logical and the absurd, the serious and the jocular, the aggressive and the conciliatory—all needing human social effort in the journey towards harmony. This effort was not without rancor, debate, factionalism, and conflict until the pathway of collective energy was found.

Therefore, in the roundhouse the effort was made to bring in different and discordant viewpoints and work until the wills of the diverse voices were blended. Then Creeks joyfully announced the closure of decision-making with the sounds of conches and horns, and the policy decisions were then administered by the appropriate civil or security representatives and functionaries in peace or war. When Creek consensus was not found, factionalism would spill over into physical confrontations wherein men and women could reenact the confrontations of the red stick/white stick legend before healing allowed the return to dialogue.

The communal fire with its companion elements earth, air, and water was kept going in the center of the roundhouse all year long, symbolic of the continuity of Creek spiritual life. The roundhouse, in the period of regional strengths, contained the central fire while each community or *talwa* or town square also had its own fire. The fire of the smaller town squares would be symbolically kept alive between meetings by using the coals and embers in companion fires in homes and then using them to assist in reigniting the central fire of the square throughout the years. Through the historical waxing and waning of regional strengths and the confederacy, however, it was the talwa, the local political community, that provided the nucleus of the Creek way of life.

THE *TALWA*, THE LOCAL COMMUNITY

Descriptions of the traditional Creek ceremonial grounds in each *talwa* (local community or township) and the central square in each ceremonial ground abound in the literature. John R. Swanton, in his monumental, primarily descriptive work entitled *Social Organizations and Social Usages of the Indians of the Creek Confederacy,* describes alternative floor plans of various ceremonial grounds in the 1920s and also summarizes previous descriptions, both oral and written.[13] Other descriptions of contemporary grounds have surfaced since Swanton,[14] but Swanton's access to older grounds makes his work far more important than more recent descriptions. What is important in this chapter is understanding the meanings of the fundamental symbolism of authority, governance, and social structure from the point of view of Creek values.

Details concerning the arrangements of ceremonial grounds, round-houses, and squares in each *talwa* in Creek history vary. Some of the differences are due to the differences in the community traditions—Euchis versus Creeks versus Alabamas. Some of the differences in the seating arrangements in the town squares were due to the local distribution of the clans. Preponderance of white sticks in peacetime or red sticks during defense efforts could also result in variances in the spirit and space usage in a town. A third source of the differences in the arrangements relates to whether the township was a regular township or whether it was a peace town or refuge or a temporary arrangement. The latter would not necessarily have the full set of buildings that a regular community would. Furthermore, a major source of variations in the structures is due to the ravages of war, removal, and the resultant attempts to rebuild elements of shattered lives. Due to these forces, local mounds, roundhouses, sweathouses, dormitories, and many other structures that surrounded the ceremonial grounds declined. As the power of Creek government waned, the struggle for spiritual survival narrowed gradually to life around the central square of each ceremonial ground. It was and remains a challenge today for traditional Creeks simply to keep the sacred fire and ceremonies going in a meaningful way.

Traditionally, each *talwa* with its ceremonial fire was autonomous in its powers of local governance. The *talwa* council met in the local *chogofa/cukofv*, or roundhouse. The roundhouse was situated within the generally circular or oval ceremonial grounds where various huts used for committee meetings, conferring, or other community tasks were located. There were sweathouses for Creek sweats, separate for men and women. The Creek sweathouses, with their interior rows of elevated seating arrangements, differed from those of the Plains Indians. There were also individual sweating arrangements. Near the ceremonial grounds were various camp houses (dormitories) for travelers and visitors who were not lodging with an immediate relative. Of course, away from the ceremonial grounds were the regular houses of the Creeks, in mostly matrilocal clusters, each with their individual fields, herbal gardens, storage bins, and women's houses surrounded by large community gardens and community storage houses hoarding surpluses for needy people and for troubled times.

At the edge of the ceremonial grounds but within the sacred area was a full field for the regular "little brother of war" stick ball games with goalposts on each end. There would be a separate pole in another area for abridged versions of the ball game. The ball would be aimed at an animal-shaped fixture at the top of the pole. Men and women could play the practice game, with the women being allowed to pick up the ball with their hands. The ball games were part of the communal participation and women participated in their own way.

The public life of the *talwas* during the May–October period centered around the ceremonial grounds, the community farms, and the community buildings. In the winter months, the families were more on their own except for the men's group hunts, the woman's supportive work, trading journeys, and pilgrimages to various mounds. At the center of the ceremonial grounds was the town square with a central "four log" fire, a pole, and other physical features—ash heaps, small "medicine" mounds, and ridges. Most squares featured four rectangular *dubbas* or beds facing each of the four cardinal horizontal directions. Some of the town squares, especially in the peace towns, had three, missing a warrior's *dubba*. In some of the grounds, additional benches and seating arrangements faced the fire and filled in the spaces between each of the arbors or beds. Some of these seats were for the women shell shakers. Usually the *micco* of a *talwa* and his assistants were seated in the west arbor, facing east. The clan seating arrangements varied widely, depending on the local distribution of clans and red stick versus white stick concentrations. It should be pointed out that elsewhere we have attempted to show that red stick/white stick labels applied to individual roles and not to clans.

Elaborate ritual rules related to various conceptions of pollution applied in the movement around the square, involving concepts of both space and time. Spatially, the medicine piles and ridges in the *talwas* could not be crossed. Directions that were left open could not be closed. Areas of concentrated medicine could not be crossed. Menstruating women did not frequent nor were they allowed anywhere near the ceremonial ground. Again, elsewhere we have shown that this was out of respect for the power of women, not to denigrate women. People who had already eaten could not enter the square during the green corn dance until the busk ended and the cycles of cleansing and fasting were broken with the eating of the green corn. People who were in their own individual vision quest, somewhat like the menstruating women in their individualized private space, could not enter the grounds either, depending on the nature of the vision. A returning warrior who had not gone through the reentry cleansing rituals would also be excluded from the immediate circle.

The *talwa* square or the community *chogo—thakko* (the big house)—in its internal spiritual sense was the center of the public life of the community in classic Muscogee life. Today, it is less political but it is still a centering place for the spiritual life of the remaining traditional Creeks, though its use is more episodic than in pre-European times. Traditionally, the *talwa*'s life cut across the full range of the political and social life of the close-knit community. Today it is a place for renewal during the busk and other stomps and a refuge from the economic, governmental, educational, and social worlds whose centers have shifted and scattered and are not easily accessible to or controlled by the Creek conceptions of morality. The dance and the spiritual synthesis of the elements of fire, air, earth, and water can now take place in more circumscribed and limited contexts of time and space.

The *talwa* square was the center of public decision-making, as we have seen. It was also the center for educational activities. Education, as is the case with other important traditional functions, was not approached in a reductionist and modern manner. Education was not conducted only in "schools," though Creek elders, medicine men, craftsmen, and beloved men often taught the young in groups and the label "schools" can be comparatively applied to these groups. The clan mothers taught the women during their menstrual isolation. The families and the clans were all involved in educating children.

Children were considered to be little spirits from the time of their first kick in their mother's womb, and the entire world of songs, rhymes, and stories would envelope the child even before birth. Within the family, the mother was the greatest teacher, then all the appropriate clan elders pitched in until the young could be turned over to an *owala* (prophet/logician), a *hilis haya* (a medicine man), a specialized *micco*, a beloved man/warrior, or a craftsman for further training.

The public square also played a central role in education. It is there that a young man was socialized into the civil and criminal laws of the tribe, and where public decision-making, honoring, rewards, and punishment took place. In the public square, the youth heard the "encouragers," the prophets, the interpreters, the oral historians, and various leaders speak and point the way to the next generation.

A lost tradition on the ceremonial grounds today is the tradition of community singing, community storytelling, competitive mind games with respect to spontaneous and creative fiction and humor, and the telling of the great legends, section by section. Between the stomp dances and the clowns, the traditional storytellers held the community spellbound as they dramatized the details of the complex creation, clan formations, and red stick/white stick and corn mother legends as well as an entire range of clan and animal stories, each with specific communal and individual lessons. The town square traditionally was also the place for general community singing, in addition to the singing that accompanied the stomps. The deep-seated musical sounds of Creek singing were developed in the town square so that all in the square could hear every syllable and every tone. Contemporary communal church singing by Christian Creeks exhibits incredibly deep tones that seem to come from the center of the earth. The foundation of that deep singing goes beyond the normal style of the Anglo Baptist and Methodist singing and is rooted in the communal singing styles of the *talwas*.

The various balances of gender and psychology were evident in the activities in the square. We have already described the logic of the stomp dances where the spirit is renewed. In addition to the all-night stomps, there were hundreds of other dances, only some of which have survived the Trail of Tears. Many of the other dancers wore elaborate masks. The late Netchie Gray, in the 1940s and 1950s, made a heroic attempt to preserve the dances and to revive those that were on the way out.

The ribbon dances of the women symbolically celebrating the hunts still survive. The current use of ribbons mirrors the earlier use of the tails of various small animals. Other dances, such as the bird dances with feather sticks, involve primarily the men. Away from the center of the square, on small elevated "mounds," were the war dances and the buffalo dances. While some buffalo dances survived, Netchie Gray, until his death, was working on the revival and the choreography of many other dances, including several "lost" buffalo dances. The formations, the choreography, and the mask-making associated with the dances involved vanishing standards of aesthetics that were part of life in the town square.

The communal system of each *talwa* made the educational and socialization system possible without the creation of bureaucratic organizations. The community farms combined with the individual farms provided balances between family effort and community effort. Each *talwa* had its own community farms. The corn, beans, and other produce were stored for hard times and used to feed the families and individuals who fell on hard times. While the individual decisions to provide assistance from the community farms and storage could be carried out by the *miccos* and other white stick assistants, the broader decisions were made in a public setting with community input.

The *miccos*, after appropriate consultations with calendar authorities, announced the timing of all the public events and supervised the distribution of counting sticks which controlled the timing for various community activities, including the busk and three other major stomp ceremonials, the communal farming cycles, and other public events. The busk was and remains the most important public event in a *talwa*. Symbolically, it was a harvest celebration, culminating with the ritual eating of the first green corn. The busk could last four days or eight days—the Creeks thought of the time span for many events in multiples of four—depending on the agenda. Traditionally, the busk not only was a time for harvest celebrations but served a variety of other important community functions as well. The busk was the grand annual community political and social convention and marked the end of one year and the beginning of another. Many utensils and objects were set afire and burnt so that a new cycle could begin. The busk was the time for legitimizing many relationships including marriages and divorces, and it provided a reference point for many other events, including mourning by widows and widowers. A busk was a time for conciliation, for forgiveness of existing grievances, and for the reentry of the banished.

The town square meetings, and particularly the busk, were times also for various appeals to be heard by the council. The appeals dealt with issues arising from civil and criminal laws which were initially administered by the families and clans. The town council was also the place where banishment and the treatment of non-Creeks, captives, and violators of the order of things with respect to tribal property were resolved. The busk, together with the other major ceremonial times, was also the time when new names were given to the youth, the warriors, and the beloved men and women. The town square ceremonially recognized the coming of age of men and women, and scratching ceremonies initiated the youth into early adulthood.

Civic participation, discussion, decisions, and public life centered around the central square in the *talwa* for the Creeks.The classic Muscogee Creeks provide a model of equity, inclusiveness, confederated respect for diversity, and participation.

THE LEGAL SYSTEM

The system of councils in the Creek government provided an umbrella for rule-making, enforcement, and conflict resolution. The Creek legal system involved a combination of arbitration and mediation as opposed to the "American" system of adjudication. Adjudication normally involves formal-ized conceptions of the individual self with sets of rights and obligations under the myth of the rule of law rather than of men. Arbitration involves rules and codes administered by specific and determinate judges whose decisions require finding of fact and of law. Mediation involves the effacement of the mediator's ego and "reconciliation" of the conflicting parties.[15] The Creeks used both arbitration and mediation, whereas currently the formalized Creek supreme court uses adjudication for building its own common law.

Under the system of arbitration, the *talwa* councils sat in final judgment on legal issues involving the *talwa*, while the larger regional and the largest tribal council addressed inter-*talwa* and intertribal issues. The *talwa* council provided the most visible source of authority, but like all working legal systems the Creeks have had their "living law," or customary law, which forms the root of the legal system. In textbook versions of the United States legal systems one learns the formal description of statutes and cases, but as every practicing lawyer soon learns, regional variations in jury attitudes, the informal power of networks and relations, plea bargaining, and discretionary justice in the hands of prosecutors and justices constitute the interstices of the system. Similarly, the tribal councils dealt with the cases that came on appeal and some of the more difficult cases that could not be arbitrated or mediated through the clans, families, or tribal committees. As we have seen, the participatory system of the tribe was infused with checks and balances and veto points in decision-making.

Two different sources of law provided the basis for the system of arbitration. One source is natural law, "the order of things" (*mahagadondos/mvhakvtontos*), which encompasses natural and ecological principles. "Do not kill a pregnant bear" is an example of natural law. The second was customary living law which translated into codification of crimes and punishment. For instance, an adulterer would be sentenced to different degrees of corporal punishment, including the loss of body parts such as the tip of the nose. These codes were administered by the relevant "authority," following the hierarchical order of family, clan, *talwa*, region, and tribe. Adultery fell under "family law" and was handled by the family first, whereas murder invoked a broader clan authority and in many cases involved the tribal council. Under the concept of living law, restitution was made to the victims among the Creeks as among other tribal groups. The aggrieved party would be compensated for the losses involved, the adequacy of which was determined by the arbitrators. Some cases would also be mediated out and the case would not reach the arbitration of the clan system or the tribal council.

The clans, families, committees, and councils dealt not only with family law, personal injury, wrongful death, destruction, and jurisdictional disputes but with natural laws as well. The bear clan was the appropriate authority for the protection of the bears. If too many bears were killed or if hibernating bears, cubs, and pregnant bears were killed, representatives of the bear clan would enforce the law and impose fines or restitution. The remedy sought would depend on the magnitude of the infraction and could take the form of compensation, corporal punishment, war games, war, or banishment. If the remedy was not acceptable to the parties after arbitration or mediation, it would end up in the *talwa* or regional council, depending on whether the relevant parties were local or regional.

Mediation could be involved at any stage in the hierarchy of offenses ranging from adultery to murder. Thus, even in murder and capital punishment cases, the "guilty" party could offer input as to the preferred manner of death and the choice of executioner. As is the case with many traditional culturally integrated groups, banishment was often feared more than death. Oral history tells the classic story of the Creek warrior who was banished from the *talwa*, but his relatives and special pleaders from the clans would repeatedly see visions of his "spirit" beyond the ceremonial fire. They finally succeeded in persuading the council to accept the brave back into the community.

The Creeks had no prisons, so incarceration was not used as a legal remedy. Restitution, corporal and capital punishment, probation, demotion, ostracism and banishment, reconciliation, and other equivalents to non-incarcerating justice were used. The offending party could agree to work for the aggrieved as an in-kind restitution. If the mediation system failed and the preliminary judgments in arbitration were not observed, then the methods of enforcement could be escalated into the "eye for an eye" dynamics of the Mosaic code variety. However, even here reconciliation during the busk could occur.

The intricate clan system of the Creeks, as we have seen, created checks and balances. There were intricate sets of joking relationships, teaching relationships, contextual in-law avoidance relationships, and age-based relationships. More than Alexis de Tocqueville knew, a Creek lived in a nexus of communitarian norms, each with a mediational and/or arbitrational mechanism for restoring harmony after infractions of the law. DeTocqueville's eighteen-month quick tour of America provided an interesting but incomplete view of the inner life and traditions of Indian tribes, including the Creek culture that existed in the Southeastern United States.[16]

The Creek traditional world, like many traditional societies, did not reduce its way of life into insulated compartments. Thus, in a sense, "government," "religion," "economics," "history," and "cosmology" were all infused throughout the Muscogee Creek world. The internal world of the Creeks was not preoccupied with the bureaucratic thinking endemic to European and some Asian ways of thought. The Creeks, instead, depend on extensive notions of balance among different virtues, qualities, and functions. Thus, one of the major balancings is the well-known distinctions in political theory between public and private worlds.

THE PRIVATE WORLD

The Creek public world was considerably communitarian. By contrast, the private world in the Creek mind was remarkably free,[17] individualistic, subjective, aesthetically rich, and magical. Much has been written about Creek Muscogee magic,[18] a subject we will address in chapter 11, but for now we will concentrate on the theme of individuality. The individual Creek has considerable leeway in operating within the umbrella of Creek norms, as long as the basic laws and protocols of Creek society are not violated and intentional harm not done to other Creeks. The individual Creek traditionally was not bound to follow his father's or mother's specialization and was free to develop his or her own gifts from nature. Children of medicine men did not and do not automatically become medicine men. While talent for a particular art and community acceptance help define the selection, the individual had the leeway to follow or not to follow the father's specialization. Individuals or groups could also leave the community and settle elsewhere as the Seminoles did in their struggle for survival.

The individual also is free to perform or not to perform a specific specialized art or function if the timing is not right. The presence of the intuitively perceived wrong spirit of things, the proximity of a menstruating woman, or the presence of bad medicine such as dog feces would be construed as a legitimate reason for nonperformance of a specialized or even widely expected act. Visions served as another source of individuality. While the visions of the *owalas*, or prophets, had a logical foundation as they envisioned and captured the essence of the state of things and predicted future states, some visions had purely individualistic dimensions, placing personal obligations on the individual independently of the community.

Young people undertook vision quests as they made their individual journeys into nature. Each individual's visions were his or her property and were highly respected. The vision could result in pointing toward a pathway in life and it could also reveal a specific wisdom, direction, or a gift such as a song. When shared, visions could waive or defer an obligation. Thus, a vision could prevent a *tustanagee* from going to a specific battle or killing a particular type of individual. Visions could also restore the lost status of an individual. A banished individual's relatives could intercede with a *micco* because they repeatedly "saw" the lonely relative's image just beyond the sacred fire.

In addition to their communitarian obligations, Muscogees hold a deep reverence for private space and solitude. The forces of nature are seen to empower individuals as well as the community. Individuals are not considered to be lonely in their solitude since the world of private visions provides the gateway to the universe. The importance of visions is evident in the network of legends. The red stick and white stick twins, in the classic formation legend, had their private space where they had visions and contemplated their existential dilemmas. Individual Creeks, like many other traditional people, have believed and do believe that nature speaks to individuals directly and gives signs and directions—one can journey through the body and mind and drink deeply in the world of the spirit. The intricate balancing of twins, *aboktas* (assistants), and forces applies to the relationship between the complex communitarian obligations of the people of the fire and the individual world of liberty where nature sings in a singular manner to a singular person as part of the movement of the spirit.

NOTES

1. David Easton proposes a broad conceptual umbrella for varying approaches to politics, which provides for a variety of theoretical, behavioral, and institutional approaches. See Easton, *A Framework for Political Analysis* (Englewood Cliffs: Prentice Hall, 1965).
2. The literature of federalism is extensive. For a comparison of Jeffersonian, Hamiltonian, Iroquois, and Creek approaches to federalism see J. Chaudhuri, *Founding America* (Dubuque: Kendall-Hunt, 1992).

3. For a discussion of epistemological issues in cross-cultural studies, see F. S. C. Northrop and Helen Livingston, eds., *Cross-Cultural Understanding: Epistemology in Anthropology* (New York: Harper & Row, 1964).

4. John R. Swanton, *42nd Annual Report of the Bureau of American Ethnology to the Secretary of the Smithsonian Institute, 1924–25*, "Social Organization and Social Usages of the Indians of the Creek Confederacy" (Washington, DC: U.S. Government Printing Office, 1928.) (See 66, 250, 307, 509 for various references to *ispokogi.*)

5. Swanton, *42nd Annual Report*, 309.

6. Scratching conceptually is related to balancing the internal energy of persons properly with the field of external energy. It is used for discipline, healing, or initiation.

7. Brent Weisman, *Like Beads on a String* (Tuscaloosa: University of Alabama Press, 1989), 28–29.

8. "Long-Lost Spanish Fort Found in St. Augustine," *New York Times*, Science Times, 27 July 1993, B-5, 7.

9. Ibid.

10. Weisman, *Like Beads on a String*, 1–36.

11. "Long-Lost Spanish Fort Found in St. Augustine."

12. Weisman, *Like Beads on a String*.

13. See Swanton.

14. James Howard (with Willie Lena), *Oklahoma Seminoles—Medicines, Magic, and Religion* (Norman: University of Oklahoma Press, 1984), 104–180.

15. For an excellent discussion of comparative jurisprudence, see F. S. C. Northrop, *The Complexity of Legal and Ethical Experience* (Boston: Little Brown, 1959).

16. See Alexis de Tocqueville, *Democracy in America*, 1830, 2 vols., Philip Bradley, ed. (New York: Alfred A. Knopf, 1945).

17. Weisman, *Like Beads on a String*, 158.

18. See Swanton; Howard, *Oklahoma Seminoles, Medicines, Magic and Religion*.

The Harmony of Nature, Norms, and Production

The previous chapters have presented an analysis of and introduction to the astronomy, physics, genesis, government, theology, ceremonial ground, interethnic and gender relations, and political systems of the Muscogee Creeks. Since each of these fundamental concepts points towards the order of things, or what are perceived to be the laws of nature, it is crucial to analyze their meanings and their impact on value formation and evil-avoidance techniques.

The Meaning of the Laws: The Order of Things

As is the case in many other societies, Creeks believed that an examination of nature would provide not only a reliable cosmology but also a normative system, that is, a way of doing what ought to be done to promote harmony. There are at least five interrelated ways of referring to the normative order, the laws (*hahagahaga*), or the order of things.[1] Each of these methods adds to the Creek concept of the laws, or *hahagahaga/vhakvhayv*, which has several important characteristics. These five characteristics are as follows:

1. *Mahagadondos/mvhakvtontos*: law in a fundamental way, the normative concept of order.
2. *Mahagabonwayhogadidos/vhakvpunvhokvtetos*: the Creator, the totality of universal energy (Ibofanga dynamically working through his assistant, Hesagedamesse, the giver of the breath of life), left this law with us; in other words, natural principles are not mere matters of subjective opinion or fantasy.

3. *Mahagamihenwados/mvhakvmehenwetos*: the truth—the laws provide the meanings of ultimate truth.
4. *Mahagafatzados/mvhakvfvtcvtos*: the laws are true and empirically confirmed. They are not hypothetical.
5. *Mahaga-ajagidos/mvhakv-vcvkvtos*: the normative order is very, very sacred.

Creek theology posits an ascending synthesis of body, mind, and spirit. While body and mind are forms of energy, only spirit is of pure energy. Ultimately, spirit, or *boea fikcha*, is purified energy (*boea fikcha* is not equal to *soul*). It is not the western spirit described by dualists and spiritualists who distinguish between Lockean and Puritan mental and spiritual atoms, entities, and souls; rather it is universal energy, the string drawing all the other elements together. The concept of law deals with how energy works and flows efficiently in specific contexts. Obeying the laws means following and showing reverence for principles of energy at work in the universe. Energy flows continuously, constantly sharing, exchanging, and transforming. The nature/culture nexus is also a place at which exchange and transformation of energy takes place. Culture, at its best, works in harmony with nature.

When describing the exchange, sharing, and transformation of energy the Creeks, like many traditional people, use gender and sometimes sexual symbolism in a denotative manner to explain their conceptions of the transformation and qualitative flows of energy. Dance and the union of male and female principles continue the dynamic circle of life. Exchanges of male and female principles are natural. Creek legends, myths, and humor are full of sexual symbolism. There is no dualism or separation between the observer and the observed and no permanent distinction between the sacred and the profane in the cosmos. Ibofanga is in process through us and there is no dysfunction ontologically. Incidentally, given the integrated Creek cosmos, direct cursing by calling the Creator's name in vain does not exist because the flow of energy is everywhere. In anger, Creeks will use some sexual or scatological epithets but there is no damnation, hellfire, or hurling the name of God in association with curses.

NATURE AND CULTURE: THE EXCHANGE OF ENERGY

In the Creek conception, the nature/culture relationship is seen as a huge circular relationship. The large circle connects the base, the round earthly community circle (*chogo biloxi*), with Grandfather Sun above the earth in the top of the circle. The sun is male and the earth is female—without the exchange of energy between the two, life would not be possible. If any link in the circle is broken, life and the cultural order would be destroyed. The middle of the *chogo biloxi* has four logs, which come from a living tree. Symbolically, this is represented by the long pole, that is, a tree in the *chogofa* (the perennial community). For the Creeks, a tree also symbolizes human life. Several tribes besides the Muscogee, such as the Iroquois, use the tree as a symbol of humanity. However, while there are parallels, Creek symbolism of the tree is unique to the Creeks and to their own epistemology and cosmology.

The tree is deeply rooted in Mother Earth and its roots are in contact with the spirit of the water (*wewafulla/yewvfullv*) which, like the earth, is female. The tree—a male principle—also draws energy from the air. Finally, there is the fiery male energy of Grandfather Sun. The four elements of air, wind, water, and fire, which are complementary forces of energy, are all needed for the tree to exist. If air is missing, destroyed, or polluted, the blending and the synergy breaks down. The same is true if the proper energy of the sun, water, and the nutrients of the soil are not available or are improperly blended. Therefore, if any of the four elements are depleted they must be restored or else the life system fails. The tree itself involves male and female elements. Different parts of trees are male, often the east side facing the morning sun; others are female. For the tree to work, the trunk, roots, branches, and leaves have to work together. Human communities, too, need to be in balance with wind, air, water, and fire; gender roles must also be balanced.

Different parts of the tree are supplied with energy through reed-like internal energy transportation systems. Symbolically for the Creeks, hollow reeds are important tools for making medicine, for curing, for soothing, and for blowing music and making medicine. It should be remembered that the white stick of the white stick "medicine" or "peace" twin was a white reed. The branches from a trunk provided the fighting stick of the red warrior twin.

The human body is also seen as containing reed-like structures which convey energy to various parts. When the flow of energy is obstructed, illness develops. It is then that the medicine man turns to the botanical world of plants and trees to find, prepare, and send "herbal warriors" (see glossary: *tustanagalgheegee-de lonee hee helizwa* or *ahhotchgee helizwa*) through the human body to battle disease. The herbal warriors are, in turn, products of the synergy of the four major elements.

In the *chogofa/cvkofv*, or community, water fills varying depressions in the earth such as a stream, a lake, a river, or a pond. Just as the tree is connected to the earth spirit and the water spirit, the water spirit, in turn, constantly renews its connection with the rest of the natural circle. In this the work of the air element is involved, as wind is also symbolically a messenger. The wind or air principle makes possible the stirring of the waters and the transportation of moisture upward. The sun accelerates the vibrancy of the journey, and the evaporative process is on the way. In Creek aesthetics the surface of the water—the female principle—is seen to be dancing with expectation of enosis with the male energy of the sun.

After the energies of the water and the sun fuse, the energy exchange creates the rain and the snow: gentle rain is female; stormy, driving rain is male. Long strands of hair on Creeks often symbolize rain. Part of the sacred storing of the snow takes place on high ground, on hills or mountains, the symbolic "mounds." On top of the mounds the special union of male and female—fire and water—takes place. Thus, the mounds are below the sun in the vertical earth/sun circle. This is one nexus for the importance of mounds in Creek classical history. We have already seen that mounds were also important for the ritual study (astronomy) or "worship" of the Muscogee Creeks.

From the transformation of mist, rain, and snow the earth is renewed by rain, and what emerges from this vertical circle into the *chogo biloxi* or natural community returns to the horizontal circle of the human community, the *chogofa*. The *chogo biloxi*—or community circle—plays a vital guardianship role in the exchange of energy. If humans do not understand the proper enosis of fire, air, water, and wind, imbalances occur in the environment and the horizontal circle of the human community. The vertical circle of nature is thus adversely affected and new destructive forces, as in bad marriages, are created. Hence, humans in the *chogofa* must connect their behavior with the natural order of things, which not only gives life but points to the appropriate values for sustaining life. The good life is at the sacred circular center where the horizontal cycles of culture and the vertical water/sun cycles meet. Thus, life is in a giant sphere where there are seven directions, spokes, or pathways (the center, up, down, north, south, east, and west); different circles connect all of them at the center, at the four logs of the ceremonial grounds where the four major elements are symbolically blended in the sacred fire.

FOUNDATIONS OF A NORMATIVE ORDER

The Muscogee Creek culture does not disengage the normative order from the natural order of things. Cultural values derive from nature. The dynamic natural energy set into motion runs through everything in the universe. The vertical cycle of water, rain, and the other natural cycles affect the horizontal circle of life in the community. In turn, what the community does with earth, fire, wind, water, and the worlds of plants and animals affects the interlinked circles of nature. Thus, for the Creek mind, community activity, environmental policy, and environmental impact are related activities. Each affects the other. Nature, therefore, is not to be "conquered" but to be understood, respected, and appropriately used.

Since energy flows through everything, the normative order must also encompass everything, hence the Creek conception of a prayer for "all my relatives, those that I know and those that I do not know." In a denotative manner, the Creek normative system attempts to achieve generality and universality. The application of the general norms to specific entities and situations takes into account the nature of each entity and the manner in which the norms are violated. Therefore, the norms are applied through the Creek conceptions of nature, the plant world, the animal world, the fundamental elements, and the human world with its relationships of family, clan, gender, white stick/red stick complementarities, confederacy, and ultimately, other groups of people.

When the normative principles are applied, preferably a gentle level of energy, the white stick element, is involved. However, when the gentle application cannot solve the ethical problem, more energy and activism—the red stick principle—comes into play. The red stick legend, the ball games, which are symbolically the little brothers of war, provide foundations of activism. However, the normative order of the Creeks does not condone violence for its own sake. The Creeks can be seen as "cruel" in some ways. A mother could engage in infanticide by drowning her baby if the new baby was so severely handicapped that it could not survive given the available resources. Killing to avenge murder was permitted. When outside bands or tribes disturbed the order of things, they could be punished if diplomacy failed. Creek women could be brutal in avenging wrongful death if the wrongdoer was brought into the community. However, nowhere in the Creek legends and in the normative order are there any directions towards a universal empire, a crusade, or total war against another society. Many aspects of Creek activism and seeming brutality that Anglo settlers sometimes perceived were reactive adaptations to what they saw as the continuous and sustained onslaught against their way of life and the "order of things." The extraordinary challenges to their existence and survival strained their attempts to maintain the balance of general principles and order.

THE GENERAL PRINCIPLE: THE DISCIPLINES

The Creek world can be subdivided into at least four or five paths, laws, or disciplines (*hahagahaga*). Each of these disciplines, in turn, has subdivisions. In the operational aspects of the normative order, the disciplines are coordinated with clan relations, gender obligations, and criminal and civil laws. A major caveat is in order before we proceed with the disciplines. The disciplines should not be interpreted in a Judeo-Christian manner. We shall see what they attempt to denote, given Creek epistemology and cosmology. We need to avoid simple dictionary definitions and equivalencies.

The enumeration of the five disciplines is the product of painstaking oral history work. In some formulations by elders, two of the five disciplines can be seen to be close to each other, so one elder may see four disciplines while others see three; nonetheless, there is remarkable consistency among elders in pointing to the common elements in Creek ethics. Since the values are closely related, the total number of fundamental values is often regarded as four, corresponding to four sacred paths. However, here we will list all five principles separately. The five general normative principles, laws (*haha-*

gahaga), or disciplines are: (1) *anoghechka* (love); (2) *yee gun bay geeta* (to be less important than others); (3) *yee yas gheeda* (to be humble); (4) *enjageeda* (compassion), and (5) *yeejagheeda* or *yeehajoyeegeegheeda* (to care for yourself). Each of these disciplines has subcategories. The subcategories describe how the disciplines apply to the classifications and subclassifications of plant life, animal life, the four families of elements in nature, gender identification, as well as family, clan, *talwa*, tribal, intertribal, and other groupings of entities in the world.

RECIPROCITY

A major operational rule in relating the disciplines to the entities is that of reciprocity. All of nature, including life in the *chogo biloxi*—the roundhouse, or the total community—is related by a series of energy exchanges and reciprocal obligations. Lack of reciprocity severs the chain of energy sharing. Engaging in reciprocity keeps the chain of energy going. Whenever something is taken, something else must replace it in the ethical energy relationship between entities. These measured exchanges inform the values of environmental protection, personal safety and development, and the communitarian responsibilities.

Reciprocity applies at the level of two-person, individual, and larger community ethics as well. At the individual level, visitors to a home or *talwa* are treated hospitably but they also have to reciprocate depending on their identity and the obligations that go with them. Since the traditional Creek world did not have hard currency, we are speaking of exchanges, barters, and in-kind reciprocity. However, to understand Creeks we should see the system as a comprehensive ethical system rather than one of modern economics. Adequacy of reciprocity is intuitively understood since each clan, each generation, and each gender has its well-defined roles and responsibilities, all of which are reinforced by the network of community value-oriented education. Inter-family, inter-clan, and inter-*talwa* relationships are likewise marked by reciprocities. Lack of reciprocity provides the foundations for quarrels and disputes.

Relationships with nonhuman nature also involves reciprocities, but these are based on the natural order of things, on the "sciences." Male and female properties and complementarities have to be balanced. The exchanges of nutrients in agriculture have to be managed. The land and the animal population have to be regenerated. Appropriate renewal of community life has to be insured. In addition to these, nature and the cardinal spirits, including Hesagedamesse, Earth Mother, Corn Woman, and Water Spirit, have to be thanked. The sacred fire that symbolically includes the energy from Grandfather Sun must be fed, traditionally with a deer tongue.

Reciprocity does not necessarily mean the loss of individuality. Many reciprocal relationships are seen as strengthening the nature of things. For example, the Creeks do not see marriage as making two entities into one; instead, two new sets of responsibilities are celebrated in the marriage ceremony during which an ear of corn is symbolically broken into two not completely identical pieces.

THE MEANING OF THE DISCIPLINES

The implications of the disciplines, as we have seen, extend reciprocally to everything in the Creek universe. A brief discussion of the values may help highlight their significance. One discipline is *anogetchka*, which represents heartfelt love. The Muscogee concept of love has a different epistemological foundation than that of Platonic idealism or Platonic love. *Anogetchka* is timeless, deeply sensual, and full of emotional feeling and a desire for unity with all nature. In Creek cosmology, all dualities and entities are held together by shared energy, that is, love. Cross-cultural comparisons are not exact and can be problematic, but in classical Greek terms, for illustrative purposes, *anogetchka* is closer to a pre-Platonic representation of eros than to logos (reason).[2]

In traditional Creek religion, the deepest experience is that of complete *anogetchka*, of communion with Ibofanga, the deep-seated principle of love which is at the heart of nature. Ibofanga is neither male nor female and the love connection is one of pure spirit when male, female, body, and mind have already been synthesized. In some aspects of nature, *anogetchka* takes on sublimated sexual symbolism in biology, geology, and physics. There are male chemicals, rocks, plants, and parts of trees and there are complementary female equivalents. The female surfaces of lakes sometimes shimmer and dance in the context of the loving energy of the sun. In marriages, of course, *anogetchka* has direct physical referents. In a community, *anogetchka* emphasizes the meeting of minds, while in theology it becomes holy communion with spirit.

In communities, clans, and families the sublimation of sexual symbolism and love is expressed by freely and spontaneously energizing the sharing and reciprocal obligations specified by the social structure of the tribe. These obligations have both legendary and customary foundations. Spontaneity and sharing are the key features of *anogetchka*. A gift that is reluctantly given is no gift at all. Enrichment by the emotions is the key to classic Creek giving and to *anogetchka*.

Anogetchka applies to relationships with non-Creeks and provides the referent for the human freedom and the absence of slavery and imprisonment in the Creek world. Even death and the freeing of an enemy's spirit was seen as preferable to slavery or imprisonment that bottled up the flow of energy in an imprisoned body. *Anogetchka* also implies loving interactions with nature—taking only what one needs and expressing thanks for the gifts and insuring the regeneration of nature.

A second discipline is *yee gum bay geeta*, which means approximately "to be less important than others." It is similar to humility and sometimes these values are seen as very close to each other. From an external perspective, they might appear to be the same. However, there are qualitative and contextual differences. To be less important suggests forgoing competitiveness in favor of being cooperative and supportive in natural and cultural relationships. However, context is the key to understanding this value. *Yee gum bay geeta* does not imply lack of athletic competition or absence of aggressiveness in war. Instead, it implies avoiding conscious displays of superior status in prescribed social relationships and, except for infractions of the ethical, civil, and criminal codes, not embarrassing others.

The third discipline, *yee yas ghee da*, is close to the last value but more directly points towards humility—not the false, self-serving humility of Uriah Heep in Charles Dickens's *David Copperfield*. It refers more to not inflating one's ego. It also represents having a sense of wonder and respect for the knowledge that the universe can provide if one is open and listening. Humility also aids in the flow of energy in a community or in a dyadic relationship. *Ye yas gheeda* is often fused with *yee gum bay geeta*, thus abbreviating five categories of values into four, such as four sacred pathways.

Enjageeda, the fourth discipline, comes close to the concept of compassion—again not in a Platonic sense of the love of the "good" or settling for "prayer," but in the context of the active heartfelt sharing of energy and emotion. *Enjageeda* enjoins social interaction and sharing one's gifts with the community and is an important foundation of civic virtue. It energizes families, clans, *talwas*, the tribe, and life itself. *Enjageeda* supports a work ethic, without Puritan guilt, without the fear of condemnation and failure. Even though one is loving, respectful, and humble, one must be engaged with the world and the system of reciprocal obligations.

Yee ha ja yee gee da represents loving and caring for yourself. This fifth discipline provides a foundation for mental health—advising one to be mindful of one's own center in the complex cycles of natural and cultural relationships. *Yee ha ja yee gee da* is intended to provide inner strength; it points toward caring for the three individualized gifts of body (*ena*), mind (*eegalba/ekvlpa*), and spirit (*boea fikcha*). Even though *enjageeda* gives us communitarian values, *yee ha ja yee gee da* points toward balanced and complementary self-reliance. In Creek values, one cannot pass the buck to the community for not taking care of one's self. This is not the individualism of the Social Darwinists, but it illustrates the reciprocal obligations of the individual to the community and the community to the individual. The self-reliant, confident individual strengthens the community in the development of the self with self-love, yet also with humility and without forgetting the values of social engagement.

The five basic disciplines are complementary in character and illuminate the intrinsic values of the Creek ethical system which are supposed to be operationally linked with the extrinsic roles, functions, and structures of Muscogee society and governance. An important reminder is that the five "disciplines" (or paths) or categories can be represented also as four sacred paths, or three disciplines, principles, or spirits since they are interrelated categories. The interrelationship all comes from the unifying theme of the exchange or sharing of energy. The sharing of energy is a positive Muscogee value, but tangling with a bottled-up or broken chain of energy is to be avoided. The avoidance of negative energy, or breaking the chain of energy, therefore is a corollary value represented by the idiomatically expressed normative principle, *gi ho ba ho gi do no wat*, avoiding the clearly obvious but unspoken bundle of negative energy, that is, energy in a person which is not directed toward sharing but toward the destruction of sharing.

After discussing the disciplines, or the Muscogee ethical principles, it will be useful in understanding the links between these values and nature by briefly seeing person/nature linkages in specific versions of three key legends—the corn woman (or spirit) legend with respect to the fundamental provider, corn—the earth woman (or spirit) legend with respect to the herbal world, and the young man in the garden who finally understands who all his relatives are.

THE GIFT OF THE CORN: ONE VERSION

A grandmother regularly would send her grandson to bring back venison, an important traditional source of meat. When he came back he usually found that his grandmother would have corn and beans ready. He was curious and would inquire about the source of the corn and beans. She would always deflect his inquiry by saying that she would discuss the source later, at an appropriate time. The young man, however, was desirous of knowledge and remained curious and watchful. He noticed that very early one morning the grandmother was gone from their dwelling.

The young man's interest was awakened and he began to search for the grandmother. He sensed some activity taking place in a nearby shed. He peeked through a crack in the logs of the shed and he was stunned with what he saw. There was a beautiful woman shimmering in an aura of light. She was wearing a transparent gown made from corn husk materials and through the gown he could see the profile of a beautiful woman. She was holding up one hand and corn was falling from the hand. She was rubbing the side of her body with her other hand and from there too corn kernels were falling. The young man was shocked, startled, and excited by what he saw and inadvertently, he made a noise.

The woman hears the noise and appears angry that curiosity had overwhelmed the young man and that he had not waited per the grandmother's instructions. The earth trembled as it often does in many Creek stories, and the young woman was transformed into the old grandmother. She comes rushing out of the shed and confronts the young man and paces back and forth. Then she begins speaking:

> Now that you know—I have always been the provider and protector of you and your kin. But now you understand part of the mystery and from here on you have to learn and find your way. You have to cut my hair and put it in a basket and you have to cut my body and put it in another basket. Then take these two baskets into the fields.
>
> Scatter my hair and my flesh in the field and remain there four days and nights. There will be a storm—there will be lightning, wind, and rain (complementary elements for the earth)—and then there will be darkness—be steadfast and remain in the field.

The young man began to cry, but reluctantly obeyed his grandmother and fed the earth as he was instructed and then took shelter under a tree as it thundered and rained, accompanied by streaks of lightning, as darkness fell. He heard the huge falling raindrops and felt the earth trembling underneath. Strange sounds vibrated through the night. Though frightened, he stayed and finally slept through the rest of the night.

> Thunder woke him near the end of the night. When he became fully awake, he was overwhelmed by the spreading fragrance of the field and the emergent beauty of the day. The field was blooming with abundance and he was astonished by the beautiful crop of corn that was all around him.

The young man began to peer at every pathway in the field until he came to the center row where there was a huge cornstalk surrounded and transformed by rays of bouncing and emerging sunbeams. He could see the image of a corn husk garment within which stood his youthful-looking grandmother with her long hair which was now the color of corn silk. She was beautifully scattering seeds of various kinds to the four cardinal directions. The young man wanted to approach the youthful and fresh-looking "grandmother," but she signaled him to stop and then spoke lovingly to him, "Now you have to take care of everything and work to deal with the responsibilities that follow from your curiosities. I wanted to tell you more about the corn and its *abokta* (assistant), the beans." At this point she was consumed by a ring of fire and she was gone.

There are many other corn woman stories among the Creeks. The version just described illuminates several cardinal points in the Muscogee framework. These include the gender identification of the earth as a caring mother who, in turn, has to be treated with reciprocal care. The importance of the work ethic in field work is also illustrated; so is the interaction of the four major elements of fire, earth, wind, and water. The reciprocal relationship between curiosity and responsibility is also evident; so is the shared cycle of human and natural energy. Also evident is the delicate twin partnership of various elements in the plant world such as corn and beans so that the balances of the nutritional chain are maintained. The matrilineal nature of social authority and the comprehensiveness (four directions) of the earthly food chain and responsibilities also emerge in the story, which captures and contains an important perspective on the nature-based values of the Creek world. The disciplined oral transmission of stories like this was an important educational instrument for understanding Creek values.

EARTH WOMAN: WATER, HERBS, AND RELATIVES

We have seen that in the Muscogee world earth and water are female principles which in union with the male principles of wind and sun give birth to all living things. No one is purely male or female since males contain some female elements, such as water, and females have some male elements. Interestingly, in Creek the label for a widow is *we-hokti*, a "water woman," since she is devoid, at the time, of complementary male support. A brief but important legend of Earth Woman again illustrates elements of the Muscogee value system and the attitudes towards relatives, herbs, and water.

It is said that one day Earth Woman came out of the water and stepped on earth and spoke to the Creeks:

> I bring you songs, herbs, and blessings. When you act and speak you must think of all your relatives—known and unknown. You must also remember the plants (*delonhi*), the animals (*anthowalgin*), the living things are separate from our group (*istulgi*) and the ancient ones—those that have gone before you (*iste-poggi*). Also think of me—your holy mother. I give you also chants and songs.

At this point, Earth Woman lifts her hand to bless everyone and as she does so, dazzling sunbeams streak through her hand. Drawing attention to the sunbeams, she begins to sing and instruct, "This is your father, this is your uncle—without them the plants and you cannot live."

Before ending her chant, she lifts her other hand and through her hand and fingers there is the dazzle of rain and thunder and the sound of conch shells blowing. She blesses the people again,

> I am the spirit of water—without it you cannot live. Look to the sun for knowledge—for he is your father—things will grow when you harmonize them with the sun—the same is true for water.

She names the families of herbs and plants and tells the people,

> They will rejoice with you and you will sing with them. You
> will use ritual water with the right herbs in them. You must
> use living water and you must sing to your plants.

She again mentions living water and how it flows through all living
things. She blows into her hand—"You must always give them the breath of
life. Without rain and sun you don't have power (*yeekchida*)." Then she
claps and clasps her hands.

> Listen to your father and mother—the living water which is
> my spirit. The earth is your home. I am giving you medicine.
> Listen and act carefully. If you don't follow the principles,
> your knowledge will be taken away from you.

Then with the end of her talk, she disappears into the water and earth, after
blessing the people.

The legend exemplifies many Muscogee values. It reinforces the gender
distinctions among the elements and illustrates how the synthesis, or
wedding, of the elements creates life. It reinforces responsibility for the environment and demonstrates the importance of water, herbs, and blowing in
healing. Finally, it shows that unused gifts of knowledge can be taken away
and lost, thereby causing imbalances, illness, decline, and ultimately death.
People are not merely observers of nature but are participants, ideally,
responsible participants in the networks of nature.

While the classical and legendary world of the Muscogees is now in
decline, the value structure continues to impact certain attitudes today. One
of the remaining contemporary mythical entities is long ears (*hachko
chapco/hvcko capko*), essentially a creature, as his name suggests, with very
long ears. He listens for the violations of natural laws and can use his long
ears for whipping violators of the natural order or to make you forget. When
people lose their moral path, the earth will tremble. "Long ears" can represent alienation and the loss of memory and knowledge which Earth Woman
stated resulted from the departure from the order of things.

One story tells how a contemporary visitor to an Oklahoma bar stated
that he was in the bar because he ran into *hachko chapco*, lost his memory,
and forgot his way. While the story may seem funny, the logic of the humor
is connected to the logic of the ethical norms given by the legendary earth
woman after she rose from the water.

YOUNG MAN IN NATURE'S GARDEN:
THE SEARCH FOR RELATIVES

Intimate human bonding with nature provides the foundation of a selfhood
which extends into the plant and animal world and provides the logic of
the Creek prayer for "all my relatives—those I know and those whom I do

not know." The following story illustrates this connection.

A young man, a *tustenagee* or warrior, found himself alone in nature. He was surrounded by beauty, but nevertheless grew bored and lonely. So he shouted to Ibofanga, "What do all my surroundings have to do with me? How am I related to what I see and who indeed are my relatives? I know that this is divine beauty but what does it have to do with me?" As is common in the Creek way, he called on the Great Spirit four times. Ibofanga was too busy with his work, so his assistant Hesagedamesse laughed and the earth shook and Hesagedamesse told the young man to go on a vision quest for four days.

The young man proceeded deep into the forest and wondered aloud why exactly he was sent here. For four days, he wandered but nothing happened and he became tired. He began mimicking a chant on relatives to pass the time. Toward the end of the fourth day, he noticed that a plant was knocked over and the dirt at the roots was dry. The young man was puzzled that anyone would knock the plant over and leave it without a life support. He shook the dirt off the roots and the act reminded him of the importance of roots and of his own roots—his grandfather, his mother, and his historian or storyteller who told all the legends. He remembered many roots.

On the fifth day, he began to look at the plants in detail. He looked at the leaves and remembered the uses of the leaves. He looked at and remembered the uses of the bark, the stems, the pistil—the good uses and the bad of each. He remembered his medicine man. He grew appreciative of what plants have done for humans.

On the sixth day, as he was walking in his vision quest he suddenly saw a heart-shaped object wiggling in the bushes. It was a white-tailed deer. There were apparently hunters around and arrows came flying. The deer leaped toward the cloud and disappeared. The young man understood the nature of the deer's warning and got out of harm's way and remembered also the role of the deer clan in controlling hunters and maintaining balance and protection of animal life in the forest.

On the seventh day, the young man picked up seeds from fallen flowers and heard an inner voice reminding him of the importance of seeds. The voice told him that Hesagedamesse would awaken all the flowers. The youth blew four times into the seeds and scattered them. In his vision he saw the flowers bloom before his eyes; however, some flowers and plants were trampled. The voice (Hesagedamesee) told him that humans are the major destroyers and that the youth was a trustee and that he must protect the plants and the trees and not destroy the medicine gardens. He was reminded that all four elements—fire, earth, air, and water—were needed in balance.

The young man turned back to the plants and spoke to them, pointing out that like the plants his roots also touched the water, a source of life. He took the roots of the fallen plant and wet the roots. The plant began to revive. The youth reflected, "We are like the plants; indeed, we are the plants, we are relatives. Different kinds, each with their nature, but all related. Even from ugliness there can be the emergence of beauty as mushrooms grow from the midst of excretion. Water connects us all." He ran toward nearby water, speaking and understanding, "I also am a plant and a deer—reciprocal energy connects us all." He bathed in a clear position of the "living" water and was refreshed and he retired for the night.

On the eighth day, the young man woke up early. He counted the days—he had been gone for eight rather than four and he had lost his way back. He called on the Breath Giver (Hesagedamesse) and asked for help. He blew into a conch shell four times. The trees weaved and parted for him and there appeared to be a beckoning pathway to crystal clear water and a waterfall with animals and plants around. However, a voice emerged and warned him that out of this peaceful scene Spirit Woman would emerge in a celebration of life—not to be afraid. There was lightning and thunder, which took over the scene, and there was turmoil and the earth trembled. Animals ran wild and even the reptiles were frightened. The young man was overtaken by fear.

A fog enveloped the entire disruptive scene and he began to hear chanting accompanying the fog, and the disruption ended. The chanting continued to move toward him through the fog. Emerging out of the fog came Spirit Woman with other spirits (energies) dancing around her. A voice spoke, "Yes we are the tree. You must nurture tree life and animal life. You must be careful like a mother is with a child." Spirit Woman submerged in and emerged from the water four times, blessed all the directions, and then chanted again with uplifted hands, "We cannot live without the solar system." He was reminded of the role of thunder and rain, the fusion of the elements, the role of sun and wind, and how Mother Earth would receive it all in a ceremonial dance. The water spirit (*wewa fulla/yewvfullv*) would recycle it all. Sunbeams danced in Spirit Woman's hands and in one of her hands raindrops also danced. Spirit Woman clapped her hands four times and the young man heard thunder and saw flashes of lightning. He remembered his grandmother, his father, the storyteller, the medicine man, and their advice. Spirit Woman chanted and spoke again, "All things depend on water—but be careful of thunder and lightning." Her voice was clear but she was moving away, toward the mountaintops, toward the mound gods, from where there was water coming down. "I must go toward the mountains now but I will replenish the earth. I will always come back to you. I am the water spirit and the roots of trees and finally all living things are interrelated and are connected to me. Remember all the spirits, including Hesagedamesse. I will come again—take care of all your relatives."

The water spirit disappeared upward and the young man was dumbfounded. He cried to Ibofanga four times. There was laughter and the assistant, Hesagedamesse asked, "What do you want and how have you done on your quest?" The young man said, "Water spirit is gone and I am only begin-

ning to know my relatives—the plants, the animals, humans, and Ibofanga."
Hesagedamesse responded:

> You knew your relatives deep inside of you but you didn't
> know how to get it out of your heart and understand. Now
> you must take care of the plants since they sacrifice to feed
> you and provide medicine for you. Carry enough seeds and
> scatter them since not all of them will grow. Make sure that
> they have the nutrients, water and sun. Take care of the
> animals since they take care of you. The deer is your elder
> brother, it tastes the plant world with its tongue, warns you
> with its tail, and also feeds and clothes you. The plant world
> and the animal world also need your help but it is humans
> who are the most destructive—toppling the plants and unnec-
> essarily destroying animal life. They are also relatives and you
> must be aware of and work toward the harmony of all your
> relatives.

The young *tustenagee*'s vision quest was now complete.

There are different versions of this oral history legend and several
spinoff stories related to it. However, the core of the story is consistent with
other stories[3] and with the implications of the Creek value system: (1) the
exchanges of energy keep the entire universe going; (2) there are male/female
couplings and reciprocal themes in these exchanges; (3) the true community
includes plants and animal life; (4) we must not ask for greater sacrifice from
plant and animal life than is necessary and we must return the loss in a
different way by protecting and caring; (5) humans are more dangerous than
plants and animals since they can unnecessarily and excessively topple the
plants and kill the animals; and finally (6) from Ibofanga to the smallest
plant, seen and unseen, indeed, we are all relatives. A just community orders
its own relationships with affection, reciprocally extends the affectionate
spirit to all of nature, and ultimately completes the cycle with Ibofanga.

Feeding the ceremonial fire with the deer's tongue, now often a cow's
tongue, caring for the herbal gardens among the last generation of elders,
recycling excess water among the herbs and plants, and giving prayers of
thanks to all the relatives, as well as Ibofanga and Hesagedamesse, are small
contemporary windows into the classic system of Creek values highlighted
in the story of the vision quest. The logic of the natural values of the vision
quest are also evident in the fundamentals of pre-European Muscogee
conceptions of agriculture and the handling of animal life.

NATURE AND PRODUCTION: HARMONY AND DISHARMONY

The Creeks interacted with nature on a cyclical basis in activities such as
agriculture, hunting, berry picking, nut gathering, and fishing. The Creek

dietary pattern was based on what was in season and notions of complementary nutritional principles of protein, carbohydrates, vegetables and
fruits. Removal and urbanization have severed this pattern and the widespread knowledge of nutrition. Many Creeks have resorted to diets of fried,
processed foods with adverse and sometimes semi-epidemic results in health
care (for example, diabetes); however, the remembered principles of Creek
foods enabled the rural Creeks, after removal and before urbanization, to
survive the stresses of Indian Territory, statehood, and the depression. By
sharing food obtained by hunting, fishing, growing herbs, and farming,
Creeks developed an informal economy and bypassed some of the ravages
of the Great Depression. The following discussion takes a look at Creek
agriculture and food practices in order to demonstrate the operational meanings of Creek values in the shared linkage between men, women, and nature.

The Creeks combined their conceptions of shared energy, the four
seasons, and principles of ecology and conservation in their planting practices. During the planting cycles, the Creeks depended on their recurrent
fascination with cycles of four—four seasons for hunting, picking, gathering,
and planting; four-day or multiples of four-day busks or ceremonies; and
four-part, or quartered, divisions of land and agriculture. Agricultural plots
were divided into four equal parts with assigned functions for each part.
One quarter-section of the land would be burned and left alone for purposes
of renewal. Given the importance of fire, burning was seen as a part of the
process of infusing new energy into and reusing whatever was left in a recycling process. The Creeks burned not only used fields, but also used clothing,
pots, possessions, dilapidated housing, and other throwaways at different
times—particularly in ending the old year and beginning the new, which was
marked by the busk or the green corn ceremonies.

Thus, one quarter of a field would be burned and left alone for at least
a year. A second quarter would be turned over, fertilized, and prepared for
future planting. A third quarter would be seeded according to the season
with corn and summer vegetables and cycles of potatoes and other vegetables during cooler parts of the year. The calendar priests, or *miccos*, together
with male and female elders, would use their judgment to try to coordinate
both the larger solar four seasons with the lunar semimonthly cycles in order
to recommend times for planting various seeds. The fourth quarter is where
plants were made ready for harvesting. After harvesting, the fourth quarter
would be burned and the four phases of the cycle would begin.

The primary calendar was solar, supplemented by the lunar calendar for
sequential counting. The inherent differences between solar and lunar days
were sublimated by the preoccupation with harvesting and planting
phenomena. Calculation of time for its own sake was less important than
daily living. The Creeks often planted things in complementary pairs, both
spatially and by reciprocal classifications. Thus, they planted different items
in horizontal rows combined with climbing plants in vertical six- to eight-

foot posts. A good example would be the reciprocal use of corn and green beans. Corn would be planted in horizontal rows while hardshell beans would be tied to vertical posts. These two plants were seen as nutritionally and chemically complementary. In today's terminology many families of beans return nitrogen to the soil, where it is then used by plants like corn. Through the introduction of corn, potatoes, squash, and other new world crops, American Indian agriculture[4] transformed and reenergized the old world. Creek agriculture is as rich and varied as the comparative experience of practically any tribe in the region now known as the United States. The four solar seasons related to planting were as follows: pre-planting activities in January, planting in the spring, harvesting in the summer followed by the green corn festival in middle summer and harvesting in late summer, and berry-picking in the fall. After the planting seasons and harvesting and picking were over, the Creeks survived on dried plant products, nuts, and meats through the winter.

The community agricultural enterprise was under the leadership of women, and the women clan elders would make decisions, guided by the calendar priests, for advice on the reference points of cosmic time, for planting, for rituals, and for celebrations. Counting sticks provided reminders for planting and other schedules. Under the women's leadership, other women and other men who did not have hunting or war assignments would collectively work the farms. "Gay" men would work side by side with women, as they were not shunned in the Creek world. Identifying the number of gays in a Creek farm could be misleading since farming clothes in the Creek world often had unisex exterior appearances. Cycles dictating the divisions of labor were in place for hunting, planting, gathering, and picking. The communitarian values of Creek society did not allow for a leisure class or its affectations. Hence, a separate business class did not exist until the coming of Europeans and the resulting impact on both blood quantum divisions and the related rise of the commercial ethic. Groups and families exchanged and traded without the existence of a business class.[5] As Thorstein Veblen has noted, there appears to be a correlation between the absence of a leisure class and the existence of efficient productivity, accompanied by non-elitist, egalitarian institutions. This was certainly true in the case of the traditional Creeks.

Each family settlement (*huti*) had its own nearby garden with usage rights that were customarily understood, not centrally dictated. The Creek conception of energy exchange kept the production system going. Just as families would get what they needed through exchange with other families, so would regional groups obtain needed items through trade. Thus, as it became more difficult to get wild rice, southern tribes would trade deerskin with more northern tribes, without creating a leisure class. However, with the coming of whites and mixed-bloods, the skin trade moved away from barter and toward an economics of manufacturing with the concomitant foundation of a leisure class, all of which contributed to the erosion of traditional Creek society.[6]

Family agriculture was supplemented with extensive community gardens, which, in their heyday, could encompass thousands of acres. Under the direction of the *talwa* government, communitarian labor-sharing kept the community gardens going. The produce of the community gardens was distributed and shared under the supervision of the *micco* and his councils, committees, and assistants. Families that faced emergencies and hardship especially were supported by the common gardens and also temporarily lodged in community housing. Finally, community storage systems offered a buffer against failures and emergencies. The Creeks traditionally stored food for at least two years and had their own styles of seed storage—sometimes animal-shaped clay seed pots with palmetto bark stoppers to keep mice out.

The production exchange involved both food and services. Visitors chipped in with their labor. Dried corn products, food items, prepared foods, and crafts were swapped for various services including visits to medicine men, various *miccos*, and other specialists. The constant exchange of various forms of energy, labor, services, goods, foods, and clothing made for a dynamic, actively participatory, and communitarian system of production. The Anglo demands for land, unregulated hunting, and the commercial, for-profit skin trade was destined to destroy the traditional extensiveness and diversity of the Creek system of production.

The Creek diet was varied, consisting of various types of berries (*gajjo faya/kvco fvyv*), including nonpoisonous sumac and black bottom berries, swamp cabbage, water cress, asparagus, artichokes, water potatoes, wild onions, and various kinds of potatoes. According to established cycles, Creeks gathered bark and roots, seeds, wild rice, nuts, mushrooms, leaves, flowers, shells, clams, fish, blackjack products, oak, and maple. In addition to corn and beans, they planted pumpkins and squash as well as tomatoes, peppers, garlic, onion, peas, soft beans, and black-eyed peas. There were also appropriate seasons for "sacrificing elder brother," the white-tailed deer, for which Creeks roamed everywhere, including all parts of Florida.[7] The Creeks did not depend too extensively on big animals for food, but elder brother deer helped take care of them. The deer was honored, remembered, and shared with the ceremonial fire and protected against excessive and improper killing by representatives of the deer clan. Other favorite meats were seasonal pheasant, quail, rabbit, turkey, turtle, and squirrel. Originally, squirrel use was ceremonial, but the practice of eating squirrel spread. The Creeks also consumed various kinds of eggs. Some were good and others bad for eating. Even the good eggs were balanced with plants and vegetables, particularly wild onions, for both flavor and balanced nutrition.

Creek food production technology included extensive drying and preserving of both plant and animal products. Several kinds of jerky, preserves, and corn products were prepared for eating and drinking (for example, the "instant" drink *obuskee/vpvske* was part of the Creek system of production). The whole production system was interlaced with rituals of sharing and thanking: thanking people, plants, animals, the earth, the fire, the wind, the water, and ultimately Ibofanga. This "production machine" was disrupted by the arrival of peoples with quite different values concerning private property and commerce. Creek theology and prophecies, however, warned about the possibilities of evil and the dangers to the system of production.

THE EVILS IN NATURE

The Muscogee Creeks do not hold the naïve belief that the world can remain a Garden of Eden. While harmony is the ideal, it is the search for harmony that characterizes the daily journey. In this journey through the natural world, there are many sources of disharmony. Many of the sources of disharmony and therefore "evil" (physical, spiritual, and mental) have already been examined in this work. The corrective path in government, health, agriculture, environmental policy, social relations, and ethics is to analyze the source of evil and to engage in activity to restore harmony.

The sources of evil, while interrelated, include: (1) inattentiveness to or violation of the "order of things" (*hahagahaga*), the key values we have examined and which are higher than codes, interests, and daily ritual; (2) violation of the laws governing plants and animals; (3) garbage, excretions, and throwaways; (4) the "trickery" of nature; and (5) evil "intentions," "bad medicine," or the magic of others. The nature of the first two sources of evil has been discussed in several places including earlier parts of this chapter. The last two, "trickery" and "magic," will be discussed in chapter 11. We now concentrate on the third source.

GARBAGE, EXCRETIONS, AND THROWAWAYS

Careless throwaways, excretions, and garbage are clearly recognized as sources of pollution and evil in the Creek value system. The seeds of evil are pointed out by good storytellers in the Creek creation legend. A focal point in that legend, as we have seen, is the evolutionary journey of the turtle as it rises from the underworld and water toward the light of the sun. From the beginning of the journey to the end, things are in process; they evolve. Among humans, this evolution is seen in the blind bumping and stirring in the womb of Mother Earth toward the light, the clearing of fog, and the identification and classification of the original clans and the clarifications of their complementary functions.

During the process of this evolution, excess matter slides off the back of the turtle and falls into the ocean. The people with their yet-to-be-perfected social knowledge pay scant attention to the disposal of this garbage. According to the oral prophecies and the oral traditions, it is this garbage

that continuously returns as evil creations in the form of dangerous, allegorically conceived sea serpents. Neglecting the proper recycling of this
energy also results in the symbolic creation of evil snakes in foul-smelling
lakes and ponds.

The literal translation of garbage into snakes and serpents in the English
language can lead to a misunderstanding of the symbolic usage of snakes in
the Creek world. Snakes symbolize great forces which are of a sinuous and
penetrating quality. The meanings are closer to that of snakelike entities than
directly to that of snakes in the world of Anglo-American sensibilities. Since
the Creek conception of time is cyclic rather than linear, the Creek legacy
warns of the interrelated cycle of unregulated garbage disposal and conse-
quent pollution and poisoning of life. Pollution and related evils are not
predestined because there are proper ways to dispose of garbage.
Traditionally, the Creeks were very careful about recycling garbage and they
had their own concepts of cleanliness. They bathed several times a day, had
elaborate protocols on who bathes where and in what part of a stream in
order to allow the proper exchange of energy to occur, isolated the women
during menstruation, returned the products to nature appropriately, and
excreted away from the camps, covering the excrement. Furthermore, they
engaged in ritual vomiting away from the square grounds, covered the area,
and prohibited people from crossing the medicine areas. They always kept
their houses and *talwa* squares clean. The contemporary deterioration of
standards that has taken place sometimes results in the debris being pushed
just outside the dance grounds rather than being completely disposed of or
burned. The Creeks systematically burned discarded personal clothing, utensils, and building materials, and cyclically burned used-up fields and structures so that new, shared cycles of energy could occur.

Evil in the Creek world is not a permanent entity, since ultimately there is
only one world, the revolving world of energy created by Ibofanga. Much is
known about the laws of the world, the "order of things" and the values that
result from this order. Not all is yet known, hence the trickery of nature and
the antics of the trickster rabbit, keeping life interesting and evolving. Even
though the rabbit creates havoc, ultimately he or she is still part of nature.

NOTES

1.   This discussion of values is extracted from primary sources in oral history,
including discussions with tribal elders conducted over more than a fifty-year period.
The acknowledgment identifies these sources. The standard literature on the tribe
deals primarily with external elements.

2.   Eros, in early pre-Platonic Greek mythology, was originally the personification of unity and later reified into a god. Gaskell points out that Eros or Phanes was
"A symbol of the higher self in its aspect of Love that which draws all things towards
unity with itself." G. A. Gaskell, *Dictionary of All Scriptures and Myths* (New York:
Gramercy Books, 1960), 252. Eros, or Love, in the above sense is used in this work

to give a sense of traditional Creek pre-Christian or non-Christian understanding of the role of love. Missionary influence superimposed the Christian quasi-Platonic connotation upon the earlier Creek conception of shared or uniformly exchanged or united energy. Another sourcebook on classical mythology initially points out that Eros often means love of a sexual kind but then goes on to quote Hesiod to mean that Eros brought about the union of the original father and mother, Uranus (sky) and Gaia (earth) and presided over all unions. Thus, Eros prior to Aphrodite was little more than a personification of generative power. See Michael Grand and John Hazel, *Who's Who in Classical Mythology* (New York: Oxford University Press, 1993), 126. The Creek conception of love (*anogetchka*) is, therefore, based on radical empiricism, i.e., directly felt, timeless love which joins all things, rather than Platonic love which is based on a philosophical realism that distances itself from feelings and the deliverance of the senses, as brought out by Socrates in Plato's Symposium. See the translation of the Symposium by Michael Joyce in *The Collected Dialogues of Plato*, eds. Edith Hamilton and Huntington Cairns (Princeton: Princeton University Press, 5th printing, 1969 [originally Bollinger Series, 1961]). Plato, as he often does, delineates differing positions before he presents his own through Socrates. In the Symposium, Plato first has Phaedrus present a non-Platonic conception, "Love is the oldest and most glorious of the gods, the great giver of all goodness and happiness to men, alike to the living and to the dead" (534). Then he has Pausanias belittle Phaedrus' definition and associates love with the later development of Aphrodite. Pausanias then speaks of two Aphrodites, the lewd, sexual, and earthly love and the male, vigorous, intellectual, and heavenly love. Socrates introduces his own rules that "love is always the love of something, and 2) that something is what he lacks." Socrates then ends by speaking with approval of Diotima's conception of love as "never be seduced again by the charm of gold, of dress, of comely boys, or a lad just ripening into manhood" (563). Platonic love is Platonic realism at work, the love of the imageless, perfect idea independent of feelings, the "ultimate beauty alone; beauty alone, absolutely simple and everlasting" (Joyce 526). Creek radically empirical, timeless love—or *anogetchka*—therefore, can complement Platonic everlasting love, but it is not the same. It is closer to the original pre-Platonic Eros prior to the Platonic, or Puritan, labeling of many forms of emotive love as lewdness. This elaborate footnote for understanding is no substitute for the deeply moving feelings of *anogetchka*, of the bonding of energy as expressed in the vibrations of old Creek songs and in the Creek stories.

3. Note the role of the elements, the jostling of ignorant living things, the fog, and finally the gift of knowledge. These sequences and demarcation points appear in the story as well as in the creation legend.

4. See Jack Weatherford, *Indian Givers* (New York: Fawcett Columbine, 1988) and *Native Roots* (New York: Fawcett Columbine, 1991).

5. For the elements of the fundamental and pioneering analysis of leisure and its functions, see Thorstein Veblen, *The Theory of the Leisure Class* (New York: Modern Library, 1934).

6. For an elaborate non-Creek discussion of the Creek skin trade, see J. Lietch Wright, Jr., *Creeks and Seminoles* (Lincoln: University of Nebraska Press, 1986).

7. See Brent Weismann, *Like Beads on a String* (Tuscaloosa: University of Alabama Press, 1989), especially 14–36.

PLACATING NATURE: MEDICINE, MAGIC, MYTH, TRANSFORMATION, AND TRICKERY

In the traditional Muscogee mind, the essential reality is Ibofanga, the one great spirit, which is the total universe and the energy spirit that connects and creates the empirical phenomena in the universe. No final ontological dualism exists within Ibofanga, for it is beyond binary categorizations such as active/passive, male/female, and observer/observed. The concept of spirit or energy should be understood in the traditional Creek way, minimizing possible distortions imposed by European values. While Ibofanga is the supreme spirit, the word *spirit* in this context implies separation between spirit and matter or mind, which are different transformations of energy. Ibofanga is basically the ultimate energy and the transformation of energy creates the temporal states of matter and mind.

Ibofanga's energy can be seen in different circumstances, and traditional Creeks give various names, such as Hesagedamasse or Pojasa, to spirit's context and function. But these are all *abokta*, or assistants, of Ibofanga. They are all instances of energy distribution in the universe. Similar to distortions that may occur when comparing philosophies and religions, the *abokta* may give an impression of a polytheism. These distortions can also feed into preconceptions of primitive aboriginal animism. However, in-depth conversations with knowledgeable Creek elders in stomp grounds who understand pre-Christian tribal ways will invariably confirm that in the Creek view, Ibofanga is all-encompassing and timeless—everything else is time bound, temporary, and often trivial. The ensuing discussion of medicine, magic, myth, and related matters should not obscure the integrating fundamental conceptions of Creek reality.

Most societies, in extending their core values, will possess elements of magic and superstition. One group's belief may be another's superstition. In the "modern" and "rational" Western world, medicine and physics label most things in order to identify and separate hypothetical events, theories, and entities. These include various viruses, "new" particles, mysterious diseases, and creation theories, including the well-known "big bang theory." For Creeks, as is the case in many tribal societies, notions of the unknown and strange are labeled magic. This could be seen as an attempt to deal with the vanishing edges of what is known about nature. The central core of nature is considered orderly and predictable, as seen in astronomy, ethics, and agriculture. At the edges of our understanding, however, magic and trickery prevail. In dealings with this domain, the Creeks have an immense and complex body of beliefs and practices that artistically and experimentally attempt to placate the puzzling and surprising aspects of nature in order to restore health, preserve or strengthen social relationships, and deal with evil created by others. However, most traditional medicine men prefer that their clients depend on rules of ethics and nature rather than magic and medicine. To manipulatively play with nature creates a double-edged sword that can cut the user. A commonly told educational tale illustrates these lessons.

THE DANGERS OF POTIONS

A young man was obsessed with the beauty of a woman who shunned his overtures. He went to a medicine man for a "love potion." The medicine man urged him to allow nature to take its course and to be patient. The young, love-struck man shopped around until he found a more agreeable medicine man. This new advisor also urged the man to be patient. Because of his patient's apparent agony, however, the medicine man reluctantly made an elixir for the young man. The medicine man directed the youth to leave the medicine by the girl's door, and instructed him to play an appropriate medicine song on his flute. The young man did his best to follow the instructions, and soon the woman appeared interested in the man. They soon began living together.

One night, the young man turned toward his beloved in bed and saw her hair transform into a ragged, brittle mess, her eyes turn fiery and strange, and her figure become hideous. He rushed to the medicine man, who again was compassionate and treated the youth with a new set of medicines, carefully and experimentally monitoring him until he recovered his strength and senses. The young man understood that dealing with the supernatural is like playing with fire.

The medicine man tried his best to be compassionate toward the impatient young man and to smooth the flow of energy. The young man painfully learned that knowledge of nature has its limits, and that the world of Ibofanga, despite science, laws, and social order, remains mysterious.

While social and educational changes can illuminate some of life's mysteries, magic remains a part of the human experience. The Creek creation legend symbolizes the evolution of humans from the material, through the mental, to a spiritual world. The legend is timeless and Creeks are waiting for the symbolic fog of the creation legend to clear so that we may discover and obtain another glimpse of Ibofanga's dynamic world.

THE LEGEND OF THE HERBS

Healing requires knowledge of all areas of Creek life, and a key legend encapsulates the fundamentals of these values. The major legends are spin-offs or extensions of the larger creation legend. As with the other major legends discussed in this work, the legend of the herbs and the healing, summarized below, are part of an integrated story exploring the logic of Creek values.

The legend begins after the clan's formation and after the structure of Muscogee society on the face of Mother Earth is in place. This is at the end of the turtle's journey through mud and water, after the fog has cleared, and once the night and day are balanced. Seismic forces, represented allegorically by giant serpents, have created the earth's mountains, valleys, plains, and rivers. These mountains, or *igan halwa*, and their ritual counterparts, the mounds, *igan halwaji*, provide platforms for knowledge. It is not surprising then, that the knowledge of herbs and healing comes from around the mountain in the form of four key medicine songs and herbs that begin the journey towards healing knowledge. The following story illustrates these ideas.

From a mountainside in Creek country came the sweet sound of harmonious singing. There were no humans on the mountainside, and it appeared as though the plants and herbs were singing. However, the plants and herbs remained indeterminate, unidentified, and hidden, despite the sweetness of their song.

A prophet or logician (*owala*) pointed the way, saying that a medicine man should accompany the people on an eight-day journey to the music's source. Prior to the emergence of man, the animals, especially the bear, understood something about the role of plants.[1] Now the medicine man, often from the bear clan, must aid in the search. The people began their journey toward the mountain.

Nothing happened for a long time and the people were quickly becoming tired and ill and decided to lie down and rest for a while near a mountain. The legitimacy of the *owala*'s insight and leadership was at stake. Before night fell, the people began recovering faster than usual. As they lay surrounded by herbs, they heard a song: "I come to you—I am *hilis hetki*— white root (ginseng). You must wait for the second day and then uproot the medicine." The medicine man realized the next day that this was not a dream, for upon digging into the ground, he found white roots.

He then went toward a river bottom, where he heard another song. "I am *micco honija*—red root (pussy willow). I, too, will help you get well." He found the red root near the bottom of a stream. The songs kept coming—in a higher dry area one song led him to a black-rooted plant that would provide the leaves and the basis for the important *asi*, the classic ingredient for the *asi lustee/pvssv*, the most important war drink.[2]

Led by a fourth song, the medicine man ended up in a valley where he found *notosa*, or angelica. The search for each of the four roots took two days, totaling a four-day journey. The orchestration of all the songs blended into one song of advice and direction:

> You must create a new medicine bundle: always accompany with a little tobacco. Know the limits of everything you use. You must sing—you have to blow—you must use living water and you must also use and respect fire. Use everything with respect. These four main healers will have many other assistants—tobacco, cedar, sumac, and others—you must always accompany the herbal medicine with singing, blowing, water, and heat or sweat from the individual.
>
> In spite of all your efforts nature may take its course and *pojassa* [the entropy principle] may take a patient away. Many diseases come from the animal families—the herbs can counter these and help people heal. Once in a while if you listen, you can hear them sing. Use them properly—understand them and their limits—otherwise they, too, will eat you up. There is energy in the rocks around you [*sabia*]—they each have their own energy. Use your knowledge wisely in caring and sharing the flow of energy [*boea fikcha*].

The song slowly faded and the *owala* and the *hilis haya*—prophet and medicine man—returned with their companions to the people in order to begin a new journey of healing and wellness.[3]

There are many relevant implications in this legend. As an offshoot of the creation story, this legend contains the fundamental codes, seeds, or logic of the Creek way of thinking. At its heart, the herb legend contains the manifestation of universal energy, or *boea fikcha*, represented by its flow, transformation, vehicle, and interruption. The herb legend also refers to the common Creek themes of the trembling or vibrations of the earth, visions, four elements, sexual balance, energy, regeneration, and entropy. All these blend to create a theory of wellness, disease, and curing. The concepts of wellness under discussion were ingrained in the traditional Creek world and provide the guiding principles among traditional elders today.

WELLNESS, ILLNESS, AND HEALING

The Creek concepts of wellness are derived from the unity of body, mind, and spirit—and the unity is created through the smooth flow of energy. Breaking this energy flow is the beginning of illness. Restoring the flow of energy is the pathway to health. Broken and coagulated cesspools of energy, and energy that works against peaceful flow, are the sources of *bothas*, or evil spirits. Appropriate blending of complementary elements and flow is important in every area of health.

The Creek clan structure, for example, contributes to a serene social flow and supports a holistic approach to health. Creek concerns about genetic health resulted in elaborate rules of exclusions and inclusions of specific clan members in marital relationships. A person could never marry a member of either the father's or the mother's clan. Further, a person could not marry into any of the spousal clans in the lineal descent from the great-grandparents on both sides down to the person at hand. At least four generations of clan-marriage exclusions were preferred. Thus, a person could not marry into any one of eight clans going back to the great-grandparents, since these clan members were considered close relatives. Like all social norms, there were bound to be gaps between and violations of the ideals, willful or ignorant. Eventually, mixed-blood offspring, war, removal, Christianization, and urbanization made severe inroads into the practice of these norms.

The exclusionary clan rules among traditionals were and are related to a series of physical, mental, and spiritual health concerns. Clan exclusionary rules historically created a core group of relatives and thereby strengthened secondary social associations. These relatives provided buffers against larger society and its governmental machinery. Relatives could represent or intercede on a person's behalf when problems arose. The clan exclusion network also created a system of honoring relationships that crisscrossed age distinctions. A younger person could be a "grandparent" because he or she belonged to the grandparent's clan. The four generations plus clan network always assured a Muscogee Creek of a home in cases of physical, mental, or spiritual crises, or during long pilgrimages and travels.

The traditional Creek concept of illness flows from the tribe's principle of wellness. Blockages and disruptions of energy were regarded, and for traditionals still are regarded, as the causes of illness, to be handled holistically. The family and clan network was the first line of defense in dealing with illness. Then, in ever widening circles, there were additional sources of healing within the family healing meetings, such as the scratching ceremonies (scratching various parts of the body, particularly the legs and hands, so that the healthy flow of energy could be restored).

When the general knowledge of family networks or standard rituals were not enough, the intervention of the *hilis haya*, the medicine man, became relevant. Generally, the medicine man did not make house calls; instead, a family sought the medicine man out. These healers even today typically spend many years in apprenticeship and have access to a semi-secret, protected herb garden. The healer possesses a collection of medications that he either gathered by himself or received as gifts. Each medicine man is an artist who often specializes in specific grievances, although patients who contract "white man's diseases," or post-Columbian ailments such as smallpox, polio, or tuberculosis, may be referred to a modern doctor. Disease can be complex and system weakness may manifest itself in both a white man's disease and an old world illness. The medicine man will work within his or her limits.

Creek medicine people treasure their own formulae and are secretive about them. In fact, many formulae were once marked out and stored as symbols marked on deerskin. The medicine man is free to accept or reject a patient often based on energy flow. If the patient's own stubbornness is preventing healing despite the healer's instructions, the medicine man might decline further intervention. Medicine men are "paid," although not always through monetary exchange, for barter and energy exchange are also important payment principles.

In Creek clan healing, there is a synthesis and representation of the four major elements in proportions appropriate to the situation. A product of the earth, often herbal, is an important part of the medicine. Fire to heat the medicine or to warm the patient, or both, is involved, as well as "living water" for blending, drinking, sweating, and other uses. The wind element— the breath of Hesagedamesse—would always be present in the medicine man's "blowing" over the relevant parts of the body and soothing the areas of disrupted energy flow or injury. The Creek medicine man also blows (in multiples of four) with reeds into medicine in a bubble pot to empower and integrate the solutions that may be taken internally or externally.

The intervention of the medicine man takes place after he speaks with the patient and/or the relatives about the history of the problem. He does not initially touch the patient while the analysis and questioning is in process. Of course, in the traditional Creek world, medicine men knew inherited and developmental histories of the patients they treated. Therefore, the questioning dealt more with the individual's problematic situation and their pathology.

After extensive listening and evaluation, treatment decisions would be made. If an herbal remedy was in order, the *hilis haya* would proceed to make the medicine and provide accompanying instructions. In addition to herbal medications, several other healing techniques were employed (and continue to be used) among stomp ground traditionals today. Nutritional and behavioral advice, vision interpretation, traditional forms of surgery, purging, special medicine bundles, sweating, and other forms of therapy were part of medicine men's repertoire. Restoration of energy flow could take place through actions such as sucking, piercing, or scratching with appropriate instruments made from a variety of sources including garfish teeth (for scratching) or animal horns (for suction).

Various forms of sweating were used among Creeks to improve health. There were family and guest sweathouses, separate and special lodges for medicine people, and tailor-made individualized wrapping and herbal sweating environments. Family and guest sweathouses have now disappeared. Medications were elaborately and exactly balanced, depending on a medicine man's experience. Complementary male and female properties of medicine had to be understood in order to achieve and maintain balance, a crucial part of the healing process. In creating herbal infusions, medicine men were always warned that wrong amounts of an herb could be addictive or poisonous, leaving a patient worse off than he or she was before. The later epidemic usage of tobacco in the Anglo world goes against the very grain of Creek health beliefs. The medicine men warned that tobacco could literally eat you up, symbolically referring to the erosion of the jawbone and tissue due to excessive chewing. The introduction of novel or unknown elements, such as hard liquor, without the internalized habits and rituals of moderation would wreak extensive social havoc in stress-ridden post-Columbian tribal worlds. Changes in nutrition accompanied by changes in the spirit also contributed to diabetes and other internal ailments. With poisons oftentimes the major causative factors of new diseases, Creek medicinal theories have expanded and adapted. However, the vanishing medicine man remains a formidable figure of authority on the entire continuum of old world illnesses and holistic healing.

Creeks had an elaborate disease classification system. Despite the lack of language describing contemporary bacteriology or virology, Creek healers understood that certain animals were responsible for certain diseases. Thus Creeks were always concerned about dogs as disease carriers. Dog excretions—saliva and feces—were considered particularly problematic. Even today, dog feces remain a powerful source of evil medicine. Birds and bird droppings, as well as mice and other rodents were also responsible for certain diseases. Symbolically, the bird diseases were wind-borne diseases, an early equivalent to what would later be labeled viral illnesses. Maggots, bad mushrooms (fungi), rotting lakes and ponds, and polluted streams were all sources of illness. Poisons from snakes were also known as threats to human health and well-being.

Certain animal qualities, including the buffalo's strength and the bear's plant knowledge, were admired. For this reason, medicine songs sought animal-like power to heal the sick. But as in the earth woman legend, the world of herbs combined with the living water, which most often countered the diseases brought by animal sickness.

Some illnesses were caused by bad medicine prepared by others. Not all examples of this are a question of "magic." Since there is a physical element to Creek medicine ways, it is conceivable that another person might chemically "poison" our food or drink, as well as the air we breathe and the objects we touch. Disease agents may be concealed in clothing, bedding, entranceways, boxes, pouches, bags, food, or drink. In extreme cases, these agents may be secretly "injected" into key areas of the body.

In Creek diagnosis, ailments were associated with alternative fixations on the heart, kidneys, throat, hair, and feet. A "broken kidney" was considered a sign of great illness, and gangrene (*liqui do*) was a disease to be feared.

The Creeks have also been fascinated by the heart since time immemorial, because it represented much of a person's spirit. Legend after legend refers to a stolen heart as a cause for concern and the restoration of the organ as the beginning of healing.

Creek stories also refer to earlier ceremonial offerings, elevated on mounds, and of youthful hearts, perhaps sacrificial, thanking the sun for its energy. In order to diffuse the energies of the enemy, the hearts of captured or dead enemies were sometimes taken and destroyed. Women played an important role in wreaking vengeance on captives who were associated with the death of a close relative. Because enemies' bodies were regarded as contaminated, purification ceremonies were conducted after battle to decontaminate warriors' minds, bodies, and spirits. There are no instances of "scalping" in Creek legends. Pending conclusive archeological evidence to the contrary, such practices may well have been introduced and spread after European contact.

In their approach to health, Creeks used the major elements to unite the body, mind, and spirit. There were physical elements to healing with specific medicines, while the mental aspect included increasing the patient's knowledge regarding the source of his problem and understanding "all his relatives" as is the case of the legend of the young man in nature's garden. Finally, the spiritual element traceable directly to the master of breath, Hesagedamesse, would be addressed. Singing and chanting would accompany the ever-present blowing on the patient and into the medicine pot. The myriad healing songs are intended to engage the spirit and build the energy of the patient so that he can be restored and reconnected to the flow of universal energy.

Even with medicine men's vast knowledge of healing and the knowledge of the historians, the prophets, and the various *miccos*, the Creeks knew that other mysteries exist and that there are limits to human knowledge. At the edge of this knowledge are strange, unpredictable transformations of energy, the cunning and trickery of nature, and the elements of a magical world.

TRANSFORMATION

All the phenomena in the Creek ontological universe are temporal manifestations of energy traceable ultimately to Ibofanga. Since the energy (*boea fikcha*) is dynamic and flowing in the long run, the transformation of energy into various temporal relational (male/female complementaries) entities is part of the physics of things. Much of the relationships and the transformations are perceived as existing in Creek astronomy, biology, agriculture, and medicine, as we have seen. However, much is still unknown. This area of the relatively unknown is real, and transformations of energy constantly take place. These mysterious transformations are part of the Creek psychic world and are seen as primitive superstitions by non-Creeks, some of whom operate from a paradigm that sees Western "rationalism" evolving and leaving behind earlier primitive worlds.

In the Creek world everything is interrelated. The appearances of trans-formations and re-transformations between males, female, humans, owls, dogs, birds, flying animals, various evil spirits (*bothas/porrv*), snakes, fish, and other entities are treated warily and carefully. The intent is to stay out of harm's way until the puzzle is resolved by further investigation or by Creek medicine and power.

The Creek world of puzzling transformations is extensive, rich, and diverse. It would be a mistake to take these transformations as evidence of ultimate ontological dualism. There is, ultimately, only Ibofanga, and the work of the single spirit is always in process. The dualism is in epistemology and knowledge, not ontology and being.

The preoccupation with transformation shows itself in every aspect of the Creek mind: the rational, magical, and humorous. A typical humorous story speaks of a rejected suitor who dearly wanted to see a girl who was sleeping in the privacy of her home. The girl had shown no interest in the young man. He begged a medicine man to transform him into a dog so he could quietly sneak into the girl's hut just to admire her. The medicine man warned him of the dangers of transformations and their unintended conse-quences. The young man, however, was in deep emotional pain and insisted. Out of compassion, the medicine man taught him ceremonial rules about man/dog transformations. The young man did the chants and changed himself into a dog and raced toward the girl's hut. In his haste, the young man did not absorb knowledge properly. He was followed and chased by an entire pack of eager dogs. To his surprise he realized—too late—that he was turned into a female dog. Even in the tribe's humor, Creek stories are morally instructive, warning of dangers of what we today might call biochemical or genetic engineering.

In addition to humorous stories there are "children's" transformation stories told to teach Creek values. One common story is about a possum and a turtle living in the days when the turtle walked erect. The turtle was an honored figure because it was a turtle that had carried living things upward to the light in the great creation myth. But even the turtle had to learn the value of humility (*yee yas gheeda*). The turtle made fun of possum because possum looked different and talked different—the odd-looking possum represented tribes with features different from the Creeks. The turtle and the possum both lost their self-control and ended in a conflict in which both were humbled. The turtle's back was cracked. The medicine man fixed them up, but turtle, in spite of his legendary importance, still has a cracked back and has to crawl humbly at ground level. Storytellers used this story to teach humility, love, respect for diversity, and honoring other living things and their capabilities. Apart from its use in humorous and educational tales, there is a serious side to transformation. Without smooth transformations, bad energy can linger, resulting in violent deaths and suicide. In more traditional times, little blowguns would shoot chemicals or poison into the throat or feet. All these acts can bring about transformations.

Given the particular conceptions of Creek space and time, the talk of transformations into owls and vultures may seem like mental illness to rigidly trained contemporary counselors. But the claims of such transformations are common occurrences in the traditional Creek world. Their roots are in the cultural mind rather than in the isolated individual psyches. The cultural transformation nexus colors some interpretations of history, particularly events taking place during the tribe's most traumatic periods. Spanish galleons can appear to be snake-like monsters emerging from the ocean's flotsam and spewing out, through the foam, venomous little invading snakes. In the oral tradition, the "radical" and rebel Chitto Harjo often spoke about Columbus being an evil spirit that returns again and again in the form of the *conquistadores* and then as Andrew Jackson, the killer of many Creeks. These *bothas* or evil spirits, must be dealt with ritually, physically, mentally, and spiritually from Chitto Harjo's perspective, or the balance of the Creek view of the world would be lost. Chitto Harjo was a full-blood Creek without a Western education. His rebellion was not rooted in European ideologies but in the Creek version of evil and transformation.

The transformation theme appears again and again in Creek legends for mature audiences. A large cluster of legends about twins in Creek mythology relates to the transformation theme. The logic of the legends shows the difference in the approach of twins to things that are at the edge of knowledge. One twin remains within the empirical and tested, and therefore intuitively rational boundaries of knowledge, while the other crosses over and is transformed. An archetypal twin transformation story goes as follows.

Two twin boys went fishing. The father pointed out that the appropriate wind clan weather authority had warned that bad weather was on the way. The mother warned them to be cautious in their fishing. The boys went to the side of a stream and built a little *chickee* hut and camped out for several days without any luck fishing in the stream. They were extremely tired and frustrated and the time for their return home was near.

From a tree near their shelter they heard a gurgling sound. The tree trunk burst open and sparkling water flowed out. The first twin cried out, "This is unnatural—let us look away." But the second twin said, "But look at the beautiful fish jumping out of the trunk with the pure-looking water." The first twin urged his brother to leave it alone—the occurrence was unnatural, irregular, and untested, and the fish were not properly examined by a knowledgeable person. He feared a transformational trick. The second twin didn't listen and got a basket and a net and collected the fish despite his brother's warnings that he needed to know the nature of the fish.

The second brother cooked the fish and fell asleep to rest before returning home. He woke up before the break of day and called to his brother. "I can't move! I can't use my legs! I need to relieve myself—my stomach seems scaly." The first twin thought his brother was teasing and went toward him. There was silence. The second twin was gradually changing into a fish and was writhing and slipping into the nearby stream. The silence was broken by the second twin's final scream. "Brother," he said, "it's bad medicine. I will have to live this way. Assure mom and dad of my love—I will still help and try to provide food." Saying this, he disappeared into the water. The first twin ran home to his parents and told the story. Some villagers assumed that the missing twin just fell into the water. But the first twin, based on his experience, warned them not to accept things without effort and knowledge—it's dangerous. To this day a sensitive person can hear the echoes of a voice near the streams in the forest—the echoes of the brother who didn't listen saying, "Don't be fooled."

TRICKERY

Alfred North Whitehead once remarked that the journey of the western mind involved a set of footnotes to Plato. The essential Plato, in his best dialogues, centered his discussion around Reason, Idea, Good, and Beautiful as essential manifestations of *logos* in the universe. This vision has provided an early foundation for the development of mathematical physics, which traditionally affirmed that reality was ordered, rational, and predictable. In Einstein's terms, God does not play dice.[4] Yet after Einstein there was recognition that predicting behavior could be problematic. In a parallel metaphor, the Muscogee rabbit is the trickster who defies the laws of nature of both Plato's *logos* and the Creek "order of things."

The Creeks are deeply reverential about the "order of things" in Ibofanga's world. To them, however, Ibofanga also possesses the gift of laughter. Ibofanga is one, but the empirical world has its dualities. Reality has its irregularities, its seeming incongruity, and even its trickery. Trickery and vision are not the same thing, but they are related in that both are manifestations of the unpredictable creativeness of nature. As soon as we understand nature, it eludes us. Therefore, true vision involves reverence for the laws of nature while also understanding the creative and seeming disparity of nature. Symbolically, we can see this in the full cycle of the stomp dance, which begins with the deep, orderly, and reverential dance and a call to Ibofanga. But in the early hours of dawn, with the rising sun and the new vision, there is the *obanga harjo*, or the vision dance, which is unpredictable and swaying, showing true spiritual intoxication and a fresh start.

The "clown" dancers at Creek stomps with their broken rhythms lead up to the last *obanga harjo* and the reinitiation into the spirit world of flowing energy and renewal. Ultimately, this points toward the gaps in the linear world and in the reason of life. In myths and stories the trickster, who appears in many cultures' stories, plays a similar role. In the Navajo world coyote is a trickster, and there are Hopi and other Pueblo clowns. For the Creeks, the most popular representation is that of the rabbit who not only runs, but also hops in unpredictable ways, linking seemingly unrelated reference points in space and time. The tricks of the rabbit can create great difficulties, yet the rabbit is part of reality, even though it has to be watched. The Creeks developed a rabbit clan and absorbed the rabbit into their worldview. However, they are mindful that creativeness and trickery are easily interchangeable. Therefore, one has to keep creative functions under the control of the social order and the disciplines as much as possible.[5] The logic of one simple rabbit story illustrates this lesson.

Rabbit was stretched out, resting under a huge tree. He wanted to be a tree, because a tree symbolized stability and respect. Trees were connected to all the elements—sun, water, earth, and air—and people respected trees. After much pleading, Hesagedamesse allowed him to be a tree with a rabbit's heart. However, the coming of a sudden storm and crashing and cracking lightning taught Rabbit that a tree has its own proper role but should not be envied. Rabbit, desiring respect, wanted to be changed into an ant, since Creek ant stories show respect for the industry and discipline of the small insect. Again, Hesagedamesse changed Rabbit into a red ant. But an army of black ants attacked the red ant and Rabbit wanted to be changed back into a rabbit.

Because of his desire and envy, Rabbit wanted to become a spider next. Spiders don't work as hard as ants, they stay out of danger's way, unlike trees, and yet they are connected to nature. After much pleading, Rabbit was turned into a spider. Once he became a spider, Rabbit was almost attacked by a female black widow. Rabbit was shocked and scared. Suddenly, he woke up and realized that he was only dreaming as he slept under a tree. The tree, the ant, and the spider have their own regularities while Rabbit has his tricks. His position and status will always have an irregular and tentative quality.

Another Rabbit story illustrates the trickster's creative powers. He had a headdress that everyone wanted. Rabbit jumped on top of a mound and there he met a beautiful woman who gave him the gift of a lover's flute so that he could play love music to bring men and women together.

Yet another Rabbit story shows him gradually fooling the Creeks in a special dance around the Creek fire. He gradually comes too close to the fire, for his tail catches. He rushes off, taking the gift of fire to the Cherokees with him. He also took fire to the Chickasaws and Choctaws. The story gently chides Rabbit and the other tribes for the theft of fire. The story's gentility also illustrates that trickery and adjustment are part of the warp and woof of life.

MAGIC AND THE SUPERNATURAL

Beyond knowledge and discipline is the supernatural and magical world of the Creeks. The magical entities of the Creek world are extensions of their view of life. Aspects of the magical entities are known; thus, they are all varying forms of energy. Other behavioral aspects are unknown and unpredictable. Since rocks and plants have energy, they can recharge a person's spirit, but this energy may be positive or negative according to Creek custom, and can strengthen or weaken a person's spirit. From earliest Creek history, Creeks have carried bags or pouches of items holding magical properties. The tribespeople also use herbs, teas, and medicine.

In cases of death, some traditional Creeks will place selected rocks in different parts of the house. Warriors going off to war would also carry small pebbles with positive energy in their pouches. A whole family of magical objects is called *sabia/svpeyv*, many of which are rocks or rock-like items. Detailed descriptions of *sabia* vary—the rocks can be crystal-like, powdery, or plant-like. *Sabia* can come in different colors: black, white, yellow, red, or blue. Some can be attracted toward a person, while others can jump away, depending on their energetic compatibility with the being. A person is indeed fortunate when he or she finds a *sabia* whose energy invigorates his or her spirit.

In the Creek world, the deer is an elder brother who looks out for humans and even engages in supreme self-sacrifice on their behalf. There is also a shining, magical little deer—*ijo micco or ijo miccoji*—who is sheer positive energy and who lives in the forest and shows himself suddenly and without warning. *Ijo micco* will never be caught—the deer is to be enjoyed as a form of sheer serendipity. When a tiny, glistening white or speckled female, or sometimes a buck, appears before you in the woods, your mind and spirit will flow smooth and clear.

While a person might welcome an encounter with *ijo micco*, he or she may not deserve to meet *hachko chapco/hvcko capko*, Long Ears. Again, descriptions of this being vary. Usually, *hachko chapko* has very long ears that can be used in whipping motions. Willie Lena, who collaborated with James Howard to write *Oklahoma Seminoles: Medicine Magic and Religion*, claimed that *hachko chapko*'s body is similar to a three-foot-tall horse.[6] John R. Swanton believed that his body resembled a mule.[7] From Jean Chaudhuri's perspective as an 'author and oral historian, *hachko chapko* is more like a powerful ogre with a huge head and very long ears. He can make the ground tremble when he is angry, and is a disciplinarian who punishes people who violate tribal codes. Children's fear of *hachko chapco* acted as an important educational tool showing possible sanctions for disrespecting nature.

Another protector is Tall Man, or *isti chapchaki/este capcvke*, a huge giant who can bump persons out of the way if they are intruding on primeval, protected areas of the forest where they do not belong or do not have a legitimate reason, by Creek standards, for being there. Tall Man is a protector of the virgin forests of Mother Earth.

In addition to Tall Man, there are various forest spirits whose descriptions varied from area to area. They were more gentle than Long Ears and warned people not to overkill animals and to respect the cycles of animal regeneration.

The Creek perspective also saw lots of Little People, or *isti lubuchki/este lobutke*, in the plants and trees. For Creeks all things were and are part of life's continuum so that the phrase *Little People* is a colorful and figurative way of speaking of the small bundles of energies in trees and bushes. The Little People, who have their own clusters and communities, can be of different ages and can be male or female. The Little People are generally fun-loving. They play games and often play with children. They are capable of playing little tricks but if they like you they can spontaneously help you. They can live in fallen logs and tree trunks and they love greenery. The Creeks left food for them in hopes of pacifying their trickery. The Little People's presence tells Creeks that the plant world is alive and well, for these Little People move when disaster is on its way.

A story tells of a hunter finding a log floating in a stream. A group of Little People were stranded on the log. The hunter gently pushed the log to the shore and helped the Little People reach land. He even fixed the injured knee of one Little Person. The Little People then invited him to stay and play with them, but he declined the invitation and went on his way. During another hunt, the hunter fell and hit his head and knee. When he awoke, he saw that the Little People in the forest had nursed him back to health. The story's logic is consistent with Creek ideas of respect for the living energies in plants and trees. Creek legend has it that the Little People helped the Creeks propagate herbs and medicine during the long and painful Trail of Tears, the forced journey to Oklahoma.

Since young people accept Little People more readily, there is a natural simpatico between the two groups. Adults can relate to Little People if they have a youthful mind. In the 1900s in Oklahoma, Little People, according to many Creeks, helped kids survive in and near trees when they ran away from boarding schools. Little People were fortunetellers in the forest and their songs told people when storms or other dangers were on the way. To keep the Little People happy, Creeks didn't and many still don't take too many fruits, nuts, or flowers, for the Little People will make the food wormy and cause sickness among the humans. One should leave plant and herbs, especially ginseng, for the Little People. They, in turn, will be silent partners on long journeys.

Children can forget themselves and play with Little People for a long time. Children are gifts of nature and they are not entirely our own. So when one leaves a beautiful area, a chant can thank the spirits of nature and help the children's spirit return to the family cycle. Some older Florida Seminoles say a prayer before crossing a bridge and leave something for a legendary woman who cries for her lost children.

Bad bundles of energy or spirit are called *bothas* in Muscogee and there can be deep fears about these evil spirits. Often *bothas* will use owls as their messengers. Therefore, Creeks will avoid owls except for some limited usage to counter *bothas* medicinally. *Bothas* can take on the appearance of different animals, and can have all the qualities of vicious barking dogs without the nobility and loyalty. Even people can transform into vicious dogs or other animals. In other words, a person can act like a dog and, indeed, at different moments look like a dog. The energies of these evil persons can act like *bothas* and symbolically appear in various forms. Medicine men can work on cures and protections against *bothas*. This bad energy can do physical harm to the mind and body. High spirituality is the ultimate defense against *bothas*, though rituals of matter and mind can point to the way of the spirit.

Another magical system revolves around serpents and snakes. Traditionally, Creeks did not eat snakes and avoided killing them. Tribal stories always urge people to be cautious around snakes. Creeks will often say, "If you let snakes into your house, you must watch them, because they can turn on you." One previously mentioned legend creates an analogy between the European invasion and a snake that devoured Creek civilization. There are many snake metaphors in Creek cosmology.

In Creek history much of the formation of mountains, gullies, and rivers was said to be the work of huge serpents that could stir the elements, creating mountains, volcanoes, snakes, and steams. Again, given the Creek perspective, the serpents represent immense undulating concentrations of energy. In Mississippian culture, there are various snake-like mounds, possibly memorializing the work of these forces. In contemporary English and geology we would call some of these forces "P" forces (because they undulate up and down), or "S" forces (because they weave back and forth), or stop-and-go forces. All three families of geological forces can be represented as snake-like because each weaves, undulates, or moves forward in repeated motions. Giant snake mounds were very possibly places of ritual honoring nature's sinuous forces.

The slithering of debris from the top of the giant earth turtle in the creation legend is the source of all evil and pollution, especially in lakes, streams, and oceans. The concentration of evil, or symbolic pollution, can take the form of a great horned snake. Pieces of the horn of this mythic snake can create powerful medicine since it represents victory over evil. Creeks will relate that a long time ago a medicine man grabbed a horned snake and cut off a piece of his horn. The shaved powders, or pieces, from this horn have been "passed" down from ancient medicine men. Since there is ultimately one universe of Ibofanga, evil can be converted to good, and the horns of serpents and the bones of some animals can confer immunity and strength.

THE JOURNEY TO THE SPIRIT WORLD

Beyond the world of magic is the final journey into the spirit world. Once the little circles of life are over, a final cycle returns the spirit to its ultimate source, Ibofanga. Because life is all a circle, Ibofanga will continue the work of creation and our energies will be recycled to serve other purposes in the great drama of life. The journey to Ibofanga, however, is not immediate. Four-day ceremonies remind us that the conversion of energy has many stages. It is impossible to understand the Creek worldview by equating a person's energy to the Christian soul. Our spirits are more akin to particles of energy in different arrangements.

For traditional Creeks, the energy of those who have died violently or who are evil will have a more prolonged journey; thus, intense cleansing rituals during their journey can help. Part of the spirit of others, the ancestors, may remain or visit around us in a temporary heaven, about four feet above the ground behind an invisible curtain. From there they can encourage us and strengthen our resolve and share in our love. The ultimate journey is symbolically westward, following the path of the sun. There, between the earth's end and the beginning of the world of the stars, is a small gap. The spirit crosses this gap and then travels along the Milky Way to the source— Ibofanga![8]

NOTES

1. Each Creek clan has its own collection of animal stories that, among other things, illustrates the functions of the particular clan associated with the animal(s). This creates a decentralized and diverse set of stories.

2. *Asi* or *asi lustee* is the black drink made from the leaves of *ilex vomitoria*. It can appear frothy white but, because the tea itself is dark, it came to be called the black drink.

3. The authors' main intention is to follow the logical interrelatedness of Creek ideas, not to deal with the detailed pharmacology or the comprehensiveness, application, or preparation and diagnosis of Creek medicine. Only the rapidly vanishing, competent, small core of truly trained medicine men can deal with technical issues.

There are at least two useful works referred to herein to supplement the philosophical discussion and the insights from oral history. The classic work of John Swanton reviews earlier sources and depends considerably on the interpretation of statements by Jackson Lewis, a traditional medicine man, and a linear ancestor of a medicine man for the major author (see Swanton, *Forty-second Annual Report of the Bureau of American Ethnology 1924–25* [Washington, DC: United States Government Printing Office, 1928]). Swanton does not say how many sources there were. For discussion of some of the major herbs see the references to *pasa* on pages 429, 547, 552, 604, 607, 608, 655, and 656. *Asi* (casine, yupon, *ilex vomitoria*) is mentioned on pages 182, 183, 185, 245, 300, 306, 485, 503, 536, 537, 538, 544, 548, 565, 584, 598, 604, 666, and 711. See also James Howard, in collaboration with Willie Lena, *Oklahoma Seminoles: Medicine Magic and Religion* (Norman: University of Oklahoma Press, 1984). Because Howard did not speak the language, his work depends considerably on a single informant, Willie Lena, whose knowledge was considerable but incomplete compared to other medicine men of major standing in traditional ceremonial grounds. Misleading and misinterpreted statements have permeated the literature by authors who lacked working knowledge of the Creek manner and language. Also, the details of usage and preparation vary from area to area and depending on the ceremonial grounds used and the medicine men practicing. Traditional elders warn against the popularization and imitation of medicine men's knowledge.

4. See Einstein's own views and commentaries on his philosophy in F. S. C. Northrop, et al., "Albert Einstein: Philosopher Scientist," in *The Library of Living Philosophers, Inc.*, vol. 7, ed. Paul Arthur Schilpp (Evanston: Northwestern University Press, 1948). For a good discussion of predictability and quantum theory, see Henry Margenau, *The Nature of Physical Reality* (New York: McGraw Hill, 1948). For a popular discussion of "reality" in physics see John Gibbin, *In Search of Schrodinger's Cat* (New York: Bantam Books, 1948).

5. The Creek rabbit stories provide the main source of Brer Rabbit and other southeastern rabbit stories. Many of these representations show up in a diluted way in the Bugs Bunny and Brer Rabbit cartoons.

6. Howard, *Oklahoma Seminoles*, 212–214.

7. Swanton, *Forty-second Annual Report*, 497.

8. Much of the analysis of the spirit world and the magical world is based on firsthand information from oral history sources. However, the major points correspond to factual references found in the existing literature. See Swanton's discussion of Creek medicine and religion, 473–672. Swanton's work involves more data collection than sustained philosophical analysis. In addition, Swanton, like most writers in the field, either did not speak the language well or did not speak it at all, depending on translators and "informants." Swanton's work was published in 1928 but refers to the works of James Adair (1775) and William Bartram (1791) on Creeks. For his bibliography see Swanton, *Forty-second Annual Report*, 855–857. Other older sources include Benjamin Hawkins, "A Sketch of the Creek Country—In the Years 1798 and 1799," originally published by the Georgia Historical Society with an introductory essay in 1848 and reprinted by Krause Reprint Company (New York) in 1971 (Lic. 5-24702). For Efau Haujo's views on the afterlife, see Hawkins, "Sketch," 80. For a self-serving but nevertheless important source of an early French European's perceptions of Creek ways, see Louis Le Clerc de Milford, *M'emoire ou Coup-D'Oeil Rapide: Sur mes differéns voyages et mon séjour dans la nation Creeck* (Chicago: The Lakeside Press, 1956). The book was first printed in 1802 and is based on his claims of living in Creek country from 1776 to the 1790s. The entire book is informative but it is clear that Milford's selfish nature, his French perspective, and his lack of knowledge of the language negatively affects his account. For "pebbles" in a war chief's bag see 219–220. On war medicine, *asi* and *pasa*, see 170–173. The most recent major work on Creek (Seminole) medicine, magic, and religion is by the late James H. Howard, who did not know Creek and relayed statements by Oklahoma Seminole Willie Lena. Howard, in collaboration with Willie Lena, *Oklahoma Seminoles: Medicines, Magic, and Religion* (Norman and London: University of Oklahoma Press, 1984). For a discussion of herbal/nonherbal remedies, magic, and witchcraft see 20–103. For supernaturals see 210–217.

CULTURE AND CONTINUITY:
A PREFACE TO CREEK HISTORY

Losers in wars seldom write their own histories. Even nonliterate societies such as the Quechua-speaking Incas usurp other tribes' memory devices, most notably the Aymara-speaking tribes they conquered. In the confrontations between literate and nonliterate societies, the dearth of Native perspectives is made worse by the work of some early Spanish, French, and Anglo scribes, recorders, and reporters who often made up a record without comprehensiveness, equity, or inclusiveness. In the end, their miswritten words remain.

Even though there are many histories of the Creeks, a comprehensive history that displays an in-depth understanding of Creek language, culture, perspective, and behavior is yet to be written. While the present chapter is not an intricate and massive history, it is a prelude to Creek history and uses a mix of time, events, and persons as traditional markers. This chapter provides a Creek perspective and links discussions of Creek ways to the tribe's historical experiences. The traditional Creek beliefs regarding time and history are not linear. Thus, rather than establish a linear chronology of standard history, it may be useful to show some Creek perspectives on major themes, including the tribe's origin, their confederacy, the Spanish invasion, the English and American invasions, Oklahoma removal, Christian influences, and contemporary tribal divisions or groups.

Traditionally, an entire class of people served as the historians and memory-keepers of events in each and every *talwa*. While some of these historians survived, the destruction of the class was massive. Spanish, English, and American forces used violence—killing people identified as intellectual leaders—to quell the dispersion of tribal history and understanding. Due to the Creek's penchant for great secrecy in religious and cultural matters, however, they were able to save some leaders.

The reliability of oral history in survivors' minds, such as the late James Scott of Alabama/Georgia and later Okemah, Oklahoma, is rooted in Creek culture. As a people without a written record, Creek culture constantly emphasized memory development and the importance of constant repetition, feedback, and practice in order to keep the mind sharp. Only those who excelled at such practices became the storytellers and the keepers of history. As this book's bibliographic and introductory discussions point out, the authors have depended considerably on the truly legendary memory of James Scott and many other traditional and respected Creeks. Transferring the content of oral history into Anglo-American concepts of space and time is not easy. Traditional Creeks can be remarkably clear on their descriptions of empirical events, but because of ideological differences in time and space continua, these accounts may seem elusive and confusing to those accustomed only to linear chronology. Oral history often uses events, sequences of events, and personalities as markers and we try to blend these markers with some key standard history dates in this chapter.

EARLY ORIGINS

Creek stories are full of discussions of mounds, both big and small. Culturally, the Creek mound culture may have been linked to Mississippian cultures through the Cahokia Mounds in eastern Missouri, the Snake Mound in Ohio, and the Great Mound in Macon, Georgia. The importance of mounds changed with migration and natural and cultural cataclysms. Vestiges of the mounds still exist in graveyards and the fire pit of the stomp grounds. Commonly, distinctions between early and late Mississippian mound builders and Creeks at the time of European contact are often made and perhaps overgeneralized. Very likely, the mound builders represent different phases in the evolution of Creek history from its Mississippian foundation. The building of the Cahokia Mounds appears to have begun around 900 AD[1] and flourished until about 1250, by which time "the center of Mississippian culture had moved south and east."[2] Moving south and east, we come across the Great Mound near Macon, Georgia.[3] The building of this mound, as well as other Georgia mounds, seemed to follow the building style of the early mounds at Cahokia. By whatever name they are called—Cahokia mound builders, early farmers, precursors of Creeks—names do not sufficiently illuminate the possible connections between these peoples and the Creeks. The mound builders' dynamics reflect different parts of Creek culture. This speculation does not contradict key known facts about Creeks.

First, Creeks, in varying degrees, were a decentralized collection of people with some key common cosmological views. They sometimes fought each other and sometimes fought other tribes. Second, the Creeks were a comparatively large tribe and therefore their pre-Columbian ancestors could have possessed the manpower for building the Mississippian mounds as well as those in Georgia. The Creeks played chunky, not uncommon among southeastern Indians, a game played by rolling stone disks, and the Cahokia mounds hold many of these disks. As an agricultural civilization, the Mississippian and Georgian cultures illustrate a balanced agricultural and hunting economy that characterized Creeks before Columbus. Third, the Creeks spoke reverentially about spiritual journeys to mounds beyond Georgia. Oral history locates the tribe in the Mississippi Valley and asserts that their journeys covered parts of the Midwest, including Ohio.

Finally, Creek culture accounts, in part, for the creation, destruction, or abandonment of various structures, providing two possible reasons for such action: religion and nature. Religious signals often led Creeks to abandon their structures, and Creek oral history repeatedly returns to the theme of a great flood. The spirit of great rivers such as the Mississippi can rise up in tremendously destructive floods, as was the case in the Mississippi region in 1993.

Creek stories from the eighteenth century trace their journey "from the west" and from the junctions of the Red and Mississippi rivers. According to the valley's topology, this junction occurs at the end of the gradually narrowing space between the eastern Rocky Mountains and the course of the Mississippi. For an agricultural river civilization, this junction would be a good place to turn east, on foot, toward Alabama and Georgia. Just as the "disappearing" Anasazi of the Southwest are the likely ancestors of the Hopi, Isleta, and other Pueblo Indians, so the ancient mound builders could have been the ancestors of the later mound builders and the Georgia/Alabama Creeks. Different bands, groups, and settlements had their own variations of the stories, but the basic cosmology symbolized by the mound as a platform to the cosmos gave them a common cultural nucleus. Arbeikas (Abhika) and Alibamus similarly may have their regional linguistic differences but still remained part of the broader Muscogee umbrella. This umbrella gradually created the sinews and tendons of the flexible and accommodating, but still distinctive, Creek confederacy.

Based on tradition, coming from the west has physical, mental, and spiritual implications. Physically, it denotes the new start of life in the southeast. Mentally, it involves issues of both peace and war, as in the ball game myth. But the Creek language is full of dual spiritual and metaphorical meanings. The word *west* also represents blackness to the Creeks, for they often used colors to identify various ideas. The land of the west and darkness was the land of visions and dreams. The journey eastward is toward the sun and knowledge. Thus, the mythical origin in the west has physical, mental, and spiritual implications for the Muscogees. Centuries later, the direction was to be reversed in the Trail of Tears and the forced removal westward to Oklahoma. This was the journey of the Muscogees toward the setting sun, or the place of dormancy and rest, and perhaps of transformation and revival.

CREEKS BEFORE COLUMBUS

Accounting for Creek events before Columbus's arrival in the "New World" is fraught with many methodological problems and difficulties. The primary aim of this section is to show Creek rendering of events in the Creek world and to point out some of the possible linkages in non-Creek literature. Inferences from the literature of this period are problematic. Early travelers in pre-removal Creek country knew little of the internal dynamics of the tribe and even less of the language. The characterization of Creek life and history is often anecdotal, and the standard problems of induction and bias apply. A classic case of a biased account is Louis le Clerc de Milford's memoirs, which are often useless when he tries to deal with chronology in Creek history.[4] While Milford's accounts may be titillating at times, his works are often plagued by inaccurate dates, directions, and locations. When he simply describes what he saw or heard, however, he can be a useful source.

The gradual creation of social contracts in Georgia, Alabama, Florida, and parts of Louisiana was accompanied by the development of complex social, cultural, and economic relations of the Creek world. None of the elements of this world were affected by European influences until the coming of Columbus. Chapter by chapter, we have explored the scope, nature, roots, trunk, branches, and leaves of the Creek tree of classic values. The pre-Columbus phase of Creek civilization was its classic stage, where the tribe had already developed and molded its earlier mound-based astronomy, biochemistry, economy, law, religion, and ethics into a cohesive system. Like many traditional societies, this involved the work of many different intellectuals, including astronomers, physicians, priests, matriarchs, war leaders, and peace leaders.

The nature of Creek values, as we have seen, provides fertile roots for an empowering confederation of compatible people, or *yeekchida* (*yekcetv*). These values became important and institutionalized in Georgia, Alabama, and Florida probably between 800 and 1000 A.D.[5] The core of the Creek groups included the Arbekas (sometimes written Arbeikhas or Arbikhas). From this center, the group began to accommodate other groups into a growing confederacy. Some groups arrived after clashing and settling their differences with the core groups, while other groups came for protection. The Arbekas remained the guardians of the northern perimeter, protecting the confederacy from later Cherokee intrusions. A small group, whose original name may have been different, survived under the Creek umbrella and became known as Tukabatchee (Tukepahce), a group and a place, or "the ones that are now crushed." Tukabatchee became one of the first four settled townships of the confederacy. Together with Tukabatchee, there was the other upper Creek *talwa* of Coosa (Koosa),[6] while toward the east were two primary lower Creek *talwas*, Casita (Kasehta) and Coweta (Koweta).[7] The Muscogee language was the lingua franca, but in the building of the confederation, leaders of *talwas* were often multilingual and had translators present for diplomatic discussions.

By the time the first Europeans arrived in the area, the Creek Confederacy had made peace with the Alibamus. The peace was later broken by several Alibamus who killed a group of nearby Creeks. Within the rules of the retaliatory code, Creeks chased the Alibamus for a protracted period up and down the Mississippi Valley into Ohio and then down again to Alabama. The final settlement occurred in the post-Columbus era, and the Alibamus once again became full members of the confederacy. The Alibamus affair is a good example of some of the confederacy's complicated dynamics. Some groups, such as the Arbeikhas, the Hitchitis, and Koasatis, remained part of the stable core. Then the circles widened to include a variety of other Muskoghean and non-Muskoghean groups. From time to time, groups would fall out and then come back into the confederacy's fold. The confederacy adopted centralist policies when external powers threatened the group; when conflicts were resolved, the confederacy reverted to local control. The confederacy's boundaries went north to the land of the Cherokees and west to the land of the Choctaws, east to the Atlantic and south to the Gulf of Mexico. At the southwestern border lived the Natchez, who later had considerable trouble with the French, as well as the Yuchis, bands of Shawnees, Yamasees, Timucuas, Apalachicolas, Tuskegees, and many other bands and groups at different times.[8] (See Corkran for names and some dates and the map at the end of chapter 8 on key locations in the southeastern United States.) When the first Europeans intruded into Creek country, the classic cosmology and values highlighted throughout this text were in place and there was peace within the confederacy.[9]

EUROPEANS BEFORE THE REVOLUTION

The Indians living in the southeastern part of what is now the United States had some of the earliest contacts with European invaders. Waves of Europeans settled in the Southeast and Southwest earlier than they did in the Northeast. It is important to point out, however obvious, that little in their past prepared the Creeks for the sheer disaster that was ahead. There is a huge amount of literature on the Indian wars, in which Native peoples were treated as pawns. While it is not our intent to rehash this historical turmoil, we do plan to highlight Creek experiences up to Indian removal.

The Euro-American world, for the Creeks, was referred to as *hetki* (white), and the Euro-American peoples were *iste-hetki* (white people); the Spanish, French, English, and Americans are generally considered subclassifications of *hetki*. We have discussed the importance of snake metaphors in describing the intensity of the colonial experience. The use of color—*hetki*—and the snake metaphors should not be construed as racism. We have discussed the Creek value system in detail, illustrating that Creeks used colors to explain experience. Further, the snake metaphors match the nature of the cultural collision that occurred. *Hetkis* of all kinds had varieties of thundersticks, or guns, and other violent technologies. They were seen as having unsurpassed greed for fountains of youth, gold, and land. They were more individualistic, commercial, and private-property oriented than anyone that Creeks had ever seen. The Southwest invasion first involved a search for treasures, since the land was barren, but the Southeast was prime agricultural real estate. It was eventually southeastern agricultural land and water that was to produce cotton, tobacco, and other agribusiness.

THE SPANISH

The first significant European threat were the Spanish, who came in waves. Juan Ponce de Leon arrived in 1513 and returned later to engage in conflict with the Calusas, Timucuas, and others. He was followed by a series of conquistadors. Diego Miruelo met the Calusas in 1516, and a year later, Hernandez de Cordoba had contact with southeastern Indians. Then came the journey of Hernando de Soto from 1539 to 1543. De Soto's wave of terror in Creek country, complete with "monster horses, helmeted harquebusmen, and musketeers," was extensive.[10] Indians were either massacred when they resisted or enslaved as porters (women were forced to become concubines). In one village alone, de Soto's people roasted and ate the entire dog population without the Creeks' consent. In the corners of Creek minds, there flow rivers and lakes of blood, devastated cornfields and homes, enslaved men and raped women.

Both the search for gold and attempts at Spanish settlement ended in bloody confrontations. In 1565 Pedro Menéndez de Arilés arrived with 1,500 soldiers and settlers, planning to set up a Spanish colony in Saint Augustine. The people were treated hospitably by a band of Timucuas, who accommodated the settlers in their large roundhouse. Soon, de Arilés tried to take over the roundhouse and initiated armed conflict with his hosts.[11] The surviving Timucuas, as was culturally appropriate, later burned the "polluted" roundhouse. The Spanish proceeded to build another fort in its place.

Spanish missionaries followed the spread of Spanish conquistadors. These people began to impose their religious values on the Creeks and Seminoles. The weakened role of Creek and Seminole women was one of the results of the Spanish sword and cross. Spirited women were carried off by soldiers and Spanish religion imposed its biased conceptions of "modesty" on women's roles and dress.

THE ENGLISH AND THE FRENCH

Following the Spanish invasion, the English and French also began to interact with the Creeks. The English, described as a nation of shopkeepers in other colonial ventures, initially arrived as traders, though they later sponsored colonization. The French, after losing to Menendez's forces in their initial attempts to settle, returned in 1701 to settle in the Biloxi-Mobile region. They began their sojourn with extermination campaigns against the Natchez. Later, the French too would become traders. The English colonial model of cultural corruption would later be taken over by the "new" Americans.

The Creek's various alliances with Europeans are understandable. The Creeks knew nothing of European lifeways. The images that they had of *hetkis*, in general, were all similar with respect to the greed for Indian property, resources, and land, as well as their destruction of Indian ways. For this reason, Creeks often chose the European group they thought the least of the evils at a given time. Out of the process of choosing allies came a temporary illusion of increased Creek "strength," but traditionals realized that the increased number of non-Indians swarming Indian Country was threatening their way of life.

The introduction of weaponry, slavery, land "sales," massive trading, and rum and liquor began to corrode—as it was intended to—the tissues of Creek life. The intrigue and great power rivalry among the English, French, and Spanish often found the Creeks aligning with the English, even though they were sporadically drawn in by the French and Spanish. Because of the divide-and-conquer machinations of European powers, none were committed to the survival of the Creeks. The history of the Europeans' weak alliances has already been extensively treated and need not be repeated here.[12] While the Creeks often leaned toward the English among the European powers they were, nevertheless, deeply disturbed about the behavior of traders and the encroachment of settlers from the Carolinas despite guarantees that settlers were not to cross the Savannah River without Creek permission.

In 1732 James Edward Oglethorpe journeyed from Charleston to Yamacraw Bluff in Georgia to found a colonial settlement. One of the minor local *miccos* was Tomachichi who, despite his friendliness toward settlers, was initially distressed by this particular intrusion. However, after meeting Oglethorpe he was party to a "treaty" that allowed Oglethorpe's colony to remain in return for a guarantee of Creek holdings. With Tomachichi's help, the English began to negotiate and make "treaties" with *miccos* from the lower Creeks, located primarily around the Chattahoochee River. The upper Creeks, centered around the Talapoosa and Coosa rivers, kept their distance from Tomachichi's relationships with Anglos. Eventually, Tomachichi became one of several figures central to British colonial divide-and-conquer logic as employed among the Creeks.

Tomachichi, along with eight other Indians, went to England in 1734 at Oglethorpe's urging to take part in the symbolic "ratification" of the treaties. During Tomachichi's visit, his reported statements appeared to articulate some basic Creek values. His toleration for different beliefs, including those of the Archbishop of Canterbury, was evident. He also claimed that though they appeared prosperous, "the English lived worse than the Creeks who were a more innocent people."[13] Tomachichi "described the evils of the rum trade and requested its prohibition,"[14] and he resisted talking about the details of the Creek religion, saying that "he had already offended the spirits by talking too much about it aboard the ship and one of his company had died."[15]

Tomachichi, in his famous speech as translated for reporters by well-known half-blood Johnny Musgrove, went on to point out the importance of eagle feathers as a sign of peace and discussed the nature of decentralized Creek debate and consensus. The feathers that Tomachichi brought with him as a gift had been carried from town to town.[16] He also complained about the unfair trading practices and ended his speech by expressing hope that there would be mutual respect. Tomachichi, despite his closeness to whites around Savannah, remained a Creek to the end.

Tomachichi was a *micco* of only one band but he was able to influence the lower Creeks with regard to initial support for the English and for the Georgia settlement around Savannah in particular. Oglethorpe used Tomachichi to deal with unfriendly Indians in north Florida. The upper Creeks, given the location of the settlement, appeared to defer to the lower Creeks in dealing with the English because of the closer initial proximity of the English to the lower Creeks. But with further intrusions by the Georgians and the Indian agent for Georgia, the upper Creeks under Hobohatchey of the Abeikas began to assert themselves against the newcomers. This added to the widening gulf between the upper and lower Creeks, for the latter were more conciliatory to Anglo intrusion. Adding to this widening gulf was the mixed-bloods' gradual rise to power as middlemen, such as Musgrove and his wife. The mixed-bloods primarily had Anglo or Scottish fathers, some of whom were traders. Others were children of violence and forced liaisons. There were a few mixed-bloods who moved around in upper Creek country, but most lived in lower Creek territory. Despite Tomachichi's good will, the sometimes tacit, sometimes explicit alliances between the leading mixed-bloods, traders, and settlers would undermine Creek traditions.

Unlike Roger Williams's style of respect for often decentralized Indian conceptions of authority and consent in Rhode Island, the English began to elevate the *miccos* to "kings," gradually weakening the role of Creek assemblies and councils. The elevation of *miccos* made the process of land transfer easier, particularly with newly empowered *miccos* who were of mixed-blood ancestry. With shallow loyalties to Creek traditions, the pace of English control over Creek lands accelerated rapidly.

The rise of Alexander McGillivray to power illustrates the role of mixed-bloods. McGillivray was only one-quarter Creek, for his mother was half Creek and his father was full-blood Scot. Through his grandmother's line McGillivray, who could hardly speak any Creek, claimed wind clan lineage, but was not socialized into the protocol of the clan.[17] McGillivray was, in part, a creation of the English and used his English connections to gain prestige and power. Though standard non-Indian histories speak extensively of McGillivray, he is hardly revered in the Creek oral traditions.[18] Instead, the oral traditions generally lionize people like Opothleyahola, (sometimes called Opeitley Mico) of Tallassee or Hobothle Mico, who tried in vain to keep the Creeks "neutral" and tried to rally them against any Europeans intruding on Creek lands. Upper Creeks, more often than not, would not agree to cessions of land, whereas the McGillivrays, the Musgroves, and later William McIntosh played double-agent roles between the Creeks and the English, and often ended by ceding various parcels of Creek land to the British.[19] In typical divide-and-conquer style, the British began to designate cooperative chiefs, including Mortar, "Great Medal Chiefs." Nowhere in Creek legend or tradition is there any basis for such empowerment of *miccos* as was given to Mortar and McGillivray. It is an example of how accurate Creek history has yet to be written. Instead, a one-quarter-blood Creek who hardly spoke the language, distorted Creek conceptions of leadership, picked up rank and honors from all the European groups, drank excessively, and was quite promiscuous (he apparently had a venereal disease) is written up as a great Creek leader.[20] Yet a traditional Creek hero like Opothleyahola is mentioned only in passing. As is often said, success has a thousand fathers while failure is an orphan. A success who is a scoundrel is more noted by scribes than a traditional hero like Opothleyahola, who recognized danger and tried to help his people, however unsuccessful. Even though McGillivray supported the English in the American Revolution, he was adept in compromising with the Americans after the war and soon was carrying water for the new Indian agent, Benjamin Hawkins, and for the Creek's archenemy, Andrew Jackson.

The English and the French employed styles of duplicity that were somewhat different. French traders went "native" more readily than the English, while the English mixed-bloods remained a more distinct class. The English relationships were more directly commercial and oriented to transfers of land ownership per English law. The French traders often became "savages" as de Tocqueville would note much later.[21] De Tocqueville failed to understand that Indian life, particularly Creek life, provided as good a model of traditional society, with its strong secondary associations and limited government, as those he admired inw traditional European societies. The equality of Indian societies made him miss the complexity and diversity of Native America. De Tocqueville correctly noted that the combination of the loss of land and the widespread killing of game—both at the hands of Anglo forces—deeply affected the economy of the Indians, leaving them destitute and dependent. He assumed that Indians would soon "perish in the same isolated condition in which they have lived,"[22] and claimed that their only hope was through assimilation, particularly intermarriage. He sorely underestimated the number of Indians who would try to retain traditional values.

Unlike Milford or de Tocqueville, both of whom visited Creek country, their countryman Rousseau, who never saw an Indian, was closer to the mark when he thought that Native peoples lived in a state of natural equality that would be threatened by the arrival of private property. Despite Rosseau's romantic notion of the "noble savage," he may have understood Creeks better than did Milford or de Tocqueville. Certainly, the French leaders who engaged in the Louisiana Purchase hardly saw Creeks as people with aboriginal entitlements to the so-called Louisiana Purchase when the French transferred their lands to America.

THE AMERICAN EMPIRE

In the Anglo-American models of aboriginal land transfer, there is a continuum from Roger Williams's recognition of basic Native title in New England and the need for in-depth Indian consent, to Jackson's policy of forced removal and ethnic cleansing in the South, with Jeffersonian "philanthropy" and removal ideas lingering somewhere in the middle. The Roger Williams (1604–1683) tradition remains, even today, a maverick and quasi-radical attitude in democratic culture. Jackson represents the racist, populist, and basically successful right wing. Jefferson attempted to define a morally and politically correct, but somewhat hypocritical, "philanthropic" and "humanitarian" middle ground.[23] But he too was for removal and eventual assimilation.

Jefferson's advocacy of universal natural rights and the contractual theory of property is well known, as is his stated interest in Indian languages and his role in the Northwest Ordinance, which shows the utmost good faith in matters relating to Indian affairs. Jefferson's secularism also frowned on missionary activity among Indians. All these noble aspects are, however, a hypocritical gulf away from Jefferson's actual policy with respect to American Indians. There is the ominous characterization in the drafting of the Declaration of Independence of Indians as cruel savages stirred up by the British on the frontiers (which included the Creeks). Jefferson was surprised and peeved that even in 1812 many Creeks sided with the British rather than the Americans, who were aggressively acquiring Creek lands.

Jefferson made little attempt to remove non-Indians from Indian lands. In fact "it was a given under Jefferson"[24] that the settlers' land hunger be satisfied, that the Indians move westward, and that the assimilation and "termination of their history" were appropriate policies.[25] Jefferson wrote to Andrew Jackson claiming that he wanted a peaceful solution to the Indian-white conflict, and insisted that obtaining land—and shifting Indian livelihood to agriculture—was his most important goal.[26]

It is ironic that the Creek economy involved a balance of agriculture and hunting. The takeover of agricultural land by settlers and the related turmoil began to destroy the balance of the Creek economy from one end. The destruction of buffalo, followed by unregulated Anglo hunting of deer and other animals to be used for their skins, began to destroy the Creek economy from the other end, driving them further and further toward hunting, trading, and a money economy. In the skin trade, again, the Creeks who benefited most were disproportionately the mixed-bloods who had the closet working relationships with the factories and trading stores.

It is at this juncture that the cold-blooded hypocrisy of the Jeffersonian approach to the destruction of the Creeks becomes evident. Jefferson appointed Benjamin Hawkins as the federal agent for the southern tribes, including the Creeks, and worked closely with Hawkins in pushing the Creeks off their lands. In working with Hawkins, Jefferson's civilization method claimed that the "government would aid the Indians by teaching agricultural methods and provide them with needed capital through the purchase of lands made extraneous by the abandonment of hunting."[27] Jefferson's profound insensitivity to the destructive potential implicit in forcing a nation to shift from a cooperative, bartering economy to the dislocations of superficially created capital is evident in his views. On top of all this is his astounding hypocrisy, for he hoped that the factories and trading posts would engage in trade in such a way that the Creeks and the other southern Indians would be so deeply in debt they would be forced to cede their lands in order to cover their debts.[28] Jefferson, through Benjamin Hawkins, also got Alexander McGillivray to cede some Creek lands that already had settlers on it and met with McGillivray in 1790 to insure the cession.[29] Even Creek cession of lands in the Treaty of New York was not enough as Georgians relentlessly pressed for more.[30]

Jefferson did little to protect the Creeks after the Treaty of New York. He was pinning his hopes on mixed-bloods who, to him, represented progress. When mixed-bloods were activists they acted on behalf of their acquired private property and did little to protect communal lands. It is for this reason that full-bloods, in frustration, complained about the McGillivrays and sometimes attacked them.[31] Some upper Creek towns and Seminoles became increasingly uncomfortable with McGillivray's activities. The mixed-bloods informed Benjamin Hawkins about the full-bloods' activities. William McIntosh, who followed McGillivray in this tradition, played a double-agent role like McGillivray, but with less skill. McIntosh, in 1805, "was one of a six man delegation sent to Washington to negotiate the sale of a strip of country between the Oconee and Ocumulgee rivers. He made the principal reply to President Jefferson and on the treaty document his was the second Creek signature."[32] McIntosh also was a spy for Benjamin Hawkins when in 1811 Tecumseh, a Shawnee whose mother was Creek, attempted to create an intertribal alliance against Americans. Tecumseh eventually failed despite his elaborate attempts at resistance.

The political use of mixed-bloods was supplemented by bribery with appropriations Jefferson had obtained from Congress supposedly to aid

Indians. Some of the federal money even made its way to missionaries as "educators" despite Jefferson's opposition to Christianizing the Indians.

In the historical collision between Euro-American and Creek civilizations, the Creeks were destined to lose given the odds against them. The cruelest odds lay with the philanthropic and supposedly moral leaders like Jefferson. If the most "liberal" wing of Anglo civilization differed only in degree in separating Creeks from their lands and hopefully from their culture, one can see the creation of the giant Jacksonian juggernaut, decorated with pious Jeffersonian hypocrisies, and driven in part by the McGillivrays and McIntoshes. In Indian affairs, Jefferson showed one of his darkest sides, blackened by his insistence on addressing Indian leaders as "children." Robert Tucker and David C. Hendrickson put Jefferson's actions in a broader context, applying it to Indian affairs: "Jefferson's dark side is also the dark side of American history, and in this too, the affinity between the man and the nation is complete."[33]

Jackson's political tenure was the worst part of the Creek's pre-removal period. Jackson was a most aggressive politician and president, riding on the backs of Indians to his political fame and success. While Jackson is remembered as a populist democrat, his circle of democracy excluded Indians, African Americans, and other minorities. His driving force, more so than populism, was to get the Indians, particularly the stubborn Creeks, out of the South. Michael Rogin's book gives a detailed picture of Jackson's apoplectic hate and anger toward the Indian world. There was no Jeffersonian hypocrisy here, but direct action and violence with respect to removal. Oral history interviews in Florida show how deeply feelings toward Jackson still run among the Seminoles. The oral history stories repeatedly tell of "red hair" Jackson killing young Creeks and even taking an Indian child and bashing his head against rocks and trees.[34]

The Creeks were in a civil war from 1811 to 1814, their factionalism led by McIntosh and other mixed-bloods on one side, and the upper Creeks and many full-bloods among lower Creeks on the other. The latter side had the "red stick" warriors at their core. Jackson, with the help of McIntosh, sought Creek allies and Cherokee volunteers for his own forces to augment his divide-and-conquer strategy. The first of two battles took place near Horseshoe Bend. Rogin summarizes the historical event:

> In January 1814, temporarily reinforced by troops and supplies, Jackson advanced again. He aimed for the Creek stronghold at the Horseshoe Bend of the Tallapossa River, seventy-five miles south of Fort Strother. The Creeks attacked at Emuckfau Creek, three miles from the Horseshoe Bend. Fighting the first battle in which they were not heavily outnumbered, they inflicted heavy casualties on Jackson's troops. Troop and supply problems forced Jackson to retreat

after the battle; the Indians followed, attacking as the whites crossed Enotachoepo Creek. Part of Jackson's line broke and only the action of a detachment under General Carroll averted a rout. Finally, with the help of Jackson's Cherokee and Creek allies, the red sticks were driven back.[35]

Jackson had originally marched into Alabama with "a militia force of 2,500."[36] He picked up reinforcements from Creek factions led by McIntosh of Coweta. "At its greatest strength, the number of effective soldiers in Jackson's force was about 5,000, including 600 Cherokees."[37]

After the January battle, with less than a complete victory, Jackson, concerned about morale, executed a seventeen-year-old recruit, reprimanded others, rebuilt his forces, and returned to the location of the first battle of Horseshoe Bend. There, 1,000 Creeks under Menawa were outnumbered two to one by 1,400 of the original 2,500 white militia force, more than 500 Cherokees, and more than 100 Creeks from McIntosh's Coweta faction. The Cherokees attacked from the rear after cutting loose Creek boats into the river. The Creeks fought almost to the last man. Jackson would gloat that he destroyed the key Creek prophets, trampled on their holy ground, and killed the key leaders of the Upper Creeks.[38] Of the original force of 1,000 Creeks under the leadership of Menawa, only seventy were able to escape with their gunshot wounds after the defeat.

General Jackson's losses were 51 killed and 150 wounded. The prevalence of arrow wounds furnished clear proof that the Red Sticks, either as a demonstration of their reliance upon Indian customs or through necessity, fought this decisive engagement mainly with their own primitive weapons.[39]

Defeating outnumbered aboriginals who were fighting for their land with bows and arrows against "thunder sticks" is the stuff that built Ol' Hickory's reputation. Scribes recorded little of the character of Menawa and his *tustenugees*. With the losing Menawa forces at Horseshoe Bend was an upper Creek youth who later came to be known as Tallassee Tustenugee, or Osceola. This young man escaped, joined his mother, and became a part of the upper Creeks' struggle to migrate away from whites into the swamps of South Florida. He helped galvanize the coalition between the Seminoles and Miccosukkees, who cooperatively worked together with other cultural kinfolk in the spirit of the Creek confederacy. But in Florida, too, the nightmare followed the Creeks, Seminoles, and Miccosukees. The battle of Horseshoe Bend involved the largest number of Indians, as well as the largest number of deaths in the United States-Indian wars.[40] After Horseshoe Bend, Jackson seized Creek lands, including sizable land parcels from his Indian allies.

THE ROAD TO REMOVAL

After the Battle of Horseshoe Bend McIntosh, in alliance with agent Benjamin Hawkins, began tinkering with Creek customary laws on the criminal code and inheritance and weakened the participatory structure of Creek government.[41] McIntosh and many other mixed-bloods picked up many white values, particularly acquisitiveness, racism against African Americans in the form of slavery, and acquisition of private property. A careful look at Benjamin Hawkins's notes shows that in Creek country most of those who owned private holdings and slaves were mixed-bloods.[42]

In regard to mixed-bloods and their role in Creek factionalism, it would be a mistake to take this as a discussion of race and genetics. The Creeks were not racists. Part of the tribe's problem was their openness to Creeks of fractional descent. It was the persistent behavior of the mixed-bloods that kept angering and disappointing the Creek traditional leaders throughout the post-Columbian period. This disappointment was felt most acutely by Opothle Micco or Yahola, in the eighteenth century; Opothleyahola, Menawa, and Osceola in the nineteenth century; and Chitto Harjo at the turn of the twentieth century. Creek factionalism would continue in Oklahoma even after statehood as the McIntosh bloc, understanding the Anglo system, captured and controlled the Creek "government," which was really a pale imitation of Anglo-American ideas. From statehood to the 1960s, the principal chiefs of the Creeks, including "Dode" McIntosh, were appointed by the president of the United States.

The traditionals tried to work with the new "government" and grumbled enough from time to time to make some changes. One result of continued activism by the Creek Centralization Committee in the 1950s and 1960s and the Traditional Indian Convention in Henryetta, Oklahoma, was that some changes involved greater participation by voters and the election of the principal chief of the Creek tribe. The grumbling can still be heard over cultural preservation issues, language, support for tribal towns, and consultation/participation.

Mixed-blood indicators are primarily cultural, not genetic. Although McGillivray and McIntosh nominally belonged to the wind clan on their mother's side, Creek culture is not limited to merely mechanically tracing the mother's clan. It involves supporting the role of the father's clan, internalizing certain obligations, and nurturing the entire clan system. Teaching and learning Creek ways and the linguistic nuances of Muscogee went unobserved by the McGillivrays and McIntoshes. Writers who do not sufficiently understand the internal dynamics of Creek culture make too much of McGillivray's and McIntosh's membership in the wind clan as the major factor in their rise to power.[43]

Even though the wind clan had important functions, no clan stands above other clans in any uniform, hierarchical political structure. The Creeks do not have a caste system. The clan system requires some exclusions to avoid incest and inbreeding, but marrying a "wind" did not traditionally improve a person's status. A focus on hierarchy and status was a learned behavior that can be attributed to English influence. McGillivray and McIntosh primarily used their immediate mixed-blood relatives in the wind clan to create factions. They reached out to other mixed-bloods, and then pulled some full-bloods into their coalition. Classic Anglo interest in aggregation politics rather than in Creek conceptions of legitimacy account for the rise of the McGillivrays and McIntoshes. In dealing with these people, the southern elite and people like Benjamin Hawkins saw willing, ready, and able (albeit slightly blurred) images of themselves. To be a Creek, one is responsible not only to a clan, but also to nurture the ways of that clan. Each clan has its special versions of the legends, the origin story, and the role of each clan in that story. Creeks passed on traditions through both maternal and paternal clans. Behaving appropriately is at least as important as clan descent in determining one's position in Creek society.

The McGillivrays and McIntoshes continued to marry into non-Indian Georgia society—even Benjamin Hawkins's descendants intermingled into an interlocking elitist directorate that corrupted Creek participatory traditions. Interestingly, Dode McIntosh, principal chief and descendent of the William McIntosh faction, was considerably proud of his Scottish heritage. He journeyed in the 1960s to a Scottish McIntosh clan reunion in Scotland and danced in Scottish kilts. In contrast, no looming images remain of Dode McIntosh leading a Creek stomp dance. Some Creeks with mixed ancestry have deeply learned Creek values, but among the mixed-blood factional leaders this was not the case. William McIntosh did not send his son, Chilly, back into the Creek socialization system, so Chilly became even further removed from his cultural roots. Of course, McGillivray's private English school education was not supplemented by an education in Creek values. His mother was a mixed-blood and there was little opportunity for him to learn these values.

William McIntosh's greatest betrayal of Creek values was in the Treaty of Indian Springs in 1824. McIntosh was not authorized by the Creek political system to enter into this treaty, which would transfer another huge amount of Creek territory out of Creek hands. The details of the process have been treated extensively in standard Creek histories.[44] McIntosh constantly sought Anglo protection because of the traditionals' concern and indignation. Opothleyahola and others repeatedly tried to explain that a Creek chief or chiefs, according to Creek ways, could not really sell communal lands. Further, the standard process of Creek governmental legitimization had not been used. McIntosh's Indian name—Tustenugee Hutkee—was strangely symbolic, as it means "the white warrior."

Opothleyahola spoke in Muscogee as McIntosh was about to sign the document and said, in part: "My friend you are about to sell our country; I now warn you of your danger."[45] Big Warrior of Tukabatchee also pointed out that chiefs could not sell land. He journeyed to Washington, D.C. in 1825 to protest against the treaty and died there. This placed even greater responsibilities on Opothleyahola, who began to speak directly as the chief spokesman for the Creek confederacy and at its assemblies and councils. Besides abrogating the Treaty of Indian Springs, the Creek nation's council made a pivotal move in its history and ordered the execution of William McIntosh for treason.[46] The action surprised and shocked people like Hawkins who underestimated the nature of the Creek confederacy and its direct democracy. The council, under Opothleyahola's leadership, condemned William McIntosh, Etomme Tustunnugee, and two sons-in-law of McIntosh—Samuel and Benjamin Hawkins—to death. The person authorized to supervise the execution was Menawa, a leader from the upper Creek town of Okfuskee. He led a Creek force to McIntosh's plantation on the Chattahoochee and set fire to the buildings. McIntosh was shot and stabbed, and subsequently died. Also executed was Etomme Tustunnugge and Samuel Hawkins. Benjamin Hawkins, not the agent himself, was wounded but escaped. This was not an assassination but a Creek tribal execution for treason, based on a Creek community and council decision.

Opothleyahola kept trying to improve the coordination of the Creek confederacy until removal to Oklahoma. He was constantly harassed and arrested on trumped-up charges in order to retard his attempts to unite the Creeks. He agreed to a compact that insured Creek ownership of their remaining land. Creek removal from Georgia had already begun but Opothleyahola resisted agreeing to removal. However, in 1829 Jackson became United States president and began pressing for Indian removal legislation, which gave blanket authorization and bypassed the necessity of authorizing each piecemeal agreement. Opothleyahola went to Washington to plead with Jackson, who would not be moved. In 1831 the twin terror of starvation and smallpox, on top of other illnesses, hit the Creeks. Sadly and reluctantly, Opothleyahola accepted removal rather than see his people die. In 1836 groups of Creeks were removed from Alabama (the Georgia removal had started years earlier). Upon arrival in Oklahoma, Opothleyahola found that the McIntosh faction had settled in choice land years earlier. He wanted to move toward Texas, but having little choice moved a little farther away from the McIntosh bloc. Incidentally, the upper Creeks, with their traditional values, turned out to be better agriculturalists than did the McIntosh group.[47]

Some writers such as Green appear to assume that Opthleyahola had developed an acquisitive instinct. From Creek oral history accounts, this is patently wrong. Whenever Opothleyahola received money as part of removal, he shared it with the less fortunate in his tribe. He protected African Americans and consistently exemplified the best Creek values as a leader. He shared what he had with the needy. Traditional Creeks generally thought that European culture was a continuous culture of violence and aggrandizement and the Creeks constantly had to struggle to survive in the midst of clashing forces. When the United States Civil War broke out, the Creeks again faced great danger. Many, including Opothleyahola, wanted to remain neutral in a white man's war, but he got involved because he thought there was a promise of protection of Creek communal lands. Given the northern rejection of slavery and this presumed promise, Opothleyahola led the way for Creek support for the North. Once again, the mixed-blood leaders, already accustomed to private property and slavery, generally opted for the South alongside their Cherokee counterparts.[48]

Opothleyahola led a large army of Creeks, Seminoles, Delawares, Shawnees, Kickapoos, and African American Creek freedmen (not slaves) from Oklahoma to Kansas. This group was ultimately defeated in the Battle of Hominy Falls by Confederate forces that included Cherokees soldiers. After the defeat, the Creek warriors had a difficult time surviving—Opothleyahola exhausted his personal resources helping his tribesmen survive. "Weakened by exposure and poor nutrition, Opothleyahola died and was buried with great ceremony in an unmarked grave in Kansas."[49] Apart from his political and military activities, Opothleyahola also played a major role in the transfer of Creek culture to Oklahoma in the startup of the ceremonial grounds and rekindled, as much as possible, Creek fire and spirit.

Opothleyahola's spirit would be seen again and again in one of his followers who had gone to Kansas during the Civil War. That man would come to be known as Chitto Harjo, who will be discussed in detail below. To keep a semblance of chronology, however, it is necessary to follow the thread of Opothleyahola's and Menawa's influence among the Creeks who fled to Florida after Horseshoe Bend. The best known and respected among them was the person who was given the name Osceola, the warrior who took the black drink and pursued the Muscogee resistance in Florida.

OSCEOLA

There is extensive "documentary" literature, as well as anthropological, archeological, and historical scholarship, on the state of Florida, Osceola, and the Oklahoma Seminoles. It is not the purpose of this essay to review, duplicate, or directly repeat this literature,[50] but to show the journey of Muscogee culture and values, with an emphasis on the oral history as a supplement to standard historical accounts. Much of what is written about Osceola is based on non-Indian hearsay. Since Osceola and the Florida Seminoles had an adversarial relationship with Americans for the most part, the standard history has considerable cultural gaps about Osceola and the Seminoles.

Osceola was a traditional Tallassee upper Creek who, under great hardship, fled with his Creek mother to Florida after the disastrous Battle of

Horseshoe Bend. The literature sometimes claims that Osceola was a mixed-blood and that his name was Powell.[51] However, there is no definitive evidence proving these claims. A trader named Powell, who was apparently kind to the young Osceola and Anglos, began to call Osceola the Powell Kid. Given the difficulties with the pronunciations of Indian names and the multiplicity of names for the same person, Anglos often would apply convenient name tags to Creeks. This was also true in Oklahoma. At the time the commercial/tribal land was chopped up into individual holdings; for example, names like Jones, Smith, and Hill were assigned to full-blood Creeks. Thus, the maiden name of the first author was Hill because her grandfather told the authorities that he was from *gun hulwa,* "high place" or hill. Hence, the name Hill stuck and has nothing to do with the equivalent English surname Hill. Osceola rejected the idea that there was mixed-blood ancestry in his family and is reported to have said, "No foreign blood runs in my veins; I am a pure-blood Muscogee."[52] The eminent Florida historian John K. Mahon verifies the lack of evidence that Osceola was Powell's son.[53] In addition, the great painter of Indians, George Catlin, also believed Osceola to be a full-blood, and it was for him that Osceola posed for hours, despite illness, for his classic portrait.

A major source of oral history was the late Billy Osceola of Okeechobee, a major leader of the Brighton group of Seminoles in the 1940s and 1950s and an elder tribal statesman until his death. Billy Osceola was a family friend of the first author's father and was interviewed many times on Seminole history and culture over almost a twenty-year period. Billy Osceola's father was Gacha, or Panther, and Panther was with Osceola in Florida and knew of his upper Creek heritage.

Osceola's father was of the panther clan. In the case of a father's absence, due to battle, hunting, or marital separation, Creek children stayed with their mother and her relatives. Unlike the McGillivrays and the McIntoshes, Osceola was nurtured by his traditional clan links; specifically, he was raised as a red stick in the Creek social system. Osceola was never a *talwa micco,* or town chief, but gradually became a *yahola* and a Talassee Tusteneggee war chief. He was able to rally other Seminoles to his cause because of his leadership qualities and compassionate character.

Like Opothleyahola, Osceola fought on two fronts. He tried to keep intruders off Indian lands and tried to prevent individual Indians from selling or ceding their lands. Having learned the dangers of fighting superior forces at Horseshoe Bend, Osceola turned to guerilla warfare given the small Seminole population, the lack of arms, and the swampy Florida terrain. Osceola knew the nature of Anglo military formations and lined up Seminoles in formation when he felt it necessary, but adopted guerilla tactics most of the time.

The Anglo forces attempted to starve the Seminoles. There are heroic stories, yet to be fully told, of the survival mechanisms of the Seminoles. Billy

Osceola quoted his grandfather about the stench of human flesh when a Seminole village was burned. In Billy Osceola's father's time, Seminoles had to develop elaborate survival methods on the run. This included eating raw fish and not leaving traces of fish bones in any one place. Billy Osceola talked of one occasion when his father and Osceola were in the swamps without any food. The group found a dried deer bone with which they began a soup, adding swamp cabbage and wild mushrooms. The soup bowl was reverentially passed in a circle and each person sipped their share with a deep reverential *maddo*—thanks to Hesagedamasse and to elder brother deer—for helping take care of them.

The Seminoles depended on their medicine. They were also trained to use hollow reeds to breathe while staying under water. They made trenches with trap doors and camouflage ground cover. Legends tell how they used alligators' backs to cross shallow water to hidden islands where they grew corn and vegetables. Even in the 1950s, the authors of this work have seen the little hideaway farms on small "islands" in Miccosukkee country, away from the Tamiami Trail. These islands were reachable only by canoe and later by airboat. Continued development in Florida has pretty well destroyed this infrastructure and ecosystem of Seminole survival.

Osceola and his people resisted removal. The final chapter in Osceola's life is well known and again shows the dark side of American history. He was captured by Anglo troops that broke the protocol of a white flag of truce. The non-Indian version of his imprisonment, treatment, death in 1838, and burial is gruesome enough.[54] The Seminole stories give a far more brutal picture of the treatment of Seminoles on the one hand and a much more admiring picture of Osceola's skills and his "medicine" on the other.

The Billy Osceola version of Osceola has him extremely solicitous about women and children. He would bring stragglers gently into his camp and take care of them the best he could. Non-Indians have commented on Osceola's plural "wives"—not understanding the Seminole social structure—particularly when on the run. As an active military leader, Osceola really had no time or interest in a "harem." In Muscogee culture, shared by the related Seminoles, it was not uncommon to have a man take care of not only his wife, but also various female relatives and needy female friends. These relations were not necessarily sexual. When on the run, Seminoles protectively would move women for purposes of safety. Since Osceola's allies included African Americans who were provided protection, African American women also traveled in the groups. Since the Seminoles did not write their history, the characterization of Osceola is full of cultural bias, unintended as it might be. In the difficulties of intercultural discourse, when missionaries spoke disapprovingly of what they thought were mistresses, many Seminoles simply would introduce a woman as a wife in order not to engage in prolonged discussion on comparative theology. In their flight, the small band of Seminoles maintained their clan rules on marriage, incest, and child rearing. Billy Osceola's picture of Osceola is that of a person with classic Muscogee red stick values.

When the Seminole removals continued to take place after Osceola's death, some of the removals were linked to embarkations out of Tampa, Florida, on ships. The word *Tampa* may be a corruption of *dimpe*, in Muscoghean Seminole dialect, which means "near something," or possibly embarkation place. The few hundred Seminole who escaped removal retreated into the swamps and their group gradually grew in size. In the process of survival and adaptation, they retained many essential elements of Muscogee culture and lost others. Being smaller in numbers, not all Muscogee clans are represented among the Florida Seminoles. The stepping times of the dances are a little different, for example, but the Florida Seminole elders retain some stories that the Oklahoma branch does not have. The Florida Seminoles also possess many "counting songs" for teaching kids numerical analysis.

THE TRAUMA OF REMOVAL

With Opothleyahola's agreement to move west and with Osceola's death in Florida, the vortex of Creek cultural and survival activities was tied to the traumatic experiences of forced removal to Oklahoma, the loss of huge numbers of people under cruel circumstances in the removal, the adjustments to Indian territory, the Civil War, the politics of statehood, and the crushing of the pre-Oklahoma statehood Indian governments, or "republics," in Oklahoma.

After Vietnam, social scientists have been more sensitive to stress and trauma. However, the trauma of an entire group—in this case the Creek full-bloods caught up in ethnic cleansing, extensive deaths, starvation, and violence—is not fully understood. The nightmare of removal left signs of deep post-traumatic stress disorder among many of the traditional Creeks. Cycles of depression, denial, anger, withdrawal, and some imitation and emulation of the victors were modalities that could be found among many Creeks depending on their family background and personal characteristics. After all, a people that was around 200,000 in number before Columbus had dwindled to around 10,000 after removal.

Indian removal was one form of "ethnic cleansing" on the dark side of US history. The document-based history of Creek removal has been told many times in scholarly literature.[55] What is missing in this literature, except for some scattered comments, is a sense of the depth of the Creek trauma created by removal and its aftermath. Grant Foreman's *Indian Removal*, with a foreword by Angie Debo, remains a decent classic review of the documentary and recorded aspects of Creek removal. Debo's *The Road to Disappearance* also remains a sensitive introduction to Creek history. While Debo attempts to include Indian viewpoints, her descriptions of the perceptions of removal are incomplete and sometimes confused because of the language barrier and because of differing concepts of space and time. This author's difficulty can be cited in interviews with Mary Hill,[56] Monie Coker,[57] and James Scott of Greenleaf.[58] All three of these Creeks were intimate members of the primary author's extended family. In fact, Mary Hill was the author's mother. She had very little formal education but was a powerful speaker and a compassionate community service person and leader. Her English was basically self-taught but powerful. In her quoted statements, she gave a sense of the pain felt by her grandmother during removal. But extended in-depth interviews could have tapped a more complete sense of the Creeks' experiences and of removal in general. Debo captures the death, dying, and suffering that Mary Hill conveyed in her interview, but the cultural dimensions hidden in the statements, particularly in regard to burials and their meanings, were not brought out. Missing also was the significance of the reeds with the eagle feathers, all ceremoniously treated by the medicine men circling the people in the march. Eagle feathers were deeply symbolic of the search for peace among the deeply troubled Creeks in the midst of their nightmarish journey.

Mary Hill, in relating her grandmother's narration, also mentioned the participatory nature of Creek society, including a particular look at women's roles. She said that at the time of her grandmother's removal, "A council meeting was mostly composed of men, but there were times when every member of a town [*talwa*] was requested to attend the meetings."[59] Debo apparently did not pursue the issues of political theory involved and missed the significance of the distinctions between a smaller council and a larger assembly at which women played a role, even at the time of removal. As we have shown, women played an even greater role in earlier times, before Creeks had to live on the run.

Monie Coker, who stayed for many years with the Hill family, spoke no English and is quoted by Debo on Creek "superstition." Before quoting Coker, Debo generalizes about Creek life as follows: "All the small details of life were regulated by quaint superstitions or formulas based on analogies."[60] This clearly shows the unintended bias of an outsider superficially trying to look into a culture she does not understand. Then, in the same section Coker is quoted as saying, "Pointing with the finger at a rainbow will make the finger crooked.... When a hunter kills a squirrel, if he will pull some of the hair ... and bury it ... he will kill more squirrels." Considerable communication difficulties are at issue here. When the traditional Creek symbolized the rainbow in hand language, one makes an arching motion which bends the fingers. In order to appreciate the rainbow's beauty, which is integrated in several legends, children were taught not to point directly toward it. Debo missed the educational significance of the remark and captured it as superstition. Also, the significance of burying a squirrel's hair is missed. It is actually part of the natural social contract, a thank-you to the squirrel and an offering to Mother Earth. Debo was near a gold mine of oral history, but linguistic knowledge and analysis were missing in her attempts.

We come now to James Scott. Angie Debo did not really understand whom she had as an "informant." The first edition of Debo's book came out in 1941. James Scott died around 1944—he was roughly 110 years old and a major resource on the Creeks. Debo briefly quotes Scott on Opothleyahola and his "flight" after his losing Civil War battle. When Scott spoke of "flight," Debo did not realize that there were many such events in Creek history and in Opothleyahola's life. Scott's comments on removal and on Opthleyahola in Kansas appear to be jumbled together in a thematic rather than linear approach. James Scott hardly spoke any English and was skeptical of Anglo interviewers. He was very careful with outsiders in a typically full-blooded Creek way and did not reveal too much of the inner world of the Creeks.

James Scott had lived "seven winters," or seven to eight years, when he was rounded up for the long Trail of Tears from the Alabama/Georgia region to Oklahoma in one of the later removal efforts. Because of clan relationships, he joined the family of Wilburn and Mary Hill—Jean (Hill) Chaudhuri's parents. Later, James Scott and the Hills lived together outside Okemah. Scott later became Grandpa Scott and was a classic Creek storyteller who maintained not only his perceptions of the Trail of Tears, but also all the major nuclei of Creek culture—the myths, legends, and stories—with the traditional accuracy of a storyteller and historian in a disciplined oral tradition. Listening to Scott's narration of his grandfather's and other relatives' accounts of the Trail of Tears, which are reinforced by other survivors, one becomes connected, at least in part, to the eighteenth-century Creek world.

Scott would change the setting of his stories, which were always told in Creek. Sometimes the storytelling would take place around a tree stump on the remaining forty-acre allotment outside Okemah. Other times the event would transpire around the family fire, or at a roadside stop while resting the horse that was pulling the family wagon. Then with Wilburn Hill's assistance, the storytelling would become dramatic, complete with shadows, screens, and lanterns. Properly plucked sunflowers and their shadows, supplemented with dexterous hand movements, became rabbits, bears, or other animals. Releasing fireflies from a jar at night portrayed the creation of the stars in a spinoff of the creation myth. Like a clan storyteller, he would be careful about details, repeating them and demanding feedback from the children to make sure Clifton, Nathaniel, Olloween, and (Ella) Jean understood the story's significance.

James Scott, at the end of the Trail of Tears, kept in close contact and visited with others from his generation and was highly respected as an elder.[61] Since he outlived most of his contemporaries, he was a major resource on Creek history and culture. With the violence surrounding Indian territorial days and Oklahoma statehood, many Creeks took their beliefs underground. Scott, together with Jean Chaudhuri's maternal grandfather and several others, incorporated Asilanabi (Greenleaf) church in 1910, a little ways from Asilanabi traditional ceremonial grounds. Scott and Jean's father, Wilburn Hill, stayed in touch with both groups.

James Scott's fading picture, in which he was holding a large old traditional buffalo horn from pre-removal days, hung on a wall of Asilanabi church until a few years ago. With the remodeling of the church, the picture was apparently taken down, weakening yet another link with the Creek traditions. At one hundred, Scott was alert and talkative. He chewed tobacco and carried his own medicine pouch. He would take the young people toward the river, sit on a tree stump with both hands on his knees, and talk about life when he was seven winters old, the time before and during removal and the struggles that ensued after reaching what is now Oklahoma. Apart from the narration or dramatization of the myths and legends, a conversation went something like this

> Know your clan ways—know who your little father (*jitkoji*), or (*jiboa*) uncle, is. Know your grandmother and others. If you lose your father or mother, your relatives and your clan people will play the same roles. I remember before removal—a hunter stopped in our village—the children ran toward him. An adult asked for the hunter's clan. He rattled out bear on one side, bird on the other, one grandfather was a deer. So his whole identity was clarified. *Naginseemaleghee dadee?* [This means, "What do you cling to?"] Two of his clans were in the village, so they welcomed him. The children were told, "this is your uncle, or little father." The hunter would give the meat that he brought with him. Then, when the time came, he left with jerky that the *talwa* had made. If the hunter's clan did not have a representative in the *talwa*, people would still be friendly, take care of him—send him on his way where there would be a relative. If an uncle came in, a kid would be sent to hunt with him and his own mother's brother. With this joint effort, he would learn a lot from his biological uncle. He would learn about the terrain, the pathways, and the local plants and animals. From his surrogate uncle he would learn about other communities and new wisdom. My own mother and father died during removal, so I was left with my clan uncle.
>
> One morning, when it was already getting cold, a runner came to our village out of breath, saying haltingly, "Talking papers. They are sending people with talking papers—people are already disappearing—what's left behind is being stolen. They are sending us to a burial ground. They keep talking about judgment day. We need to either hide or mix with other

tribes up north. These demons are shooting *istejadis* [Indians, or literally, "red people"] if we resist. I have to warn the next village." He left and, even though I was just a boy, I knew that something very bad was about to happen—a dark cloud hovered over us. I don't know how many days went by. We started gathering provisions, we talked about other *talwas,* the earth trembled, and even the trees seemed to be shaking. The hovering dark cloud brought the evil men sooner than we expected. The soldiers started shooting. The whites rounded us up like cattle and put shackles on the strong men.

There was a silent cry—no words—so devastating—silent prayers—then low humming of the chant of communal encouragement: *we he na wehena.* Gun butts were hitting mouths. That morning cold winds blew—like judgment day. We did not know where we were heading. There were talking papers—more talking papers—the whites would keep on bringing talking papers, and tragedy always followed. Along the trail, they split us up. I lost my mother and father and ended up with an uncle. Little babies sometimes would have their head smashed against a tree. Strong shackled men were used for pulling wagons and chopping wood. Those who got sick were left or dumped by the soldiers. There was hardly any food—people were hungry, cold, and frostbitten. The whites roasted meat and the aroma made you want to die. Each time someone fell, they sacrificed, saying, "take my blanket—I am going home." The chilling wind never left us— we have seen blizzards—now we were in one. Even strong buffalo would not have survived such a winter. Somehow, Hesagedamesse was with us. Most of the time, children walked; however, sometimes they would be allowed to ride in a wagon with older folks. About that time we reached Indian territory. There were very few of us—mostly older children and shackled men. After our walk, there were no babies left; they had killed the babies. Hardly any women made it. I only had one uncle left. We began with about 500 in our group and we wound up with fifty and we wound up near Okemah, Asilanabi, Greenleaf, the places where we finished growing up. These places were near some Christian Indians who had already got there before us. Nitaspoki—the last day—I was always looking for it, but it did not come. It took twenty years for the nightmares to lessen.

You've got to know your relatives. I am a bear and your mother is a bear, so I am here. Be watchful of the whites. The snake you welcome will be the one that destroys you. They will sell their own mother—they will leave their burial grounds—they have no roots—they don't know where their umbilical cord is buried. That is why they are restless. If you allow one in—you can't get rid of him. Acquisition, private property, and trickery, that is their way. There is nothing you can do. They multiply like flies and they keep coming when they want something—they use talking papers. They came to me with talking papers after they gave me 160 acres of allotment land. Then with papers they said that if I gave the land I would have food for my relatives and myself. I signed over three-fourths of my land in exchange for a guarantee for food. I got tricked again. I had become Christian and I had forgotten how deceptive they can be. I thought they were friends. But I lost—we don't have any beans or flour. Whatever little land you have, hold on to it. If it takes the rest of your life, learn about talking papers. It's full of trickery. For your own survival, transplant pecans and water them. I am old—I can't do it. See those berries? Those are the poisonous kind. If you know what is what out there, you won't be hungry. Look at your mother Mary; she sold food in the depression. Always identify the plants. Know the woods and don't be wasteful.

Once there was a prairie fire. The Hill kids ran toward the house because there was a shape in the fire—then the house collapsed. The parents thought James Scott had died, but he came out from the west side of the building. The shape was just a water barrel. Scott was in the outhouse, and he scolded everyone because he had asked them to dampen the ground around the house for fire prevention because it was dry. Everyone was happy that Scott survived the fire. He reminded them "not to be attached to the house or anything else except your relatives and your *boea fikcha*—your spirit—if that is strong—you will make it. But you have to watch the white world—they will sell their mother." He pointed out that German prisoners kept in Okmulgee during World War II were treated better than the Creeks ever were.

When James Scott died around 1944 or 1945 there was a big funeral for him at Greenleaf. It was the end of an era as he left the seed of the Creek world around two Asalanabi, the church and the stomp ground, so that he would live among both Christian and non-Christian Creeks. He was known and respected among both people. Though gulfs exist between these two worlds, Creeks go back and forth between them. Even though the dance grounds are closer to the old traditions, the church grounds have some elements of Creek values, including fellowship and cooperation, traditional language use, and singing. To different degrees, they attempt to retain their values as much as possible, though the economic infrastructure and the communal lands are eroded while "modernization" marches on.

CREEK HEROES AND LEADERS

The Muscogee Creek tradition suggests that leaders possess not only courage but also humility. Consequently, the most revered Creek leaders have been quite self-effacing. Unfortunately, the existing literature has given greater attention to McGillivray, the so called "Creek Talleyrand," and even to non-Indian adventurers like Bowles. There indeed have been revered Creek role models despite the fact that not much has been written about them, with the possible exception of Osceola. However, the real generosity, traditionalism, and character of Osceola are often emphasized less than his supposed mixed ancestry, some of his military exploits, and his death.

In this, we have touched on Opthleyahola I (Opothle Micco) of the late 1700s, Opthleyahola of the removal era, and Osceola. We will soon add Chitto Harjo to this list. In addition, other genuine heroes must be written about before the oral history surrounding them fades: Billy Jo Cypress, a Miccosuki, younger than Osceola, who in the late 1800s encouraged Seminoles to hold on to their land; Buffalo Tiger's father in the late 1800s held the Miccosukees together; Billy Panther, in the early 1900s, was a Seminole medicine man who kept traditional pharmacological knowledge alive; Billy Osceola's brother kept the Florida Seminole intact against state encroachments in the 1940s; in the 1830s the Creek prophet Yahola was a precursor to Chitto Harjo; the prophet Chitto Obothleyahola from the 1700s; the Creek prophets from the 1820s, including Lumhi Harjo and Dimithwa Yahola; Jackson Knight, in the mid-1800s, and Jackson Barnette in the early 1900s started economic development efforts with mixed results because of federal bureaucracy; Montezuma Jackson who in the late 1700s led a health battle against alcoholism and other white man's diseases; Thomas Brown, Euchee, who at the turn of this century worked hard on cultural preservation and the Duck Creek grounds; Aaron Grayson, an African American son of a slave who was adopted by the Creeks in the 1920s and helped preserve the blending of Creek and African American music and goodwill; Tom Wesley, who in the early 1900s was an advocate and supporter of Chitto Harjo; Menawa, who led the Creek forces despite overwhelming odds against Jackson's forces in the battles around Horseshoe Bend and who carried out the execution of William McIntosh; and Micconubbi in the 1830s, who—as a result of his vision of admiration and friendship between Creeks and African Americans, or *iste lustee*—told the Creeks, "We do not know where he comes from. We don't know whether he is a white man in a black body. But he is in so much agony and pain. We can kill him or take him. I suggest the latter—he is in too much pain to be white. Let's treat him like a brother."

As in every other society, deciding on contemporary heroes is more controversial than dealing with historical figures. On the traditional side, the late Netchi Gray should be remembered as a person on the forefront of preserving Creek music and the elaborate Creek repertoire of both spiritual and social dances. On the church side, the late Wilburn and Mary Hill, who founded many Creek missions in an effort to retain a sense of community, worked hard to bring elections to Creek tribal government.

CHITTO HARJO AND BEYOND

From a standard public policy standpoint, the post-removal period between the US Civil War and Oklahoma statehood is full of incredible historical events, including the following: (1) the forced shrinking of Indian lands as punishment for some Creek factions' sympathies with the southern cause (in spite of Opothleyahola's self-sacrifice and the Creeks loyal to the Union); (2) the coming of Indian allotments, or the forcible break-up of Creek communal lands; (3) "Grant's Peace," which carved up federally approved sectarian zones for missionary and advisory input activity—the Creeks got the Methodists, the Presbyterians, and an abundance of Baptists; and (4) the abolition of any semblance of tribal elections of "chiefs" and the end of meaningful tribal government. The standard public policy history has been done many times and is not attempted here. In the spirit of this work, it seems most useful to see the landscape from a Creek traditionalist perspective, since each of these landmarks further eroded Creek institutions.

The most important Creek traditionalist to rise after the death of Opothleyahola until the creation of the State of Oklahoma is Chitto Harjo, also known as Wilson Jones, a full-blood possibly from the bear clan who was not fluent in English but was one of the greatest orators in the Creek tradition.[62] Chitto Harjo remains a genuine hero among many full-bloods and is to them a treasured symbol of the last historical attempt to preserve the completeness of the Creek world. Many acculturated Creeks, however, regarded and some still regard him as a renegade. Creek activism continued and still continues sporadically after Chitto Harjo, but he remains a person of heroic proportions. If he had lived at an earlier time his status would be comparable to that of Osceola and Opothleyahola. Already hemmed in by post-removal forces, Harjo had a more restricted power base than other Creek heroes.

Chitto Harjo was a great orator. Even in translation his speeches are powerful. Those who heard him in Creek thought he was analytical, incisive, and poetic in his use of the flow and symbolism of the Creek language. Among the many people who heard him were James Scott of Okemah/Asalanabi and Micco Elmer Hill of Fish Pond. Micco Hill was one of Harjo's supporters and was listed by federal sleuths as a member of Harjo's so-called Snake Group.[63] Many other traditional Creeks attest to the style and content of Harjo's orations and prophecies. He was an imposing man with powerful eyes. He looked magnificent when he rode into town or stepped up to speak.

Chitto Harjo had been a young solider in Opothleyahola's army during the Civil War and made his way back to Creek country after the collapse of Opothleyahola's forces. He went quietly to work, attempting to build a network after seeing the Creek lands shrunk by the federal government as "punishment" for southern support, despite many Creeks' support for the Union. What really galvanized Harjo's activity was the emergence of the forces of allotment, or the breaking up of communal lands and the impending conversion of Indian territory into the state of Oklahoma and the end of meaningful tribal government. Chitto Harjo is often translated as Crazy Snake. However, as we have noted, Creek can be easily mistranslated. Harjo, when used with respect rather than contempt, means "visionary" or "with vision," as in *obanga harjo*, or the vision dance, the early morning dance at the end of the night with the first rays of the sun, which to whites can look wild and crazy.

When Chitto Harjo spoke, he often used an editorial "we" in a mystical way. His style symbolically used transformation of persons and collapse of time. He would speak as though he was there when Columbus came, and he would repeatedly mention this coming as an evil watershed. Columbus was symbolically transformed into the conquistadors and then into Andrew Jackson. He would berate whites on broken treaties, pointing out that these treaties with the Creeks did not authorize allotments by unilateral congressional action. He emphasized that the whites were breaking their word again and again.

He was arrested on trumped-up charges several times and was taken to an Arkansas prison where his long hair was cut off, a major indignity to a traditional Creek. He went to Washington, D.C., several times, trying to prevent allotments and the end of tribal government. He was befriended and then cheated by lobbyists who took his money, promising falsely that they would work to influence Congress. Each setback deepened his conviction that Anglo civilization had fallen from the sacred path of nature's moral laws.

In speaking to Creeks, he repeatedly urged them to: (1) recover control of their own government; (2) reject allotments, as he did; (3) hold on to their lands; and (4) follow the sacred Creek path of values. Anglos will sell their mother, he orated, speaking specifically of Mother Earth. They will divide, subdivide, and fragment the land. They will put a price on air and water. Creeks, if they sold land, would not have a place to set their feet— they could not even go to their toilet without being prevented or being forced to pay for it.

In spite of being a full-blood with little or no modern education, Harjo was a keen observer of the two cultures and was able to articulate the distinctions between them. He also knew that without a land base and a connection with Mother Earth, fire, and spirits, Creeks would have a difficult time and would end up in the bottom of a hierarchical society. That was the essence of his message and why he fought hard against allotment, land sales, and Oklahoma statehood. Many elder full-blood traditional Creeks proudly remember the Chitto Harjo trails as he went into the backwoods and traveled to and from select traditional grounds, including Hickory and Fish Pond. Harjo knew that he had a two-headed enemy: the people who wanted Indian lands and those Indians (with many mixed-bloods among them) who preferred immediate gain enough to ignore the long-term ramifications of lost land. Opothleyahola I had his McGillivray, Opothleyahola II had his William McIntosh, and Chitto Harjo had his Pleasant Porter, the formal principal chief of the tribe.

The chief, ironically, often was a pleasant porter for the private property interests in Indian Territory and often took a different road than the traditional Creeks. Porter, in 1906, agreed to end elections for chiefs and continued to act as chief, appointed by the United States president.[64] This appointment system and the absence of any democracy continued until the 1960s when Congress was persuaded to permit the election of the chief. Among the forces that worked toward restoration of choice was the Creek Centralization Committee, based mostly in Okmulgee, but active throughout Creek country.[65] Oklahoma Congressman Ed Edmondson was the sponsor of the legislation that brought about this change.

Pleasant Porter opted for supporting Oklahoma statehood.[66] He did not think that Creek freedmen (African Americans) needed any special protection,[67] nor did he find fault with the federal handling of Creek affairs.[68] Porter's constituency included many of the mixed-bloods who played a disproportionate power role in tribal affairs because of the close connection between them and the important non-Indian power brokers in Indian Territory. The nature of Porter's legitimacy can be seen from the fact that rather than depending on Creek support, he called on the US Marshall and a phalanx of non-Indian enforcement authorities for protection against the Snakes, Chitto Harjo's supporters.[69]

Harjo's "violence" was highly exaggerated by his enemies. Though he helped create a regiment of Creek lighthorsemen, the new red sticks, they were not involved in pitched battles. Harjo knew who had the military power, and it wasn't the Creeks. The lighthorsemen wanted to enforce the wishes of the new tribal government that Harjo had formed as an alternative to Pleasant Porter's administration. The enforcement was to be involved in individualized Creek cases rather than engaged in territorial or federal affairs.

Chitto Harjo articulated major Creek values in his speeches. These values included openness to and acceptance of African Americans who sought protection with the Creeks. He opposed other African Americans who entered Oklahoma outside the Creek fraternal system seeking individualized Indian lands like the whites. Harjo provided mutual support and protection for Creek freedmen and many of the full-bloods supported the inclusion of freedmen in decision-making and in communal living.

Hickory Grounds was a classic Creek peace town, and groups of blacks who found protection there rallied to Chitto Harjo's cause. Even now in the Hickory Grounds—rebuilt after the destruction of the old one in Harjo's time—there are only three *dubbas*, beds or arbors; the fourth, which is symbolic for warriors, is purposely missing. Harjo unsuccessfully tried to persuade the federal government to submit the treaty versus unilateral congressional legislation issues to international arbitration by an independent tribunal of other European representatives. Instead, because of his rising power among full-bloods, he became the issue. He became the hunted. He was able to rally at one time 3,000 angry Indians in Henryetta.[70] More than 500 Indians and protected blacks tried to create a traditional peace town in Hickory Grounds (outside Henryetta) in 1900. Previously, under Isparecher, more than 2,000 Creeks, mainly full-bloods, had clearly voted in an assembly against allotments and Harjo was further developing this momentum.

Law enforcement authorities found an excuse to raid Hickory by following up on a white farmer's complaint that smoked meat was stolen from his property by people at Hickory, hence, the peculiar label "The Smoked Meat Rebellion." A deputy was turned back from Hickory by armed African American freedmen. The white Henryetta deputy came back with reinforcements and attacked the Hickory group and captured and jailed more than forty people, mostly African Americans. Chitto Harjo was not even present at the Hickory Grounds at the time but he got blamed anyway; this gave the authorities, who feared an inter-ethnic coalition of blacks and full-bloods, an excuse to move against Chitto Harjo. The target of destroying meaningful Creek leadership emerged once again as it did with the Spaniards, Andrew Jackson, and with the army against Osceola under the flag of truce.

Initially a posse formed at Checotah in McIntosh County, which in 1909 surrounded Harjo's home and opened fire. Several people were wounded and killed, including two deputies. Chitto Harjo escaped, skillfully picked up on a horse by a supporter. It is possible that he was wounded and sought the services of an Indian medicine woman. Oklahoma Governor Haskell called out the militia in McIntosh and Okmulgee counties and under Colonel Ray Hoffman, an organized but unsuccessful manhunt commenced. They never found Chitto Harjo. The common story is that he disappeared into McCurtain County. Harjo had a following among full-bloods in neighboring tribes. He was reported to have died two years later from his wounds in the home of Choctaw Daniel Bob. Contrary stories emerged, asserting that Harjo and a few of his friends escaped into Mexico. Further, rumors still circulate that he came back quietly, at least once, to assess the situation and visit with friends.

Chitto Harjo had used notions of confederacy symbolically and literally in his networking. He used hidden trails and "runners" between the various ceremonial grounds such as Hickory Grounds, Fish Pond, and Asilanabi, covering his tracks and taking measures against hunting dogs. He would meet with people at these *talwas* and confer with each of the *miccos* there. In turn, people on these grounds helped by providing him with food, shelter, and security. They would go out and wet the road where Harjo traveled so that sniffing dogs could not easily follow him. Even people in church groups helped him. The Chitto Harjo affair was one of the last hurrahs—possibly the last major hurrah—before the return of activism in Indian Country in the late 1950s through the 1960s. However, quiet underground movement of traditionals in the snake tradition continued into the 1930s with letter-writing campaigns and delegations sent to Washington, D.C.[71]

After the Chitto Harjo affair, it was a relatively quiet time in terms of politics in Creek country, until the rumblings against the appointed principal chief, Dode McIntosh, and the movement for "free elections" began to be heard. To Creek full-bloods, direct democracy comes naturally. Indirect representative democracy, on the other hand, with its interest groups and registration manipulations, turnout (including absentee balloting), balloting, and counting, is a different matter. With his knowledge of the system, Dode McIntosh became the first elected chief in the state of Oklahoma. The position of chief still primarily remained ceremonial until the coming of the social program beginning with Lyndon Johnson's Great Society, the rediscovery of tribal sovereignty, and the income from smoke shops and bingo.

Current Creek government has very little traditional flavor, since its formal structure is very much defined by Anglo-American jurisprudence. Consequently community input and participation levels have their ups and downs in contemporary politics. The fragmentation that Chitto Harjo feared has occurred to a large extent. With the loss of land, and the rise of missionary activity, new public policies, urban forces, boarding schools, public schools, new sicknesses, and intermarriages, rapid changes have occurred in Creek country. The loss of allotment lands, the decline of farm employment, and relocation policies drove full-bloods away from rural areas. Today, Oklahoma City and Tulsa, with the influx of Creeks as well as other tribes, have become large centers of urban Indian populations. The result is the development of different demographic Creek groups with some overlapping membership in such organizations as the Baptist or Methodist church circuit, the traditional ceremonial grounds people, the ranchers, the professionals, and the bureaucrats. Each has taken bits and pieces of Creek ways without always understanding the linkages.

The churches have transformed Creek symbolism into quasi-Christian meaning. Rather than facing west, the Christian dead are buried facing east. Yet there are little mounds and houses over some of the buried dead, vestiges of past traditions. Hesagedemesse has become the Christian God and the meaning of love has somewhat shifted. The *gun halwa*, the mound and the call to higher ground, has been transformed into a heavenly journey. But some of the sharing of energy and food and communal ways are still there.

Families hold onto the clan stories that elders have told them, though they might miss the tale's significance. Despite "modernization," Creeks remain curious about their ways, and many would like to know more about their origins. The search for roots is human. Those who are curious will find that the Creek way was caring, communal, egalitarian, and knowledgeable about nature's way.

Counting Indians, over time, is difficult due to a lack of records and varying definitions of an Indian. There is little question, however, that in the Mississippi Valley days the Creek cultural groups were large in number—perhaps around 200,000. With diseases, wars, and removal they shrank to around 10,000 in the late 1830s and rose to around 14,000 in Oklahoma in the 1890s.[72] Currently, there are about 36,000 Creeks, of whom at least around 35 percent are full-blooded.[73] Besides the Oklahoma Creeks, some Creeks remain in Alabama. The Oklahoma Seminoles, who in 1977 numbered around 9,000, are a much larger group now. The Florida Seminoles, from the small groups who escaped removal, had grown to more than 2,000 by 1985.[74]

In fundamental community institutions, divisions exist between traditional and Christian gatherings. Among the Creeks alone, prior to removal there were almost one hundred key ceremonial fires and over forty-three tribal towns, each with their own spinoff settlements and communities. Now there are fourteen to sixteen key ceremonial fires still going and some other grounds where the dancing is more social and the rules less stringent. There are about one hundred Creek churches with the Baptist being the largest, followed by the Methodists and the Presbyterians. Of the one hundred Creek churches, approximately sixty-seven are Baptist. In the 1930s, beginning with Willie King, Oklahoma Creek missionaries began to spread the Baptist faith among the Florida Seminoles. However, in the process both the Oklahoma and the Florida Creeks and Seminoles adapted their own songs and symbolisms to the Christian faith.

However, it is in the ceremonial grounds with the beginning call to Ibofanga and the concluding vision dance that Creek values still live. Through Ibofanga's assistant, Hesagedamesse, one feels his breath as he goes on with the work at hand—as Creeks continue to struggle with the incredibly rapid pace of western values and change. Much of the western political and social philosophy—the Lockeans, Jeffersonians, Hamiltonians, Marxists, and Hegelians—have worked within a paradigm of "progress." In such a paradigm, aboriginal ways are primitive and must give way to the idea of progress. Yet the Creeks are one aboriginal people whose values were extensive, logically interrelated, and developed outside the European evolutionary models of progress. They valued community, freedom, and equality.

Their major hardships occurred after the coming of Europeans, with the resulting weapons of violence, the erosion of tradition, and the influence of the idea of "progress."

Most European ideas have done little to help the Creeks. In fact, both Jeffersonian and Jacksonian values had an immensely erosive and regressive impact on the tribe, introducing slavery, social hierarchy, possessive individualism, alcoholism, and a host of other physical and social diseases. With the march of technology, the impact of "progress" on Creek and Seminole ways has accelerated rapidly during the last few decades.

Hegel, despite his European perspective, once pointed out that learning, philosophy, and social science come too late to change the march of "progress." According to him, the owl of Minerva, symbolizing wisdom, flies only at dusk. The owl, to the Creeks, symbolizes not a message of wisdom, but of fear. In Creek prophecies of things yet to come, when one strays from the sacred path, they no longer live in harmony with nature.

NOTES

1. For a good discussion, analysis, and review of the mounds, see Ray A. Williamson, *Lighting the Sky: The Cosmos of the American Indian* (Norman: University of Oklahoma Press, 1987), 240–256.
2. Williamson, *Lighting the Sky*, 241.
3. For a history of the Creeks that attempts to place the tribe in its own context, see David Corkran, *The Creek Frontier: 1540–1783* (Norman: University of Oklahoma Press, 1967).
4. Louis le Clerc de Milford, *Memoir, or A Cursory Glance at My Different Travels and My Sojourn in the Creek Nation, 1802*, trans. Geraldine deCourcy, ed. John Francis McDermott (Chicago: Lakeside Press, 1956).
5. Corkran, *The Creek Frontier*, 4.
6. See adapted map of Creek country in Corkran, *The Creek Frontier*, 50.
7. Casita, as it is now called, may be a later Spanish corruption of Koasati.
8. For a list of some of the names of the bands and groups, see Corkran, *The Creek Frontier*, 4–7.
9. Corkran, *The Creek Frontier*, 42.
10. Ibid.
11. See "Long Lost Spanish Fort Found in St. Augustine," *New York Times*, 27 July 1993, sec. B, 5, 7.
12. Corkran, *The Creek Frontier*.
13. Ibid., 87.
14. Ibid., 89.
15. Ibid., 88. See also C. C. Jones, Jr., *Historical Sketch of Tomochichi: Mico of the Yamacraws* (Savannah, Georgia: The Oglethorpe Press, 1998).
16. Corkran, *The Creek Frontier*, 87.
17. Milford, *Memoir*, 16.
18. John Walton Caughey, *McGillvray of the Creeks* (Norman: University of Oklahoma Press, 1938). Also see Michael D. Green, "Alexander McGillvray" in *American Indian Leaders*, ed. R. David Edmonds (Lincoln: University of Nebraska Press, 1980), 41–63.
19. Corkran, *The Creek Frontier*, 239.

20. McGillivray's father was Scottish and his mother was French and Creek (Caughey, *McGillvray of the Creeks*, 5). For information on his medication for vene-real disease, see ibid., 4; for McGillivray's lack of knowledge of the Creek, see Milford, *Memoir*, 16, 21; for his lack of warrior skills, see Milford, *Memoir*, 29. McGillivray was, at times, simultaneously receiving Spanish and English salaries while accepting gifts from the English (see Caughey, *McGillvray of the Creeks*, 55).

21. See Alex de Tocqueville, *Democracy in America*, vol. 1 (New York: Alfred A. Knopf, 1972), 331–335.

22. De Tocqueville, *Democracy in America*, 356.

23. For Roger Williams's and Jeffersonian political theory, see Joyotpaul Chaudhuri, *Founding America* (Dubuque: Kendall-Hunt, 1992). For additional contradictions in Jeffersonian politics, see Robert Tucker and David C. Hendrickson, *Empire of Liberty: The Statecraft of Thomas Jefferson* (New York: Oxford University Press, 1990). See also Chaudhuri, Review of *Empire of Liberty: The Statecraft of Thomas Jefferson*, in *American Political Science Review* 85:3 (September 1991): 1009–1010. For a critical but still sympathetic treatment of Jeffersonian Indian policy, see Bernard W. Sheehan, *Seeds of Extinction: Jeffersonian Philanthropy and the American Indian* (Chapel Hill: University of North Carolina Press, 1973). For a vivid portrayal of Jackson's attitude toward Creeks, see Michael Paul Rogin, *Fathers and Children: Andrew Jackson and the Subjugation of the American Indian* (New York: Vintage Books, 1975). See also Anthony Wallace, *Jefferson and the Indians* (Cambridge: Harvard University Press, 1999).

24. Tucker and Hendrickson, *Empire of Liberty*, 304.

25. Ibid.

26. Ibid., 305.

27. Ibid.

28. Ibid., 304, 312. See also Michael D. Green, *The Politics of Indian Removal* (Lincoln: University of Nebraska Press, 1982), 47.

29. Coughey, *McGillvray of the Creeks*, 40–46 and 276.

30. As Jefferson's opposition, the federalists were hardly protectors of Indian rights either. The federalist judiciary under John Marshall outlined several of the key decisions of Indian law, including *Johnson v. McIntosh* (1823), *Cherokee Nation v. Georgia* (1831), and *Worcester v. Georgia* (1832). Johnson represented a low point in Indian sovereignty and strengthened the plenary powers of Congress. Worcester appears to provide the strongest elements of sovereignty while Cherokee logic is often used for treating tribes as dependent nations, outside state jurisdiction. While some of these decisions helped tribes later, none would help the Creeks at the time, since the Jeffersonians basically wanted to appropriate lands in a decentralized way while the federalists wanted to exercise more direct federal leverage. See Joyotpaul Chaudhuri, "American Indian Policy: An Overview," in *American Indian Policy in the Twentieth Century*, ed. Vine Deloria (Norman: University of Oklahoma Press, 1985), 15–34.

31. Sheehan, *Seeds of Extinction*, 162.

32. Green, *Politics of Indian Removal*, 54.

33. Tucker and Hendrickson, *Empire of Liberty*, 8.

34. See Rogin, *Fathers and Children*, 151, specifically the reference to the attack by Jackson's forces at the Coosa River: "They attacked and burned the Creek village of Tallushatchee killing warriors, women and children alike. Six days later, Jackson himself led his troops in a victory." The Creeks were greatly outnumbered in this battle.

35. Rogin, *Fathers and Children*, 154.

36. Edwin McReynolds, *The Seminoles* (Norman: University of Oklahoma Press, 1957), 60.

37. Ibid.

38. Rogin, *Fathers and Children*, 156.

39. McReynolds, *Seminoles*, 61.

40. Rogin, *Fathers and Children*, 156.

41. Antonio J. Waring, ed., *Laws of the Creek Nation* (Athens: University of Georgia Press, 1960).

42. Benjamin Hawkins, *A Sketch of the Creek Country in the Years 1798 and 1799*, in the collections of the Georgia Historical Society, vol. III (New York: Kraus Reprint Company, 1971).

43. Green, *Politics of Indian Removal*, 33, 54; and J. Leitch Wright, Jr., *Creeks and Seminoles* (Lincoln: University of Nebraska Press, 1986), 116.

44. Green, *Politics of Indian Removal*, 69–125.

45. Ibid., 88.

46. Ibid., 97.

47. Grant Foreman, *The Five Civilized Tribes* (Norman: University of Oklahoma Press, 1934), 170.

48. See *A Warrior for the Confederacy: The Autobiography of Chief G. W. Grayson*, ed. W. David Baird (Norman: University of Oklahoma Press, 1988).

49. Noah Long, "Opothleyahola to Be Enshrined," *Muscogee Nation News* 22 (Okmulgee, Oklahoma), 8 August 1993. This story describes the 1993 induction of Opothleyahola in the Indian Hall of Fame in Anadarko, Oklahoma with the endorsement of Bill Fife, the then-principal chief.

50. For a standard history of the Seminole wars, see John K. Mahon, *History of the Second Seminole Wars, 1835–1842* (Gainesville: University Presses of Florida, 1967). Professor Mahon supervised Jean Chaudhuri in her Seminole oral history fieldwork in the 1970s. For an introduction to Seminole "ethnohistory," see Charles H. Fairbanks, *Ethnohistorical Report of the Florida Indians*, Indian Claims Commission, Dockets Nos. 73, 151, 1957 (New York: Garland Press, 1974). For additional information, see bibliographies in Brent Richards Weisman, *Like Beads on a String—A Cultural History of the Seminole Indians in Northern Peninsular Florida* (Tuscaloosa: The University of Alabama Press, 1989). See also Patricia Wickman, *Osceola's Legacy* (Tuscaloosa: The University of Alabama Press, 1991). For an introduction to Oklahoma Seminoles, see James H. Howard with Willie Lena, *Oklahoma Seminoles* (Norman: University of Oklahoma Press, 1982). For a standard chronological history, see Edwin C. McReynolds, *The Seminoles* (Norman: University of Oklahoma Press, 1957).

51. McReynolds uses the name Powell interchangeably and a popular biography assumes that Osceola was of mixed ancestry (William and Ellen Hartley, *Osceola: The Unconquered Indian* [New York: Hawthorn Books, Inc., 1973]).

52. Quotation from James Piece, cited in Hartley, *Osceola*, 24.

53. Mahon believes that Osceola had instead a Scottish great-grandfather. The evidence for this is also skimpy (Mahon, *History of the Second Seminole Wars*, 91).

54. See Patricia Wickman, *Osceola's Legacy*.

55. See Grant Foreman, *Indian Removal* (Norman: University of Oklahoma Press, 1972); id., *The Five Civilized Tribes* (Norman: The University of Oklahoma Press, 1934); Angie Debo, *The Road to Disappearance: A History of the Creek Indians* (Norman: University of Oklahoma Press, 1941); and id., *And Still the Waters Run* (Norman: University of Oklahoma Press, 1984).

56. Debo, *Road to Disappearance*, 104–105.

57. Ibid., 299.

58. Ibid., 151.

59. Ibid.

60. Ibid., 299.

61. Donald Dee Sullivan, *Hillabee to Weogufkee* (Corpus Christi: Del Mar

, College, 1989). This book is a photographic essay on the Creeks and gives a "quotation" from Jim Scott, full-blood Creek who lived to see his fifth generation and died just recently at the age of 117. The Reverend Roley Hanes, Creek Indian, provides the translation. The translation of Scott's statement is as follows, "Times have changed and even the sound of the birds is different. There was a certain kind of bird that used to make noises or chirp just before winter time. You don't see or hear them anymore. Times are different now. Some of the birds are gone."

62.   For a general discussion of Chitto Harjo, see Debo, *And Still the Waters Run*, 54–55, 135, 154–156, 290, 294–296. For a good review of documents and newspapers regarding Harjo, see Mel H. Bolster, "Crazy Snake and the Smoked Meat Rebellion of 1909: A Study of Creek Unrest Among Full Bloods in Oklahoma," (MA thesis, University of Arkansas, 1952).

63.   Micco Elmer Hill of the wind clan was Jean Chaudhuri's paternal grandfather and is listed as a Snake in the files of the United States Superintendent of the Five Tribes. See Bolster, "Crazy Snake," 113 and 148. Micco Hill was the *micco* of Fish Pond and was a noted medicine person.

64.   Debo, *And Still the Waters Run*, 64.

65.   Some of the members of the Creek Centralization Committee included Joe Fife, London Coker, Cindy Hill, Jimmy Harjochee, Tom Henry, Marie Henry (one of the last members of the snake clan), Winey Bell, Wilburn and Mary Hill, and Robert Marcey as an adviser.

66.   Debo, *And Still the Waters Run*, 147.

67.   Ibid., 136.

68.   Ibid., 146.

69.   Ibid., 55.

70.   Bolster, "Crazy Snake."

71.   Debo, *And Still the Waters Run*, 296.

72.   Debo, *Road to Disappearance*, 33.

73.   Conversation with tribal social services administrator, 29 July 1993.

74.   Howard and Lena, *Oklahoma Seminoles*, xv.

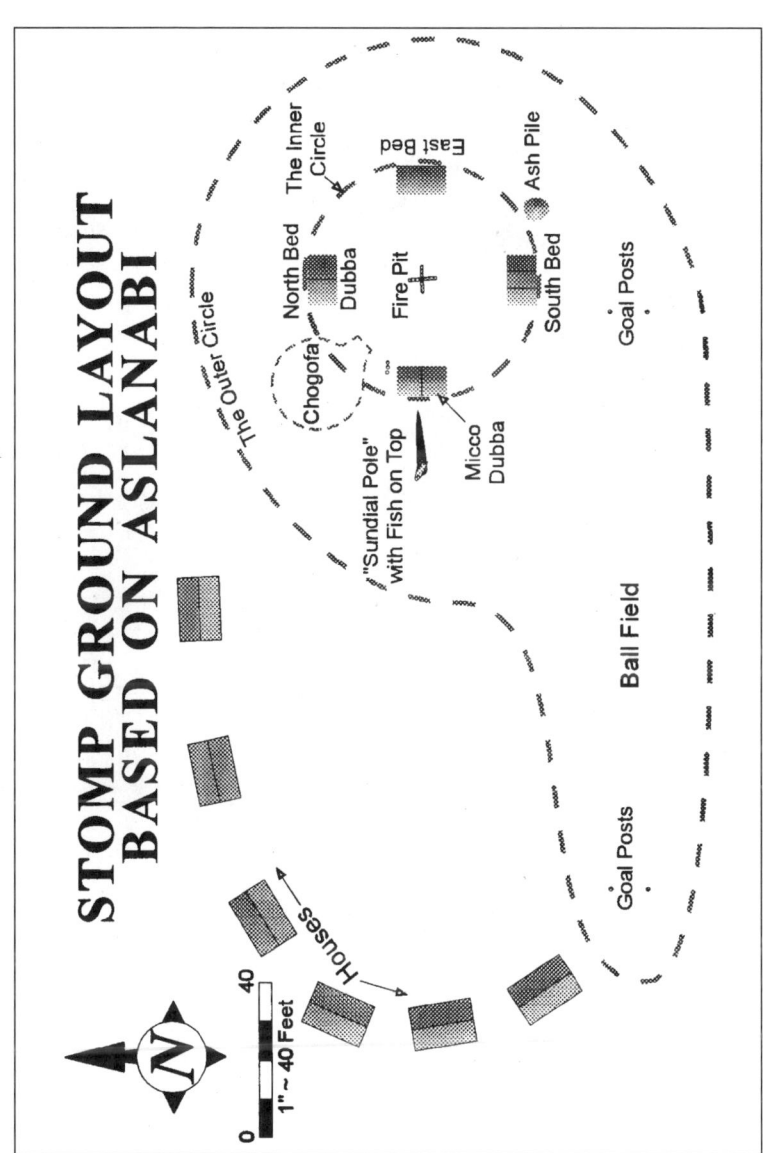

A stomp ground layout: based on Aslanabi grounds, Oklahoma (*notes by Joy Chaudhuri; map by Byron Schneid*)

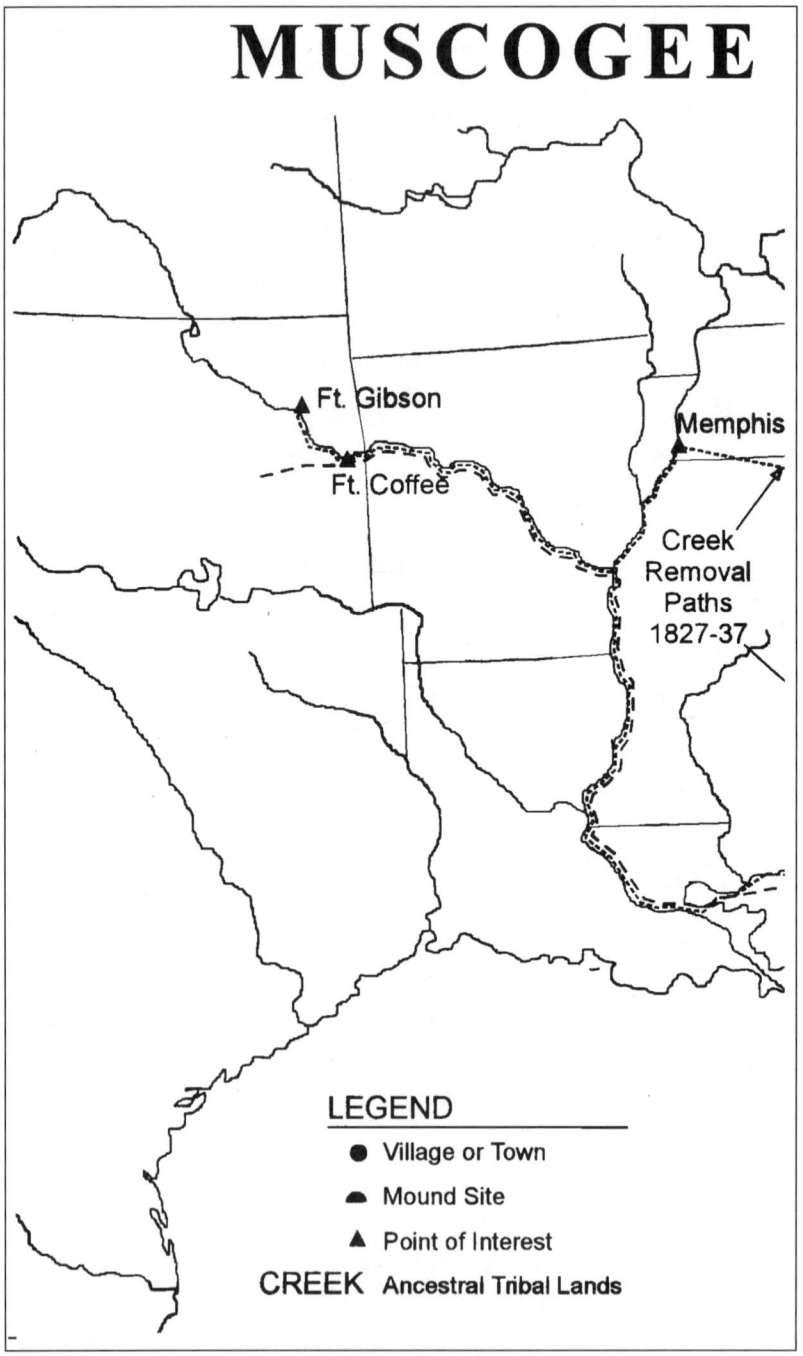

Muscogee sites in the southeastern United States (*map by Byron Schneid*)

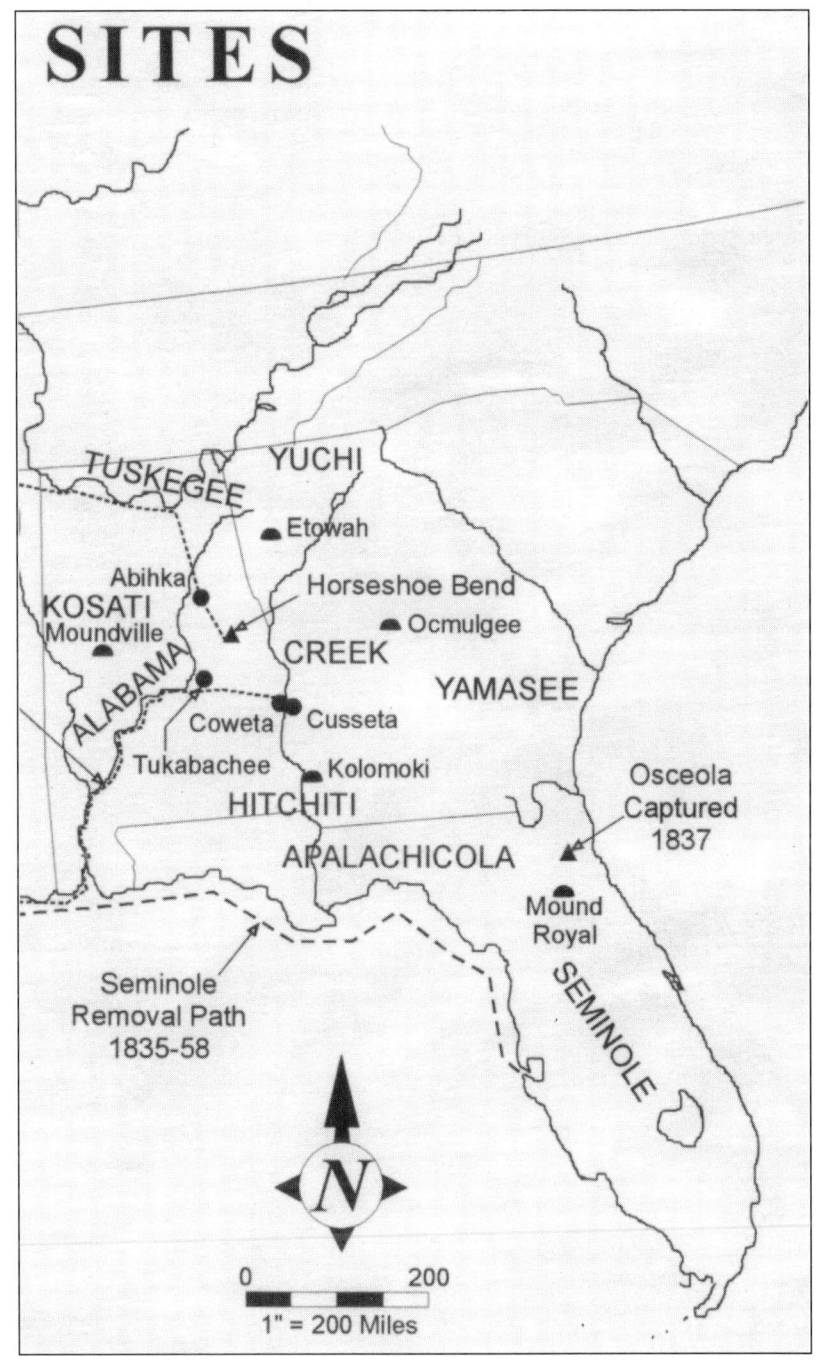

SITES

TUSKEGEE
YUCHI
Etowah
Abihka
Horseshoe Bend
KOSATI
Ocmulgee
Moundville
CREEK
ALABAMA
YAMASEE
Coweta   Cusseta
Tukabachee   Kolomoki
Osceola
HITCHITI   Captured
1837
APALACHICOLA
Mound
Royal
Seminole
Removal Path   SEMINOLE
1835-58

N

0   200
1" = 200 Miles

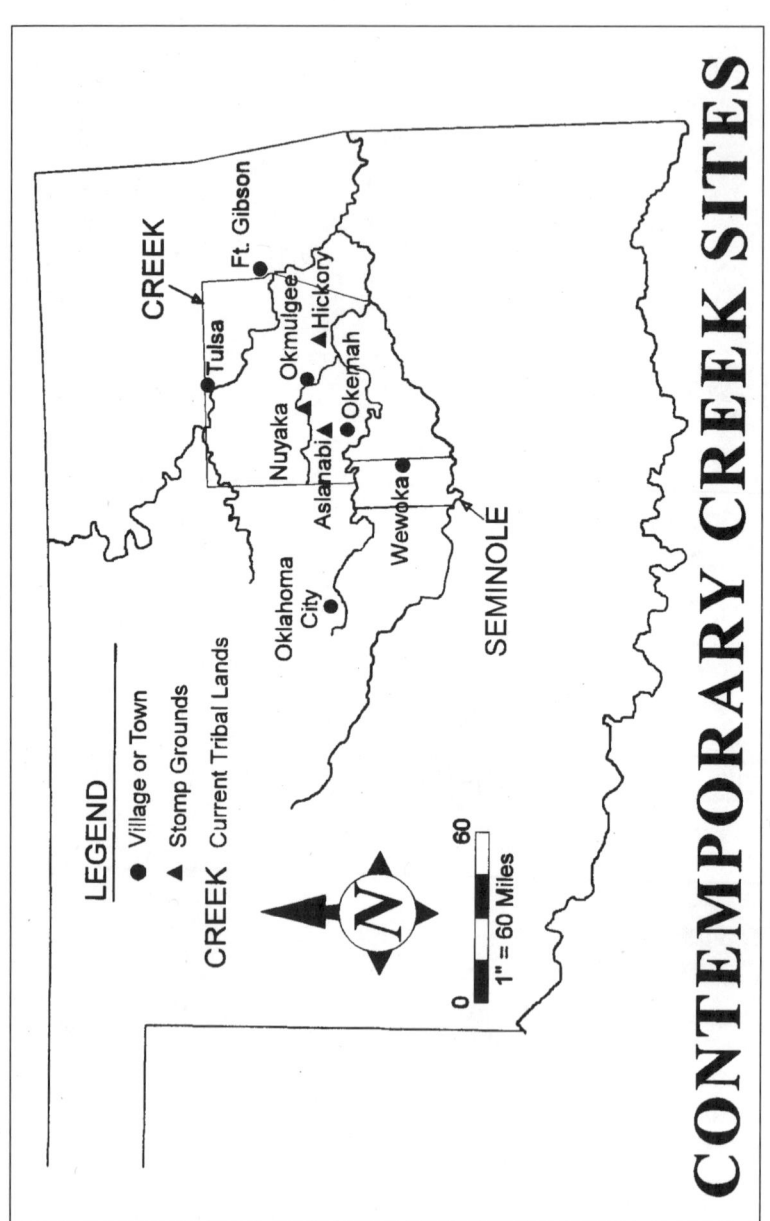

Contemporary Creek sites, Oklahoma *(map by Byron Schneid)*

James Scott of Okemah, Oklahoma, more than
100 years old, storyteller and survivor of the
Trail of Tears (*Hill family collection; photo
provided by Catherine [Hill] Foreman*)

From left: Billy Osceola's wife, Jean Chaudhuri with infant
son Jon, Billy Osceola of Brighton Seminoles; *in front:* Jean's
nephew Lance Sands and son Paul, Florida, 1972
(*photo by Joy Chaudhuri*)

Hickory Grounds in Oklahoma, a peace town, with Jean Chaudhuri in front
of the arbors at the stomp grounds, 1993; part of the Chitto Harjo trail
(*photo by Joy Chaudhuri*)

Jean Chaudhuri in 1985 in Las Cruces,
New Mexico (*Chaudhuri family collection*)

An old Etowah Mound in Georgia
(*courtesy of Georgia Department of Natural Resources*)

Statuettes at Etowah Mound area in Georgia
(*courtesy of Georgia Department of
Natural Resources*)

The four seasons of a Creek woman's life (*copyrighted poster by Jean Chaudhuri*)

Obanga. A contemporary social stomp (*artwork by Joydev "Paul" Chaudhuri*)

EARLY MUSCOGEE ALPHABET AND ENGLISH EQUIVALENT

A	broad "a" as in mar
C	che as in check
Ē	drawn-out "ee"
E	short e, as in tin
F	F
H	H
I	long "I" as in twine
K	K
L	L
M	M
N	N
O	long "o"
P	P
R	HL
S	S
T	T
U	"oo" as in food
V	u as in hut
W	W
Y	Y

A Glossary of Terms

Historically, Creek was an unwritten language. Prior to removal, there were some scattered early attempts to capture a written version of the language. The full development of a Creek alphabet with a modified English type of alphabet began to occur after removal. There are several ways to write Creek and several Creek "dictionaries." This glossary is not intended to teach Creek but to give a list of the Creek terms used. The English rather than the Creek alphabet is used to approximate the sounds phonetically. Wherever relevant, the word in the "Creek" alphabet appears after the English spelling, for Creek readers or speakers. Throughout the book, the Creek spelling is usually provided after the first appearance of the English spelling. Creek words have multiple layers of meanings depending on both the explicit/implicit and idiomatic rules as well as variations in intonations. A brief meaning is provided and the sense of the word is given in the places in the text where it is used. (Many words have been given a different meaning by missionaries and Christianized Creeks compared to the pre-Christian meanings.) I gratefully acknowledge the assistance of Amos McNac, the *empunayv* (speaker) of the Nuyaka Ceremonial Ground.

Abokta (*vpoktv*): Assistant or twin

Abokat (*vpokvt*): Assistant or twin

Ajiboea fikcha (*vcepuyvfekcv*): Corn spirit, corn mother

Anogetchka (*vnokeckv*): Heartfelt love

Anthowalgin (*vnrawvlke*): Animals

Asalanabi (*vsselanvpe*): Greenleaf (also a ceremonial ground)

Asi (*vsse*): Tea (many varieties)

Asi lustee (*vsse lvste*) (*Pvssv*): The black drink

Asi yahola (*Osceola*): A senior commander or dedicated war chief (who has [*vsse yvholv*] taken the war drink)

Asimbonaya (*vsempunayv*): Medicine speaker

Boa (*pauwv*): Uncle

Boea fikcha (*puyvfekcv*): The spirit within, or spirit

Boja (puca): Grandfather, as in grandfather wind—tornado

Botha (porrv): Evil spirit

Buskida (posketv): The green corn harvest fast and ceremonial

Casita (Kasehta): Lower Creek town

Chafigi (cvfeke): My heart

Chefigi (cefeke): Your heart

Chogo biloxi (cuko polokse): Roundhouse: community circle

Chogofa (cvkofv): The real community

Chogo thakko (cuko rakko): "Big House," location of a community ceremonial area on mother earth

Coosa (Koosa): Upper Creek town

Coweta (Koweta): Lower Creek town

Dahopgee (tvhopke): Very skillful

Delonhi (yvlunkv): Plants

Dimithkosi (temerkuse): Poor people and poor area

Eegalba (ekvlpa): Mind

Egan jadi (ekum cate): Red earth

Empenaya (empunayv): Speaker

Ena: Body

Enjageeda (encaketv): Compassion

Fakka jadi (fakk cate): Red dirt

Figi (feke): Heart

Gajj o faya (kvco fvyv): Berries

Gun halwa (kvnhvlwv): Mountain, high place, mound

Gun fuski (kvnfuske): Peninsula (Florida)

Hachko chapko (hvcko capko): Long Ears, a disciplinarian

Hahagahaga (vhakvhayv): Laws

Hassi (hvse): Sun

Haya-atke (hiyvtke): First light of dawn

Heniha (henehv): Administrator of public works

Hesagedamesse (hesaketvmese): The giver and taker of breath (Christians use the term for God)

Hetki (hvtke): White

Hilis hetki (heleshvtke): Ginseng, white root

Hilis haya (*heleshayv*): Healer, medicine man

Hithkida (*hvtketv*) or (*Vcaketv*): Sacred Place

Huti (*hute*): Extended family settlement (matrilocal)

Ibofanga (*Epohfvnkv*): Ultimate energy or spirit in the universe

Igana (*ekvnv*): Land

Igana dilesas (*ekanvtelesvs*): Earth come together

Igana faski (*ekvnvfuske*): Land that goes sharply out

Igana jaga (*ekvnvvcakv*): Holy mother earth

Igan halwa (*ekvnhvlwv*): High place, hill or mountain

Igan halwaji (*ekvnhvlwuce*): Small hill or mound

Ijo Micco (*ecomekko*): Magical deer

Imalas (*emvra*): Coordinators of rank and file

Ispokogi Micco (*espokoke mekko*): The last of the sacred priests, those who are gone (who brought sacred things for the people)

Iste (*este*): People

Iste jadi (*este cate*): Indian people (red)

Iste poggi (*este pokv*): Ancient ones; those who have gone before you

Isti chapchaki (*este capcvke*): Tall man

Isti Lubuchki (*este loputke*): Little people

Istnlgi (*estvlke*): Our people

Italwa micco (*etvlwv mekko*): Civil chief of a particular town

Iyabi (*Eyvppe*): Chant, call to the great spirit

Jada (*catv*): Blood, red

Jadi (*cate*): Red/blood, basic flow of life

Jiboa (*cepauwv*): Your uncle

Jitkoji (*erkoce*): Little father, clan way

Labotskalgi or *Lahootskalgi* (*Rvhoskvlke*): Mature *Imalas*, most trustworthy warriors

Liquido (*lekweto*): Gangrenous, or rotten

Loja (*loca*): Turtle, the transporter in the creation legend

Lustee (*lvste*): Black

Maddo (*mvto*): Thanks

Mahagabonwayhogadidos (*Vhakvpunwvhokvtetos*): The laws that the creator has left us, beyond subjective

Mahaga-ajagidos (*mvhakv vcvkvtos*): They are very, very sacred laws

Mahagadondos (*mvhakvtontos*): The order of things, natural law

Mahagafatzados (*mvhakvfvtcvtos*): Empirically true, beyond conjecture, confirmed laws

Mahagamihenwados (*mvhakvmehenwetos*): That is the truth, the basis for the laws

Mamagee (*mamoce*): Little mother, aunt

Micco (*mekko*): Chief

Micco honija (*mekko hoyvnecv*): Red root

Micco thakko (*mekko rakko*): A principal chief

Muscogee (*mvskoke*): Creek language, also people

Muskokalgi (*mvskokvlke*): The Creek people

Nagin geemaleghee dadee: Where do you stick to? What clan do you belong to?

Notosa (*notossv*): Angelica

Nuyaka: A specific ceremonial ground

Obango hadjo (*opvnkv haco*): Vision dance; dance with appearance of unusual rhythm, drunk-like (no alcohol involved)

Obuskee (*vpvske*): Dehydrated corn-based drink

Ojboya fikcha (*vcepuyvfekcv*): Corn mother

Opothleyahola: Highly intelligent war chief

Osceola: The war chief who has taken the sacred *asi* or black drink

Owala (*owalv*): Prophet

Pojasa (*pucasv*): Grandfather spirit which takes back the spirit or energy

Sabia (*svpeyv*): Magical rocks, crystallish

Sofki (*sofke*): An entire class of corn kernels or hominy; soupy drink filtered through special wood ashes

Talwa (*tvlwv*): A township

Tasikayalgi (*tvsekvyvlke*): Young warrior recruits in early pre-removal period

Tastanagi simiabaiya (*tvstvnvke sevpayv*): Military diplomat

Thakko (*rakko*): Large, grand

Tukabachee (*tukepahce*): Those who now have been crushed (Shawnees fleeing south sought refuge with the Creeks). A specific Upper Creek township name

Tustanagalgheegee (*tvstvnvkvlkoce*) *Delonee hee helizwa* (*telenake heleswv*) or *Ahhotchgee helizwa* (*ahoceheleswv*): Herbal warriors; the role of herbal medicines

Tustenagee (*tvstvnvkke*): Reliable core warrior in shock troop

Tustenagee thakko (*tvstvnvke rakko*): Officer, mature warrior

We hokti (*oye hokte*): Water woman; widow

Wewa boea fikcha (*wewv puyvfekcv*): Water spirit (also *wewafulla/yewvfullv*)

Yahola (*yvholv*): A war chief, high ranking warrior

Yatika (*yvtekv*): Interpreter of traditions and encourager of proper action

Yee gun bay geeta (*ekvncvpeckv*): To be less important than others

Yee yas gheeda (*Eyasketv*): To be humble

Yeehajagheeda (*cecayecv*): To care for yourself

Yeekchida (*yekcetv*): Power, or empowerment (gathering of energy such as in the confederacy)

APPENDIX

A Muscogee Journey

Oh warrior! On your last journey
Tarry a little under that tree
Gathering strength with the black drink
In your vision quests, you were always free

No race, age, or gender escapes the struggle
Or the celebration of busk
The poisoned spirits of battle now are cleaned
Head lying eastward awaiting the dusk

Kind to relatives, seen and unseen
For pangs of hunger, mother earth had been kind
Prayed to seven directions and fed the fire
Now you must leave the last dance behind

Oh warrior on your westward journey
An older Beloved Man you will never be
But at the end of the day you'll climb to the Milky Way
From where grandfather sun meets the shining sea

—Joy Chaudhuri

ABOUT THE AUTHORS

Joy and Jean Chaudhuri in Hanover, New
Hampshire, 1993, prior to Jean delivering one of the
graduation speeches in Dartmouth chapel

The late Jean Chaudhuri (or Ella Jean Hill or Haya-atke/Hiyvtke) was a full-
blood Muscogee Creek who brings to bear an in-depth, informed,
"insider's" view to this work. She belonged to the bear clan on her mother's
side (the late Mary Hill). Her father, Wilburn Hill, was a member of the bird
clan. Members of her extended family—including her late parents, her late
brothers Clifton and Nathaniel Hill, and her sister Richinda Sands—have
been active participants in the Creek world. Jean's paternal grandfather, said
to be related to Opothleyahola ("Very Intelligent War Chief"), the late Elmer
Hill (wind clan), was knowledgeable in Creek medicine and culture and was
the *micco/mekko/*chief of Fish Pond ceremonial grounds. A grand-uncle,
Tony Hill, was *micco* until his death at Asalanabi ceremonial grounds. A
distant uncle, the late John Davis, was a principal chief of the tribe.

Jean was born outside of Okemah on the original James Scott allotment,
where her umbilical cord is buried in the Creek way. Her remains were
returned to her birthplace. Creek was her first language. She spoke it fluently
all her life and could converse in it in depth with others. As a child, she also
learned some Cherokee as part of neighboring interactions, but she did not
speak English until public school age. Given her family's network, her Creek

186

language skills, and her interest and persistence, she grew up at the cutting edge of the Creek storytelling and oral history tradition. She attended Eufala Boarding School, attended Tulsa schools, and then graduated from Oklahoma City public schools. She has taken college courses at several universities. "Grandpa." Scott was a major source of information and education daily for Jean on the Scott allotment.

In addition to being in constant touch with the Creek world of values, Jean was very active in the "outside" world. She did community organization work in several cities, including Oklahoma City, Tallahassee, Tucson, and Phoenix. She was a field interviewer for the Doris Duke Seminole-Miccosukee Oral History Project for the University of Florida. In addition to serving on many boards, councils, and committees, she worked extensively in administering tutorial, employment, alcoholism, and cultural enrichment programs in Tucson, Arizona (1972–1979). She was an executive director for the Tucson Indian Center and later the Traditional Indian Alliance. She served from 1986 to 1994 as chairperson of the Native American Heritage Preservation Coalition, which was involved in issues related to the closing and land transfer of the Phoenix Indian School. She was awarded the Jefferson Award and gold medal for public service in a local community—first in Tucson, then in an auditorium in the United States Supreme Court Building in Washington, D.C. in 1977 with Justice White presiding. Jean was honored posthumously as "Outstanding Native American Leader" by the Annual Native American Recognition Days awards in Phoenix, Arizona on October 20, 2000. In addition to her legacy of public service, storytelling, and preservation of Indian cultures, she left behind an unedited collection of Creek stories.

As a traditional storyteller she had a great ability for listening to elders and the memory and ability to recall minute details from her lifelong quest in gathering the oral history of the Muscogee Creeks and the related Seminoles. For this book, she dictated the legends, the stories, the interviews, and her interweaving of the ideas in almost daily early morning sessions through most of 1993 to her husband and coauthor, Joyotpaul Chaudhuri. She corrected the written results. The foundations of her work included the disciplined storytelling of James Scott until his death around 1944, her parents, family, and tribal elders until the sixties; lifelong conversations with knowledgeable tribal cultural sources; formal interviewing of Florida Seminoles (1969–1972), sponsored by the University of Florida; and her own yet uncatalogued lifelong collection of notes, tapes, literature, and artifacts. In spite of a busy public life, she quietly and constantly worked toward understanding the body of her work and gathered and articulated all of this in her disciplined dictations in 1993. For citation purposes, the 1993 dictation provided the major basis for the oral history narrations. Jean Chaudhuri, until her death in 1997, repeatedly checked for inaccuracies in full drafts of this work and also approved the full interpretation of *A Sacred Path*.

Her husband, Joyotpaul Chaudhuri, is a professor of political science at Arizona State University (ASU). He also was an associate dean of liberal arts and sciences at ASU, a department head at New Mexico State University, and a faculty member at several universities including the University of Oklahoma, Central State University (Edmond), Florida State University, and the University of Arizona. His central discipline is political philosophy and theory but he has also taught and published in the fields of American Indian politics and public affairs and comparative politics. He was a member of the (American) Indian Studies committee at the University of Arizona and the Institute of Indian Studies at the University of South Dakota. "Joy" Chaudhuri has a Ph.D. (1964) from the University of Oklahoma and has been a visiting fellow of Silliman College at Yale University (1968–1969). The extended cooperation and synergism of Jean's insider work, blended with outside experience and Joy's outsider's discipline and distance and inside experience, makes this work possible, together with the contributions of the Creeks whose names are mentioned in the acknowledgments. Correlating the pieces of the larger system of values, and discovering and presenting them in a coherent way, has been an exciting but difficult journey.

Two of the most important reasons for the book are to provide a resource to young Muscogee people regarding the "sacred path" and to share with readers a sense of the values of the Creek world as a supplement to the standard, mostly "external" descriptions of Creeks. The analysis and description of the basic Creek values provides a reference point for understanding the clarity and depth of an aboriginal worldview and the process of change that has occurred, and points the way to issues of the future. Hopefully, this will stimulate similar studies of other Native peoples.

INDEX